Analyzing
NARRATIVE
REALITY

Analyzing NARRATIVE REALITY

Jaber F. Gubrium
University of Missouri

James A. Holstein
Marquette University

SAGE

Los Angeles • London • New Delhi • Singapore

For information:

SAGE Publications, Inc.
2455 Teller Road
Thousand Oaks,
  California 91320
E-mail: order@sagepub.com

SAGE Publications Ltd.
1 Oliver's Yard
55 City Road
London EC1Y 1SP
United Kingdom

SAGE Publications India Pvt. Ltd.
B 1/I 1 Mohan Cooperative
  Industrial Area
Mathura Road, New Delhi 110 044
India

SAGE Publications Asia-Pacific
  Pte. Ltd.
33 Pekin Street #02-01
Far East Square
Singapore 048763

Printed in the United States of America

Library of Congress Cataloging-in-Publication Data

Gubrium, Jaber F.
Analyzing narrative reality/Jaber F. Gubrium, James A. Holstein.
    p. cm.
Includes bibliographical references and index.
ISBN 978-1-4129-5219-4 (pbk.)
    1. Ethnography—Methodology. 2. Discourse analysis, Narrative.
3. Storytelling. 4. Oral tradition. 5. Narration (Rhetoric) 6. Participant
observation. 7. Written communication. 8. Culture and communication.
I. Holstein, James A. II. Title.

GN345.G83 2009
301—dc22   2007052846

This book is printed on acid-free paper.

08   09   10   11   12   10   9   8   7   6   5   4   3   2   1

Acquisitions Editor:	Vicki Knight
Associate Editor:	Sean Connelly
Editorial Assistant:	Lauren Habib
Production Editor:	Sarah K. Quesenberry
Copy Editor:	Teresa Wilson
Typesetter:	C&M Digitals (P) Ltd.
Proofreader:	Theresa Kay
Indexer:	Ellen Slavitz
Cover Designer:	Glenn Vogel
Marketing Manager:	Stephanie Adams

Contents

Preface

Narrative analysis crosses several borders. In literary studies, long-standing interest in the organization of stories has dealt with epistemological issues, the structure of folktales, and the shape of characterization, themes, and emplotment, among other organizational matters. Interest has moved into the social sciences and been applied in research projects that utilize stories to understand personal experience as it relates to work, family life, the community, and nationhood, for example. A further crossing enters the domain of rehabilitation and reform. Here narrative analysis features how the restorying of experience can be used to recover from personal ills or to reframe the way we think about disadvantage and social betterment. The narrative landscape is exceptionally broad, and its borders have been porous enough to make for extensive cross-fertilization.

Analyzing Narrative Reality deals with one region of this landscape. Following important contributions in anthropology, communication, folklore, oral history, sociolinguistics, and sociology, the book presents a working vocabulary for making explanatory sense of storytelling practice, the everyday uses of accounts, and the situated shaping of narrative composition. While it draws extensively upon these contributions, the book is innovative in the way it combines analytic sensibilities into a unified framework. *Analyzing Narrative Reality* targets stories and storytelling as these operate within society. As simple as that may sound, this concern still lurks at the outskirts of narrative analysis. The book locates the concern more centrally in the narrative landscape by laying out its challenges and explanatory utility.

Contemporary narrative analysis in social research has engaged all kinds of accounts—formal and informal, written and told. Typically, stories are recorded and analyzed as transcripts or texts. Typically, they are considered mainly for their internal organization. This is hardly surprising, since it has drawn extensively and profitably from the humanities and literary studies. *Analyzing Narrative Reality* suggests that researchers systematically consider the communicative mechanisms, circumstances, purposes, strategies, and resources that shape narrative production. This requires ethnographic sensibilities, which resonate throughout the book.

Narratives reduced to transcripts are flat, without practical depth or detail, even while textual organization has been shown to relate in important ways to factors such as gender and social status. While portions of a transcript might refer to narrative occasions, the settings of storytelling are often taken for granted or missing. For example, a transcribed story from the workplace might reveal a worker's assessment of challenges encountered on the job, but may not tell us much about the setting's discursive conventions or the linguistic resources commonly used to construct the challenges. One gets little sense of how people usually talk or don't talk and remain silent about challenges. The issue of what is not uttered or storied as opposed to what is communicated encourages us to consider the surrounding conditions of storytelling. Such information can only be discerned from direct consideration of the storying process within the circumstances in which it unfolds.

Analyzing Narrative Reality targets researchers who are drawn to the study of storytelling in vivo, be they veteran researchers newly interested in narrativity or students learning the trade. It is aimed especially at those who have found text-based forms of analysis lacking in concern for narrative production. The book also should appeal to those interested in social interaction and the diverse contexts of, and situated demands on, communication. It draws extensively on primary and secondary narrative material from a variety of settings to illustrate how researchers can conceptualize and analyze narrative practice across the disciplinary landscape.

The book's primary goal is analytic. Most social researchers end up with some form of narrative material in hand—interview tapes, transcripts of life stories, field notes of talk and interaction, and personal documents such as letters and diaries. This book presents a way of approaching, viewing, and analyzing this material as it relates to its construction and distribution. Having an analytic mission, it is concerned with how to think about and provide understanding of the storytelling process and the organization of accounts. Explicit analytic guidelines are provided, which lead the way to illustrations of their application. While the book offers suggestions for research procedure, it isn't especially about the nuts and bolts of data collection. Nonetheless, the diverse narrative material presented bears on the entire research enterprise.

Undeniably, *Analyzing Narrative Reality* reflects the authors' sociological perspective, but it is truly multidisciplinary in its intent. It should be valuable, for example, to researchers working in academic disciplines as varied as sociology, anthropology, social psychology, oral history, folklore, women and gender studies, family studies, and communication, as well as to narratively focused researchers in nursing, education, public health, social work, management/organization studies, and counseling. It touches base with the variety of qualitative research methodologies developed in these disciplines and taps into the growing cross-disciplinary interest in narrative practice.

The book is organized around a distinctive analytic vocabulary. Each chapter begins by orienting the reader to a significant concept and follows that with a specific guideline for research. Each chapter then ventures "into the field" to illustrate how the concept can be used empirically. The chapters are pedagogic, build on each other, and are not overly conceptualized. In this way, we demonstrate concretely a way of analyzing stories as not simply reflective of experience, but as integral parts of society.

Acknowledgments

The book bears the imprint of the friends, colleagues, and students who have shared with us their insights regarding narrative analysis. We are enormously thankful for their contributions. We also are grateful to those at Sage Publications who helped bring this project to fruition: Lisa Cuevas Shaw for launching the book, Vicki Knight for seeing it through to completion, the initially anonymous reviewers for their helpful suggestions, and the editorial, production, and marketing staff for their skillful input.

We want to mention two very special influences who are no longer with us. While we were working on this project, Spencer Cahill and Melvin Pollner passed away. Spencer and Mel were good friends and inspirational colleagues. This book is a small tribute to their legacy as it attempts to advance the traditions of sociology they so masterfully represented. Our lives and work have been enriched by their friendship and scholarship.

Sage Publications gratefully acknowledges the contributions of the reviewers:

Rachelle D. Hole, *University of British Columbia Okanagan*

Sky Marsen, *Victoria University of Wellington*

Kevin D. Miller, *Huntington University*

Mandy Morgan, *Massey University*

Jennifer Rowe, *Griffith University*

Amy Shuman, *Ohio State University*

About the Authors

Jaber F. Gubrium is professor and chair of the Sociology Department at the University of Missouri. He has taught at Marquette University and the University of Florida, was a Fulbright scholar at Tampere University, Finland, in 1996, and has been a visiting professor at Tampere, at Lund University in Sweden, and at the Universities of Copenhagen and Odense in Denmark. His areas of specialization are aging and the life course, social interaction, identity, qualitative methods, and narrative analysis. Gubrium works empirically at the border of ethnography and narrative analysis, combining them in new ways to deal with the perennial problems of linking observational data with transcripts of stories, speech, and other narrative material.

James A. Holstein is professor of sociology in the Department of Social and Cultural Sciences at Marquette University. His research and writing projects have addressed social problems, deviance and social control, family, and the self—all approached from an ethnomethodologically informed, constructionist perspective. He has published over three dozen books on topics including mental health and illness, social problems theory, and qualitative research methods. Recently, he was the editor of the journal *Social Problems*.

As collaborators for 20 years, Gubrium and Holstein have developed a distinctive constructionist approach to everyday life in a variety of projects, including *What Is Family?, Constructing the Life Course, The Self We Live By, Institutional Selves,* and *Inner Lives and Social Worlds.* They have outlined the conceptual, theoretical, and methodological implications of their approach to qualitative inquiry and narrative analysis in several other texts, including *The New Language of Qualitative Method, The Active Interview,* and *The Handbook of Interview Research.* Their most recent project is the *Handbook of Constructionist Research.*

Introduction

A Point of Departure

As qualitative inquiry becomes increasingly sophisticated, narratives, stories, and accounts of all sorts are being reconsidered as forms of social practice. Charles Briggs (2007, p. 552), for example, invites us to consider how interview narratives "produce subjects, texts, knowledge, and authority," especially in relation to other social activities and circumstances. Briggs is especially interested in how interviews and their stories are assembled, communicated, and circulate in the various fields in which this transpires. His concern points to the social life of stories, which are worked up and presented in particular settings, perform different functions, and have varied consequences. If stories are about our lives, the world, and its events, they also are part of society.

That is the point of departure for *Analyzing Narrative Reality*. The book presents a view of narrativity and its storied by-products as operating within society. As refined and insightful as narrative analysis in the social sciences has become, its purview remains rather narrow. The tendency is to orient to stories as multifaceted textual windows on the world, even while assuming that those windows are dressed up by storytellers for the viewing. Researchers collect stories about the course of living, about growing up in particular places or circumstances, about families and communities, about protest and politics, about an endless variety of things. The stories are transcribed and analyzed for the way they emplot, thematize, and otherwise construct what they are about. If the conventional idea is that storytellers actively assemble the messages that become story texts, the unfolding and ongoing activeness of the process is frequently shortchanged.

The accent on the transcribed texts of stories tends to strip narratives of their social organization and interactional dynamics. Narrative is framed as a social product, not as social action. As Mary Douglas (1978, p. 298) noted decades ago, "We now realize that we have unduly privileged the verbal channel and tended to suppose that it could be effective in disembodied form." As Paul Ricoeur (1981, p. 203) added later, "A text breaks the ties of discourse to all the ostensible references" it could have in various social contexts. Paul Atkinson (1997), among others, has suggested a shift in focus:

> The ubiquity of the narrative and its centrality . . . are not license simply to privilege those forms. It is the work of anthropologists and sociologists to examine those narratives and to subject them to the same analysis as any other forms. We need to pay due attention to their construction in use: how actors improvise their personal narratives. . . . We need to attend to how socially shared resources of rhetoric and narrative are deployed to generate recognizable, plausible, and culturally well-informed accounts. . . . What we cannot afford to do is to be seduced by the cultural conventions we seek to study. We should not endorse those cultural conventions that seek to privilege the account as a special kind of representation. (p. 341)

Atkinson is encouraging us to look more carefully at the social dimensions of narrativity. To that end, and following from the related contributions of researchers who focus on everyday storytelling, this book expands narrative analysis to consider the circumstances, conditions, and goals of accounts. We are especially concerned with how storytellers work up, and what they do with, the accounts they present. We are particularly interested in the functions stories serve in different situations. Adapting familiar phrasing from philosopher Ludwig Wittgenstein (1953), storytellers not only tell stories, they *do* things with them. What speakers do with stories shapes their meaning for listeners, as well as the consequences of their communication.

But this is not just a book about how to view stories as they operate in society. Certainly, we discuss, explore, and exemplify aspects of this operation. Throughout the book, we consider various facets of storytelling, from the social production of accounts, to considerations bearing on the quality of stories. The main contribution of the book is providing a framework for viewing these matters analytically. The book's key question is how to analyze narrative reality as a matter of everyday life. If storytellers not only talk the talk, but also walk the talk, so to speak, how can researchers analyze the process and the results? While we are interested in the data-gathering end of things, our primary concern is with how to think about what comes into view in the process of interpreting and analyzing narrative data. Indeed, as we will show, how one conceptualizes things actually affects what comes into view, as much as empirical material shapes our understanding (see J. F. Gubrium & Holstein, 1997).

The discussion is divided into four main parts, which follow from each other. Since each part sets the analytic stage for the part that comes next, it is important that the book be read sequentially. Part I presents the sense of narrative reality we are dealing with. The empirical material to be analyzed is not simply stories, as if they were self-evident texts with plots, themes, points, beginnings, middles, and ends. To be sure, this view of story is present in the production, communication, and appreciation of accounts. But there is more, and this something more requires explanation before we turn to the question of how to analyze it. One reason for this is that, in the context of narrative reality, plots, themes, beginnings, middles, and endings may be completely beside the point. As we will show in Part I and through-out the book, the beginnings of a story may be widely dispersed in a variety of sources other than the storyteller's experience or a particular text. Similarly, endings might be multiply consequential, implicating a variety of others and having diverse outcomes. The articulated part of a story might be as apparently short as a single utterance, such as "Yeah, that's the way it is." Or it might be as lengthy as the combined and continuing narrative contributions of several individuals who meet together every Wednesday evening to play cards and share thoughts and feelings. The sense of story and story-teller under consideration centers on the social organization of narrativity. This expands story's operating horizons well beyond what narrative analysts—who are generally concerned with the internal organization of texts—commonly bring on board.

Part II takes us into the field of narrative reality. While we continue to elaborate our perspective, we now begin to demonstrate how the approach operates in practice. Part II deals with what we call "narrative work"—the interactional activity through which narratives are constructed, communicated, and sustained or reconfigured. The leading questions here are "How can the process of constructing accounts be conceptualized?" and "How can the empirical material be analyzed?" Chapter by chapter, we build an analytic vocabulary that highlights facets of narrative work as well as the ways that researchers can orient to it.

Part III shifts empirical and analytic gears. Here we turn to what we call "narrative environments"—contexts within which the work of story construction and storytelling gets done. The emphasis is more on the *whats* of narrative reality than on the *hows* of Part II. A leading question is "What does it matter for the meaning of a story that it is told in a particular setting, with its understandings, rather than in another setting, with different understandings?" Another leading question is "What are the purposes and consequences of storying experience in particular ways?" A turn to the narrative environments of storytelling is critical for understanding what is at stake for storytellers and listeners in presenting accounts or responding to them in distinctive ways. What people say or hear in specific settings can have significant consequences.

Part IV takes up the issue of quality control. The chapters pose two questions—"What is a good story?" and "Who is a good storyteller?" The answers are not as clear cut as they might be if the search for answers were limited to story texts. In the context of narrative reality, no simple list of quality indicators or set of characteristically good stories or good storytellers will do. Rather, as we will show, "narrative adequacy" relates directly to what is good enough in the circumstances. Adequacy is contingent both on the work of storytelling and what is at stake for participants. While standard-issue quality indicators are important reference points for evaluating narratives and storytelling—for whether what is communicated is true, compelling, or complete, for example—they tell us very little about how elements of goodness are understood and applied in practice.

From our perspective, the most important feature of narrative reality is that its chief operating components—narrative work and narrative environments—are reflexively related. We touch upon this throughout the book, and offer some final observations in the afterword, which is titled "Stories Without Borders?" In practice, narrative work is undertaken in specific settings under particular circumstances. Viewing narrative work as having a separate and distinct logic of its own shortchanges its substantive and moral bearings—the varied purposes, functions, and consequences that unfold in everyday life. Similarly, in practice, narrative environments—their social forms and understandings—are not simply "there" empirically, operating as if they shaped narrativity on their own terms. Conceiving environments this way would obviate the ongoing work that constructs them and their meaning and relevancies. Such a view would turn storytellers and their audiences into automatons of received accounts. From our vantage point, it is more fruitful to orient to the reflexive interplay between narrative reality's operating components than to force empirical material into either analytic compartment.

In this context, it would be counterproductive to define a priori what is meant precisely by "story" and "storyteller." Rather, loose commonsense understandings are assumed as a basis for unpacking and paying empirical attention to how story and storyteller are discerned, defined, and responded to in practice. Throughout the book, we use the terms *narrative, story,* and *account* interchangeably to refer to spates of talk that are taken to describe or explain matters of concern to participants. This vocabulary implicates descriptive, interactional communication of one sort or another, but the length, structure, and content of what is said are notably variable. What narratives and stories might possibly amount to becomes apparent as our argument unfolds—simply because what they are arises out of circumstances and social interaction. To define a narrative or story in axiomatic terms would be antithetical to this.

Accordingly, we ask readers to move ahead into the book with whatever received sense of story and storytelling they are comfortable with, along with an open mind, of course. For example, initially, the idea that a story is an extended account, or that it is an explanation or description of something that makes a point, will work. The sense of the storyteller as one who provides an account of experience or event of his or her own that is more or less credible is equally suitable to start. As readers move through the chapters, we hope to show how these accounts are socially organized and how the process of storytelling is circumstantially shaped.

This request relates to the approach to theory that undergirds our perspective and presentation. Theory, in our view, best informs analysis when it works incrementally and in close relation to empirical material. The "story" theory tells should not prematurely overshadow or overshoot the material in view. As Herbert Blumer (1969) once put it, concepts are meant to sensitize us to the empirical world, not to construct it on their own terms. In our case, concepts should help us to understand how stories develop and operate in social context, but should not predetermine what we choose to look at or how we apprehend the empirical. This minimalist approach to theory has pragmatist bearings (see Putnam, 1995; Shalin, 1986; Skidmore, 1975). We expect it to suit us well as we introduce the concepts of the following chapters and, in the process, build a framework for analyzing narrative reality.

Finally, on a personal note, we have occasionally inserted our own experience into the discussion. We haven't done this simply to be friendly or to show that we're all in the same boat analytically. Certainly, we have no qualms with friendliness nor with sharing research experiences. Rather, we have interjected the personal to help make unconventional observations more accessible and to ease the way into unfamiliar territory. This is especially pertinent when we introduce unorthodox ways of viewing narrativity. For example, we will argue that inanimate objects and nonrational beings have their own stories, which can emerge seamlessly and competently in the right interactional environment. This would seem unusual or magical in the commonsense scheme of things. But as we will show, these stories also can be analyzed as a matter of narrative practice, materializing in the give-and-take of social interaction. Personal illustrations help make that sensible.

PART I

Narrative Reality

Much of narrative analysis centers on written texts. The texts may start out as spoken accounts, but these eventually take transcribed textual form. For example, veterans of recent wars might be interviewed for their life stories, with special attention being paid to how particular war experiences figure into the accounts. The interviews are transcribed and the texts analyzed for various purposes. Researchers might wonder how popular wars such as World War II, as opposed to unpopular wars such as the Vietnam War, play out in the soldiers' stories (see Hynes, 1997). In particular, they might ask whether popular wars figure more positively than unpopular ones in soldiers' identities. Typically, the analytic strategy is to compare texts for similarities and differences, specifying these in terms of distinct vocabularies, plotlines, or themes, for instance.

In this approach, textual material is drawn from individuals' accounts on the occasions they are asked or in some other way prompted to convey their stories. The accounts may be autobiographical, historical, or even literary. As open as the empirical horizons of such narratives might appear to be, boundaries are erected around the experiences as the stories are turned into concrete texts, beginning where the recorded and/or transcribed text starts and ending where it finishes. Characterization, emplotment, themes, inscription practices, and other textual matters are identified and then compared for omissions, organization, and the like. The features of stories, in other words, are found within the confines of their texts.

Part I of this book paves the way for a different view and an alternative form of analysis oriented both to the internal and especially to the external organization of stories. Rather than limiting the empirical horizons of stories to the boundaries of texts or transcripts, the horizons are expanded to include the diverse everyday contexts in which stories are elicited, assembled, and conveyed. The term *narrative reality* is meant to flag the socially situated practice of storytelling, which would include accounts provided both within and outside of formal interviews. The term suggests that the contexts in which stories are told are as much a part of their reality as the texts themselves. The narrative reality of the stories of WWII and Vietnam veterans, for instance, would not only include narratives elicited in research interviews, but extend to other circumstances in which such stories were incited and told. It could extend, for example, to occasions such as veterans' reunions, therapy groups, or the exaggerated "war stories" that some circumstances encourage. Stories not only are told in interviews, but they also wend their way through the lives of storytellers. They are boundless in that regard, are told and retold, with no definitive beginnings, middles, or ends in principle, even while a sense of narrative wholes and narrative organization is always in tow. This obliges us to analyze stories and storytelling in an extended framework, with the aim of documenting what the communication process and its circumstances designate as meaningful and important, together with the various purposes stories serve.

The chapters of Part I locate narrative reality in everyday life. Chapter 1 orients to stories *in* society. The discussion is initially set against the background of the historical aim of social researchers to obtain narrative material from subjects themselves, in their own words. Of particular interest is how the practice of storytelling and the resulting features of stories relate to what is at stake on the occasions stories unfold. We introduce Clifford Shaw's (1930) classic examination of a juvenile delinquent's own story to illustrate various aspects of narrative practice. The study serves as an analytic touchstone throughout the book. The other two chapters of Part I expand on the orientation to stories in society. Chapter 2 compares forms of narrative analysis and suggests an innovative ethnographic approach. Chapter 3 elaborates narrative reality's empirical terrain, discussing the procedural implications for studying narrative work, narrative environments, and their reflexive relationship.

1

Stories in Society

S tories have captivated social researchers ever since Henry Mayhew (1861–1862/1968) and his associates conducted observational surveys of London's "humbler classes" in the 1850s. In the preface to Volume 1 of the study report, Mayhew indicated that, until then, what was known about the poor and their labor had been drawn from elite and administrative accounts. Those in the know provided information about the lives of those ostensibly without the knowledge or wherewithal to do so on their own. Members of the humbler classes were viewed as incapable of offering useful opinions, much less sensible descriptions of their circumstances. They were considered ignorant, if not incommunicative and irrational, subject to whimsy and exaggeration. Why ask them about their social world when others could provide more cogent accounts?

Mayhew's strategy was to turn this around and, instead, begin by assuming that, while perhaps crude in the eyes of their betters, members of the humbler classes could speak for themselves. Like others, they could provide their own accounts of experience, even while the accounts required professional polish to turn them into public information. The humbler classes' own stories, in other words, could be the basis of knowledge about their lives and labor. Referring to this unconventional perspective, Mayhew described his study as "curious for many reasons."

> It surely may be considered curious as being the first attempt to publish the history of a people, from the lips of the people themselves—giving a literal description of their labour, their earnings, their trials, and their sufferings, in their *own* [italics added] "unvarnished" language; and to portray the condition

of their homes and their families by personal observation of the places, and direct communion with the individuals. (Vol. 1, p. xv)

Continuing to underscore the study's novel approach, Mayhew was compelled to justify his research. He explained that the study filled a void of solid information about "a large body of persons," meaning the London poor, whose existence wasn't officially recognized.

It is curious, moreover, as supplying information concerning a large body of persons, of whom the public had less knowledge than the most distant tribes of the earth—the government population returns not even numbering them among the inhabitants of the kingdom; and as adducing facts so extraordinary, that the traveler in the undiscovered country of the poor, like Bruce, until his stories are corroborated by after investigators, be content to lie under the imputation of telling such tales, as travelers are generally supposed to delight in. (Vol. 1, p. xv)

If curious, the portrayal offered in the volumes of *London Labour and the London Poor* is described as nonetheless valid in its empirical claims.

Be the faults of the present volume what they may, assuredly they are rather short-comings than exaggerations, for in every instance the author and his coadjutors have sought to understate, and most assuredly never to exceed the truth. . . . Within the last two years some thousands of the humbler classes of society must have been seen and visited with the especial view of noticing their condition and learning their histories; and it is but right that the truthfulness of the poor generally should be made known; for though checks have been usually adopted, the people have been mostly found to be astonishingly correct in their statements,—so much so indeed, that the attempts at deception are certainly the exceptions rather than the rule. (Vol. 1, p. xv)

Mayhew concludes the preface on a moral tone. This will resonate in the future with similar indigenous studies of the disadvantaged on both sides of the Atlantic. These studies aimed to bring into view for purposes of social reform the stories that may have frequently been told, but that were largely unheard.

My earnest hope is that the book may serve to give the rich a more intimate knowledge of the sufferings, and the frequent heroism under those sufferings, of the poor—that it may teach those who are beyond temptation to look with charity on the frailties of their less fortunate brethren—and cause those in "high places," and those of whom much is expected, to bestir themselves to improve the condition of a class of people whose misery, ignorance, and vice, amidst all the immense wealth and great knowledge of "the first city of the world," is, to say the very least, a national disgrace to us. (Vol. 1, p. xv)

"Own Stories" and Social Worlds

In the first excerpt above from Mayhew's preface, we emphasized the word "own" to make a point. While truthful portrayals of the unseen world of London's poor were rare, it was important that those eventually produced were faithful to the poor's unvarnished words and their own accounts of life. This launched a tradition of research that oriented to what American sociologist Clifford Shaw (1930) later would refer as "own story" material. Shaw believed that stories conveyed by those whose experience was under consideration were more telling, truthful, and useful than stories drawn from other sources. In a sense, Shaw assumed that those in question owned their stories and should be treated as proper proprietors. Their lives should not be conveyed by outsiders, if such accounts existed at all. Stories of indigenous life told in people's own words were more authentic than stories offered in others' words. The phrase "in their own words" would thus add to the significance of their "own story," encouraging researchers to seek native accounts of indigenous life. This required that such accounts be sought in situ and as unobtrusively as possible. The researcher should listen to and faithfully record "their own stories," avoiding "contamination" at all cost. It posed quite a challenge, as the individuals being studied were often portrayed as dangerous inhabitants of mysterious and threatening social worlds.

Shaw's own work is exemplary. Writing of the "value of the delinquent boy's own story," Shaw (1930) describes his initial contact with Stanley, the subject of his book *The Jack-Roller*. The book is a "case-study of the career of a young male delinquent, to whom we will refer as Stanley." It provides an inside glimpse of Stanley's social world. The term "jack-roller" was part of the vernacular of the times, referring to the mugging of "jacks" or drunk working men. Younger males took advantage of the jacks' inebriation to rob them of their money, especially at the end of the workweek on payday.

> The case is one of a series of two hundred similar studies of repeated male offenders under seventeen years of age, all of whom were on parole from correctional institutions when the studies were made. The author's contact with Stanley has extended over a period of six years, the initial contact having been made when Stanley was sixteen years of age. During this period it was possible to make a rather intensive study of his behavior and social background and to carry out a somewhat intensive study of social treatment. (p. 1)

The value of Stanley's story is made clear as Shaw continues.

> The case is published to illustrate the value of the "own story" in the study and treatment of the delinquent child. As a preparation for the interpretation of

> Stanley's life-history, which comprises the major portion of this volume, a brief description of the more general uses of "own story" material, along with illustrations from a number of different cases, is presented in this chapter. (p. 1)

Echoing Mayhew, Shaw addresses the "unique feature" of own story material. We again hear references to their "own words" and the importance of recording them in what Mayhew called "unvarnished language." Shaw is palpably excited at the scientific prospects of using this "new device of sociological research," affirming that social truths be conveyed according to their subjects.

> The life-history record is a comparatively new device of sociological research in the field of criminology, although considerable use has been made of such material in other fields. The life-record itself is the delinquent's own account of his experiences, written as an autobiography, as a diary, or presented in the course of a series of interviews. The unique feature of such documents is that they are recorded in the first person, in the boy's own words, and not translated into the language of the person investigating the case. (p. 1)

A decade later, sociologist William Foote Whyte (1943) continues the emphasis on indigenous stories in his classic study of the Boston Italian immigrant slum he calls "Cornerville." The opening paragraphs echo the "we–them" distinction resonant in Mayhew's plea for accurate knowledge of London's poor. As Whyte initially addresses his reader, it's evident he assumes that there is a story there (in Cornerville), but one that, because of broader social attitudes, remains untold. It is Cornerville's own story, one that, like the story of London's humbler classes, is silent in the face of the immense wealth and great knowledge of the elite Boston community.

> In the heart of "Eastern City" there is a slum district known as Cornerville, which is inhabited almost exclusively by Italian immigrants and their children. To the rest of the city it is a mysterious, dangerous, and depressing area. Cornerville is only a few minutes' walk from fashionable High Street, but the High Street inhabitant who takes that walk passes from the familiar to the unknown. (p. xv)

The subsequent parallel with Mayhew's prefatory comments is remarkable.

> Respectable people have access to a limited body of information upon Cornerville. They may learn that it is one of the most congested areas in the United States. It is one of the chief points of interest in any tour organized to show upper-class people the bad housing conditions in which lower-class people live. Through sight-seeing or statistics one may discover that bathtubs are rare, that children overrun the narrow and neglected streets, that the juvenile delinquency rate is high, that crime is prevalent among adults. (p. xv)

We are eventually told in a tone of surprise that this world has its own moral order, the inference being that it is as regulated and comprehensive as the familiar haunts of fashionable High Street. The punch line leading to "their own story" is clear. As if to say that human beings, unlike cardboard figures, have stories of their own to tell located in the integral scenes of their lives, Whyte concludes:

> In this view, Cornerville people appear as social work clients, as defendants in criminal cases, or as undifferentiated members of "the masses." There is one thing wrong with such a picture: no human beings are in it. Those who are concerned with Cornerville seek through a general survey to answer questions that require the most intimate knowledge of local life. The only way to gain such knowledge is to live in Cornerville and participate in the activities of its people. One who does that finds that the district reveals itself to him in an entirely different light. The buildings, streets, and alleys that formerly represented dilapidation and physical congestion recede to form a familiar background for the actors upon the Cornerville scene. (pp. xv–xvi)

Whyte moves on to present Cornerville's story in its own unvarnished language, featuring racketeers, "big shots," and the gangs he calls the corner boys and the college boys. Whyte's interest in indigenous accounts reflects that of his predecessors, Mayhew and Shaw. He is keenly attuned to unrecognized social worlds, told in terms of inhabitants' "own stories."

Stories such as those relayed by members of the humbler classes, by Stanley and other delinquents, and by the corner and the college boys, were taken to portray social worlds. Individual accounts were not as important sociologically as what individuals told about the worlds they inhabited. While *The Jack-Roller* is all about Stanley's life in poverty and his experience as a juvenile delinquent, through his story we learn about the world of juvenile delinquency as it plays out in a great metropolis, in this case in the city of Chicago. Whyte's book, *Street Corner Society*, is about gang leaders Doc, Chick, and their boys, but the individual stories are presented as comprising "the social structure of an Italian slum," the subtitle of Whyte's book. Individual accounts add up to something more than biographical particulars, namely, stories of social worlds on their own terms.

Narratives of Inner Life

Psychological interest in individual stories moves in another direction. While continuing to emphasize their own stories, narratives in this case are viewed as windows on inner life rather than on social worlds. Eschewing indirect methods such as projective techniques and psychoanalysis, ordinary life stories are taken to reveal "who we are" as persons; they are the way individuals construct their identities as active agents of their lives. Inner life is a product of "narrative knowing," as counseling psychologist Donald Polkinghorne (1988) puts it. The first sentences of the introduction to his exemplary book *Narrative Knowing and the Human Sciences* set the stage for this perspective.

> Experience is meaningful and human behavior is generated from and informed by this meaningfulness. Thus, the study of human behavior needs to include an exploration of the meaning systems that form human experience. This book is an inquiry into narrative, the primary form by which human experience is made meaningful. (p. 1)

As if to say that inner life comes to us by way of stories, Polkinghorne outlines how the "realms of human experience" are constructed through narrative expression. The last chapter of the book actually identifies narrative with human experience. If human experience is viewed as narrative, our stories become our selves; narratives structure who we are as meaningful beings in the world.

> The basic figuration process that produces the human experience of one's own life and action and the lives and actions of others is the narrative. Through the action of emplotment, the narrative form constitutes human reality into wholes, manifests human values, and bestows meaning on life. (p. 159)

There is a parallel between this "inner lives" approach to narrative and the "social worlds" perspective on stories. If Mayhew, Shaw, Whyte, and other sociological researchers point to social worlds by presenting members' accounts of experience, Polkinghorne and those with a psychological interest in stories view the presentation of narrative accounts as the hearable embodiments of inner life. As William Randall (1995) implies in the title of his book *The Stories We Are*, we *are* our stories. The book is an "essay on self-creation," which is its subtitle. Narrativity looms in importance in both views. It is a conduit to, if not constitutive of, domains of social and psychological experience that are otherwise hidden.

A key text representing the inner lives perspective is psychologist Dan McAdams's (1993) book *The Stories We Live By*. Asking what life stories are about, the author directs us inward rather than to our social surroundings, the viewpoint apparent in the book's opening paragraphs. It's telling that the word "own" appears again, this time resonating with individual uniqueness rather than with social distinction.

> If you want to know me, then you must know my story, for my story defines
> who I am. And if *I* want to know *myself*, to gain insight into the meaning of
> my own life, then I, too, must come to know my own story. I must come to see
> in all its particulars the narrative of the self—the personal myth—that I have
> tacitly, even unconsciously, composed over the course of my years. It is a story
> I continue to revise, and tell to myself (and sometimes to others) as I go on
> living. (p. 11)

This is a story that changes, rearticulating the developing inner life it
represents, paralleling the sociological view that changing social worlds are
constructed in their unfolding narratives. For McAdams, the storied possibilities of inner life are endless, limited only by the narrative imagination.
Describing the personal myth, McAdams leads us within to the created
domains of the self.

> First and foremost, [personal myth] is a special kind of story that each of us
> naturally constructs to bring together the different parts of ourselves and our
> lives into a purposeful and convincing whole. . . . A personal myth is an act of
> imagination that is a patterned integration of our remembered past, perceived
> present, and anticipated future. As both author and reader, we come to appre-
> ciate our own myth for its beauty and its psychosocial truth. (p. 12)

Certain of personal narrative's ultimate reference point, McAdams refers
us to a "secret" place within, sometimes shared with others, and known
most purely in epiphanic moments of truth.

> Though we may act out parts of our personal myth in daily life, the story is
> inside of us. It is made and remade in the secrecy of our own minds, both con-
> scious and unconscious, and for our own psychological discovery and enjoy-
> ment. In moments of great intimacy, we may share important episodes with
> another person. And in moments of great insight, parts of the story may
> become suddenly conscious, or motifs we had believed to be trivial may sud-
> denly appear to be self-defining phenomena. (p. 12)

Stanley's Story *in* Society

As insightful as these perspectives are, they provide limited information
about the occasions on which their respective stories are told, about what
Alan Dundes (1980) stresses are the "folk" features of folklore and Richard
Bauman (1986) might call the "performative environment" of narratives.
Certainly, chance utterances in an account might indeed refer to occasion
or circumstance. An interviewee, for example, might ask the interviewer,

"Do you mean when I'm at home or at work?" Or an informant might say "Things are like that during the week, but it's a different place on the week-end." Otherwise, significant details about storytelling settings are often missing in individual accounts either of inner life or of social worlds. Transcripts, for example, usually don't reveal a setting's discursive conventions. They don't specify what is usually talked about, avoided, or frowned upon. They often are silent about the consequences (for storytellers and others) of communicating stories in particular ways. While there is no strict line of demarcation between stories and storytelling, we need to know the details and working conditions of narrative occasions if we are to understand narrative as it operates within society.

Stories are assembled and told to someone, somewhere, at some time, for different purposes, and with a variety of consequences. These factors have a discernible impact on what is communicated and how that unfolds—whether that is taken to be about inner life or about a social world. A life story might be told to a spouse, to a lover, to a drinking buddy, to an employer, to a clergyperson, to a therapist, to a son or daughter, or to a team member, among the huge variety of audiences. The occasion might be a job interview, part of a pick-up line, a confession, or a recovery tale. The consequences might be amusing or life threatening. The point is that the environments of storytelling mediate the internal organization and meaning of accounts.

Let's revisit Shaw's presentation of Stanley's story as a pathway to considering how stories take shape within society. Direct references to storytelling occasionally do appear in *The Jack-Roller* as Stanley describes his world. But Shaw's focus on the content of the story and his decided interest in the social world of juvenile delinquency eclipses what could otherwise come into view. Shaw understandably overlooks what Stanley is *doing* with words as Stanley tells his own story. Shaw's focus is on insider information for its value in understanding the delinquent life. As Shaw notes at the start, case studies, especially in the form of subjects' own stories, serve to reveal with greater depth social worlds on their own terms. According to Shaw, case studies are ideal for getting beyond and beneath the surface facts provided by official statistics.

In considering what Shaw overlooks, it is important to keep in mind that Stanley conveys some of his story in the context of his experience in the Illinois State Reformatory, to which he was sent when he was 15 years old. Shaw explains that this "institution receives commitments of youthful male offenders between the ages of 16 and 26" (p. 103), so Stanley had many other delinquent youths to look up to or look down upon on the premises. Status, apparently, was an important feature of inmates' social ties, something that is glaringly obvious as Stanley tells his story. If Shaw argues that the delinquent boy's "own story" compellingly reveals his social world, he fails to notice that Stanley's account is descriptively variegated, that Stanley actively shapes his story to fit the circumstances. More generally, Shaw fails to notice that stories operate *within* society as much as they are about society.

Consider how Stanley describes the daily round of life in the institution, an environment that poses distinct challenges to how Stanley stories himself. We begin with his first days in a cell, which make him "heartsick." We also hear about the role his cell mate plays in helping him "get used to things."

> When the whistle blew for breakfast the next morning I was heartsick and weak, but after visiting with my cell mate, who took prison life with a smile and as a matter of course, I felt better. He said, "You might as well get used to things here; you're a 'convict' now, and tears won't melt those iron bars." (pp. 103–104)

Stanley looks up to his cell mate Bill and, interestingly enough, Stanley virtually steps out of his story to inform the listener/reader that what one says about oneself is narratively occasioned. Referring to his cell mate, Stanley explains,

> He [the cell mate] was only seventeen, but older than me, and was in for one to ten years for burglaries. He delighted in telling about his exploits in crime, to impress me with his bravery and daring, and made me look up to him as a hero. Almost all young crooks like to tell about their accomplishments in crime. Older crooks are not so glib. They are hardened, and crime has lost its glamour and becomes a matter of business. Also, they have learned the dangers of talking too much and keep their mouths shut except to trusted friends. But Bill (my cell partner) talked all the time about himself and his crimes. I talked, too, and told wild stories of adventure, some true and some lies, for I couldn't let Bill outdo me just for lack of a few lies on my part. (p. 104)

Given the situated nature of this account—which narratively orients to Stanley's relationship with other inmates and what that means for his social status—it is apparent that this is far from simply being Stanley's "own" story. Stanley actively shapes what he says to enhance his standing with Bill and other inmates. The account is evidently sensitive to its circumstances. The content and the theme of the story are as much a matter of what Stanley does to enhance his position with cell mates as they are faithful renditions of his social world. At this point in his narrative, Stanley can be viewed as telling us that he occasionally does *status work* when he recounts his experience. His storytelling has a purpose beyond straightforward description.

We might figure in this regard that a particular narrative environment (the reformatory) and narrative occasion (a recollection within an interview) mediate the content and emphasis of the story being told. The environment and the occasion "own" the story as much as Stanley does. And there is no reason not to believe that other narrative environments and narrative occasions would do the same. Stanley's storytelling responds as much to the practical contingencies of storytelling, as it reflects Stanley's social world. In his way, Stanley knows that the organization of his story and his circumstances as a storyteller are narratively intertwined.

There is other evidence that Stanley's presence in the reformatory prompts accounts that not only shape his social world but implicate his inner life. In the following excerpt, notice how Stanley laments his lack of narrative resources and what that means for who he is within.

> So I listened with open ears to what was said in these groups of prisoners. Often I stood awe-struck as tales of adventure in crime were related, and I took it in with interest. Somehow I wanted to go out and do the same thing myself. To myself I thought I was somebody to be doing a year at Pontiac, but in these groups of older prisoners I felt ashamed because I couldn't tell tales of daring exploits about my crimes. I hadn't done anything of consequence. I compared myself with the older crooks and saw how little and insignificant I was in the criminal line. But deep in my heart I knew that I was only a kid and couldn't be expected to have a reputation yet. I couldn't tell about my charge, for it savored of petty thievery, and everybody looked down on a petty thief in Pontiac. I felt humiliated in the extreme, so I only listened. (pp. 108–109)

A bit later, Stanley refers to a different narrative environment. The context this time isn't storytelling among reformatory inmates, but rather banter among male peers who gather on a city street corner. This now is Stanley putting his narrative skills and his story to work for a different purpose. The representational needs of this occasion entail the construction of both status and masculinity. Once again, the circumstances of storytelling are taken into consideration in shaping what Stanley's story turns out to be, the internal and external organization of the account interrelated.

> I went out to look for work, but it was scarce at the time. After a week of fruitless effort, I began to loaf around with the corner gang. These fellows were all working and doing well, but they had the habit of hanging around the corner and telling dirty stories about women. We took pride in telling about our exploits with such and such a girl, and tried to outdo each other in the number of women that we had conquered. (p. 118)

Conclusion

These extracts from *The Jack-Roller,* and Stanley's keen attention to the narrative reality in which his stories are embedded, turn us to how stories operate within society. While the content and organization of stories such as Stanley's are an abiding concern, a focus on narrative reality also directs us to how social circumstances figure in storytelling. This leads us to the important questions we will take up in this book: How are stories activated and put together in practice? How do circumstances mediate what is assembled? What are the strategic uses of storytelling? And how do the personal and social purposes and consequences of storytelling shape their accounts?

2

Forms of Analysis

Stories in society deploy a distinctive narrative reality along with a preferred form of analysis. Because the reality in view is about *both* the substance of stories and the activity of storytelling, it is imperative that in addition to what is said and recorded on any occasion, researchers go out into the world, observe and listen, and document narrative's everyday practices. If stories in society reflect inner lives and social worlds, society has a way of shaping, reshaping, or otherwise influencing stories on its own terms. The texts of accounts are important for narrative analysis, but so are the contexts, which we take to extend from interactional to institutional environments.

Narrative reality is not limited to the mechanics of communication. Stanley, for example, tells us about his experience in and out of a reformatory. He refers to his thoughts and feelings in the company of others. He describes his desires, his self-conception, his progress in life, his contacts with the underworld, his sense of being an outcast, and his placement in the private households that were part of his "social treatment." He is a skilled storyteller to be sure, but he also knows that there is something at stake in what he says, to whom, and for what purpose. These contextual matters are morally, not just procedurally, consequential for Stanley. While Stanley aims to tell a good story in the company of others, he has an eye on matters that extend beyond the immediate give-and-take of talk and interaction.

As text, Stanley's story is mostly about the substantive details of his own inner life and social world. The depiction is limited in scope, because the beginning and ending of the text that contains these details exist within the confines of the monograph reporting them. This provides little information about how the story is shaped for purposes other than Shaw's research needs. In narrative reality, however, the substance of a story is elastic, pulled and influenced by communicative circumstances. There is substance, and that is altered or recast from time to time and from place to place, including the differences between what Stanley would present to Shaw as opposed to various peers.

The substance of stories and the circumstances of storytelling supply the categorical and moral horizons of narrative reality. The distinction between inner lives and social worlds, for example, makes it sensible to story experience in ways that reflect one more than the other. The comment "I was pressured into it" rests on the substantive distinction; inner motivation or personal will is claimed to be trumped by the social world surrounding it. Or experience might be storied in terms of being caught in the clash between inner life and a social world, as suggested by the assertion that "my heart tells me one thing and the situation tells me another." Which way this goes and how that is worked out are matters of circumstantial contingencies and ongoing social interaction. This returns us reflexively to the mechanics of communication, whose artful and strategic work provides the motion toward narrative outcomes.

The substance of stories is the basis for noting similarities and differences between lives and worlds, as well as for conveying preferences. The substance of one articulated inner life may differ in both kind and degree from the articulations of another. To the extent these are categorically differentiated, we are likely to hear tales about, and accounts of, distinctive types of persons. By the same token, the substance of one social world can differ in both kind and degree from the substance of another. Here, too, the extent to which they are categorically differentiated is the basis of tales about types of social worlds and how they differentially affect individuals.

Stanley's is a story that, in Shaw's judgment, is enlightening for the window it provides on a particular social world. Like the Cornerville world that Whyte (1943) describes in *Street Corner Society*, Stanley tells the story of a social world with its own rules of description and narrative preferences. It is a world, in that regard, that privileges particular accounts and disparages others. It is a story that, from the outside, conveys moral shortcomings. It is about a "delinquent," after all, which resonates with marginality, disadvantage, rule breaking, and the need for reform, according to Shaw's sense of the moral worthiness of the story under consideration.

Narrative reality is also a matter of work, of the activity of storytelling. Stories aren't simply conveyed, but they are given shape in the course of social interaction. How things are put or unfold is as important as what is said and in what circumstances. Stanley was well aware of the effort needed to secure proper membership in the delinquent world of which he was a part. He was an active, purposeful storyteller, not just a purveyor of information. The agency of storytelling is certainly an integral part of narrative reality.

We emphasized "both" at the start of the chapter because, in practice, narrative reality centers on both the substance and the activity of story-telling. To focus on substance alone, as Shaw does in *The Jack-Roller*, pro-vides the rich detail of Stanley's own story and, by extension, his social world, but it leaves the situated shaping of the account undistinguished. To be sure, Stanley provided glimpses of how his storytelling was designed for various recipients, of what was at stake for him in his social world, and the possible consequences for his identity of telling his story in particular ways. But Shaw's book is decidedly less concerned with this as it is with portray-ing the social world of juvenile delinquency from the inside out.

Narrative practice brings what is told and the telling together to deploy a rich empirical terrain. The particular form of analysis required to describe and understand this reality takes account of both the substantive and the performative, drawing together diverse stories of selves and social worlds on the one hand, with the concerted work of storytelling on the other. The pro-cedure of choice for opening this to view is ethnographic fieldwork oriented to texts and textualization. It is a method with sufficient alacrity not only to take note of the substantive dimensions of accounts but also to document the accounting process in the various circumstances that shape it. This method of procedure is at the heart of *Analyzing Narrative Reality*, extending con-cern with storytelling texts to their communicative contexts.

Analyzing Story's Internal Organization

Before we turn directly to field methods, it will be helpful to have the form of narrative analysis centered on texts in the background for purposes of comparison. In the text-based approach, the internal organization of stories, typically their characterization, modes of emplotment, themes, and other textual features, are of central concern. The contrast with the analysis of nar-rative reality comes with the latter's decided interest in both the internal and external organization of accounts, especially how the two relate in practice to produce situationally adequate stories.

Several books offer guidelines for how to conceptualize and analyze the internal organization of stories (see Bertaux, 1981; Clandinin & Connolly, 2000; Cortazzi, 1993; Daiute & Lightfoot, 2003; Herman & Vervaeck, 2005; Kenyon & Randall, 1997; Lieblich, Tuval-Mashiach, & Zilber, 1998; Riessman, 1993). Some are out of print and many are heavy on theory. Two are exemplary because they are readily available and provide practical models for, and illustrations of, the analysis of life story texts—Amia Lieblich and her associates' (1998) book *Narrative Research* and Catherine Riessman's (1993) book *Narrative Analysis*.

Lieblich and her associates distinguish three uses of narrative texts in social research. One is for exploratory purposes. When not much is known about a particular topic, narrative inquiry can be used to identify researchable questions. Small or strategic samples of stories from focal populations might be collected as a prelude to the identification of variables that can later be operationalized for further study. For example, narratives can provide a preliminary in-depth view of the lifestyle of an unfamiliar group such as a gang or a social movement. This was Shaw's aim in producing *The Jack-Roller*.

A second use is for research on stories themselves. This deals more with the organization of stories than with the subject matter. Vladimer Propp's (1928/1968) analysis of Russian folk tales was pioneering in this regard. Propp noticed similarities in otherwise diverse stories and argued that the fairytale had a narrative form common to all storytelling. Actions and characters functioned in limited ways despite the diverse subject matter. For example, a witch or a dragon provided the evil force in tales of struggle and victory. From this perspective, a dragon that kidnapped the king's daughter could serve the same function as a force of evil as the witch who snatched a baby from its mother's arms. While dragons are not witches and king's daughters are not necessarily babies, it could be argued that they played identical narrative roles in the accounts. As Terence Hawkes (1977, p. 69) explains, "The important thing to notice is that [Propp] is dealing with discernible and repeated structures." Note that the functions under consideration here are functions served within the story, not functions served within storytelling circumstances.

A third use of narratives that Lieblich and her associates identify is philosophical and methodological. Inquiry in this case centers on what narrativity can contribute to a deeper knowledge of individual and group experience, which is juxtaposed with the typically thin contributions of positivistic methods. For example, Polkinghorne's (1988) book *Narrative Knowing and the Human Sciences* speaks to the growing debate about the place of narrativity in a variety of fields, including, oddly enough, the sacrosanct narrative contours of scientific inquiry.

The rest of Lieblich's book is devoted to a discussion of four strategies for analyzing the internal organization of life stories. The strategies result from the intersection of two analytic dimensions: whether the whole story or a part, such as an utterance or theme, is under consideration; and whether content or form is of primary interest. A holistic-content reading of narrative material deals with entire stories and their contents. For example, one might compare the content of stories of recent versus long-time immigrants for the extent to which they deal with adjustment issues. This is the kind of analysis that W. I. Thomas and Florian Znaniecki (1918–1920/1927) undertook in examining the content of letters written by Polish immigrants in America to relatives in Poland, as well as letters received by the immigrants from their homeland. Thomas and Znaniecki viewed the letters as a window on the immigrants' social world. A second strategy is a holistic-form reading of narrative material. In this case, stories might be compared for whether they progress along a continuum such as from scene setting, characterization, and plot elaboration, to climax and wrap-up. A third strategy entails a part-content reading. In this case, specific parts of stories are examined, such as beginnings or endings, for the presence of particular substantive usages, such as distinct wording and self/other references. The fourth strategy involves a part-form reading. Here one might study the relationship between narrative coherence as a facet of stories, on the one hand, and how coherence relates to the form of emplotment, on the other.

The other exemplary text focused on the internal organization of accounts is Riessman's (1993) book *Narrative Analysis*. Riessman begins by explaining that we do not have direct access to experience, but rather our sense of who and what we are, as well as the character of our social worlds, is constructed by formulating these into stories. The analysis of narratives thus becomes a way of analyzing experience. Inasmuch as storytellers are active in shaping their accounts in addition to communicating information, stories re-present inner lives and social worlds. While Riessman's constructionist slant on narrativity is clear, this does not extend to the situated practices of storytelling. The activeness she assigns to the storying process centers on the agency underpinning intratextual matters. The book is nonetheless valuable for the models it provides for doing this form of analysis.

One model Riessman highlights is Faye Ginsburg's (1989) study of the lives of 35 women activists in Fargo, North Dakota, who were divided in their views on abortion. Riessman describes how Ginsburg explored the ways the women constructed their positions narratively, comparing the linguistic and substantive differences between pro-choice and right-to-life activists. The analysis showed that the women developed very different plot lines for their experiences. Referring to excerpts from pro-choice activist Kay Ballard's story, Riessman describes Ginsburg's approach.

Kay illustrates the typical pro-choice plot line [absent in right-to-lifer stories]: being different in childhood (Excerpt 1); questioning the confines of motherhood through a particular reproductive experience (Excerpt 2); a conversion upon contact with feminism in the 1960s and 1970s (Excerpts 3 and 4); and a subsequent reframing of understandings of self, women's interests, and ideals of nurturance (Excerpts 4–7). (p. 30)

Riessman illustrates another model using Susan Bell's (1988) research on the stories of DES (diethylstilbestrol) daughters. Bell explored how these women understood the risk of developing reproductive tract problems, including infertility and vaginal cancer, from using DES. She was especially interested in what might have led the women to become politically active in response to the adverse medical consequences of the drug. Bell used William Labov's (1972b) structural categories and method of transcription in her analysis, coding stories into an initial *abstract* reference to the problem (for example, "that sort of brought the whole issue of DES much more to the forefront of my mind"); followed by *orienting* information (for example, "when I was around 19"); to *complicating* action (for example, a discussion of what happened to the storyteller as a result); and finally to a *resolution* (for instance, "and that's when I um began to accept the fact, y'know, once it made sense"). Such stories might be analyzed further for the point at which the voice of medicine is incorporated into the plot, or when and in what way resistance to medical discourse develops. Alternatively, one might ask whether those who resist medical discourse and develop counter-stories preface this so that a triumphant resolution follows. The point would not be that DES daughters engage in narrative machinations, but rather that differences in experience have discernable narrative contours.

Riessman herself (1990) applies a version of this approach in her important work on accounts of divorce. She analyzes divorce stories not only for the way plots depict social life, but for how distinctive themes and the internal shape of accounts differentially construct the divorce experience. Her book, *Divorce Talk*, shows how "women and men make sense of personal relationships"— in this case divorce—through storytelling. It emphasizes the way divorce is differentially emplotted by men and women. Riessman's analysis of the internal organization of the accounts reveals not only what those experiences are like for each group, but how each group puts this particular experience together narratively. The analysis indicates that gender differences serve to inflect divorce in distinctive ways. As the back cover of the book points out,

To explain divorce, women and men construct gendered visions of what marriage should provide, and at the same time they mourn gender divisions and blame their divorces on them. Riessman examines the stories people tell about their marriages—the protagonists, inciting conditions, and culminating events—and how these narrative structures provide ways to persuade both teller and listener that divorce was justified.

Narrative Reality and Ethnography

As we noted earlier, analysis of the internal organization of stories is based on accounts typically elicited in interviews. The storytelling process is mostly hidden from view. Analysis is limited to textual by-products. In contrast, our interest in narrative practice takes us outside such accounts and their transcripts to varied storytelling occasions, raising new concerns. While the substance and the internal organization of accounts continue to be of interest, this now extends to concern with how the circumstances of storytelling—which range from interviews to street corners and households—mediate what is said and how that is assembled for the telling. Would Ginsburg's women activists, for example, have constructed their accounts the same way in circumstances different from those in which their accounts were elicited for Ginsberg's study? Would Riessman's men and women divorcees have featured the same recollections, explanations, and emphases in divorce talk conveyed, say, within groups of sympathetic friends or skeptical strangers? These kinds of questions require an immersion in narrative reality. As Francesca Polletta (2006) explains, "Stories are differently intelligible, useful, and authoritative depending on who tells them, when, for what purpose, and in what setting" (p. 3).

We are fortunate that Shaw's text does reveal some of the circumstances that shaped Stanley's life story. But these come to us mostly by way of Stanley's offhand observations, not Shaw's research design. What would we have learned had we been present in the reformatory or on the street corners or in the urban neighborhoods in question? How might others' accounts have affected what Stanley talked about and how Stanley told his story? We do know from bits and pieces of Stanley's account that he was occasionally encouraged to enter particular conversations and to embellish certain stories. We also know that there were other occasions when he was reluctant to do so. His story apparently occupied a salient position in some social worlds and was unheard in others. It is evident, too, that Stanley's feeling about himself and his identity as a young male delinquent and hanger-on were affected by the circumstances.

All of this suggests a different research method and form of analysis, which turn directly to narrative practice. Method needs to take account of what Stanley says and how he says it, but also should be sensitive to the narratively contingent conditions of assembling an account. This is undertaken with an eye to the consequences for the storyteller of storying experience in particular ways. Significantly, it would also consider stories told by others about Stanley, extending narrative analysis into complex networks of accounts.

Moving in this direction, we would want to avoid judging the adequacy of Stanley's and others' accounts simply on the basis of individual memory, rationality, or representational fidelity. Certainly, these affect what we know about people's lives and how we evaluate their accounts. Some people remember very little, while others appear to have photographic memories. Some seem eminently reasonable and straightforward in their accounts, detailing step-by-step what they have been through and what experience might mean to them. Others meander. There are those whose stories hardly conform to what is otherwise known to be the truth of the matter, which might prompt us to figure that they are, perhaps, lying or "denying" reality, as some put it. But evaluating stories on individual grounds would fail to take account of the profoundly social influences on narrativity, which, if known, can cast an altogether different light on such ostensible shortcomings. We return to this in Part IV of the book, where we address the issue of narrative adequacy.

It is the practical dimensions of narrativity that we spotlight and that call for a form of analysis and related research procedure that take us outside of stories and their veridical relationship to storytellers and experience. The method of choice might be called "narrative ethnography," that is, the ethnographic study of stories (see J. F. Gubrium & Holstein, 2008). Unfortunately, the term "ethnography" has taken so many meanings and usages in recent years that it now is almost synonymous with qualitative inquiry (see Atkinson & Hammersley, 1994). Not abandoning the term, we have something more specific in mind, a method attuned to discursive contours and old-fashioned naturalistic observation. It is a method of procedure and analysis involving the close scrutiny of circumstances, their actors, and actions in the process of formulating and communicating accounts. This requires direct observation, with decided attention to story formation. The approach clearly resonates with contextually rich work done in the ethnography of communication (Hymes, 1964), the study of orally performed narratives (Bauman, 1986; Briggs & Baumann, 1992; Ochs & Capps, 2001), and ethnographically grounded studies of folk narratives (Glassie, 1995, 2006).

Being on the scenes of story construction and storytelling, and considering how stories are shaped by the contingencies of communication, is not simply window dressing for the form of narrative analysis that is centered on texts. Settings are integral parts of narrativity. Whoever heard of a story being told nowhere, at no time? Even stories told to researchers like Shaw, or to therapists or in job interviews, are occasioned and conditioned by storytellers' and listeners' descriptive agendas and substantive objectives. Erving

Goffman (1961) put this succinctly when he wrote of the need in his own work for ethnographic access to experience. Writing about the ostensibly irrational, even the mad, he explained:

> My immediate objective in doing fieldwork at St. Elizabeth's [psychiatric hospital] was to try to learn about the world of the hospital inmate, as this world is subjectively experienced by him. . . . It was then and still is my belief that any group of persons—prisoners, primitives, pilots, or patients—develop a life [story] of their own that becomes meaningful, reasonable, and normal once you get close to it, and that a good way to learn about any of these worlds is to submit oneself in the company of the members to the daily round of petty contingencies to which they are subject. (pp. ix–x)

Concern with the production and reception of stories in society requires that we step outside of narrative texts and consider questions such as who produces particular kinds of stories, where are they likely to be encountered, what are their purposes and consequences, who are the listeners, under what circumstances are particular narratives more or less accountable, how do they gain acceptance, and how are they challenged? Accordingly, we might ask how Stanley's story is told in the context of inmate talk at Pontiac as opposed to the bravado of the street corners he frequents. We might wonder how the "daily round of petty contingencies" of each occasion for story-telling shapes Stanley's accounts. This would require us to examine the narrative organization of these occasions. It would turn us to stories as they are being put together, told, and received (or not told and received, as the case might be). We would need to listen to and take account of how stories are taken on board, consider what might be preferred tellings in particular circumstances, and explore the risks and outcomes of storying experience in conformity, or out of line, with what is expected. We would need to pay serious attention to the possibility that narrative occasions and circumstances have privileged stories.

A growing body of ethnographic studies has begun to address such questions. For example, Gale Miller's (1997) book *Becoming Miracle Workers: Language and Meaning in Brief Therapy* is a historical account of the shift in institutional discourse that led to altered ways of conceptualizing selves and doing therapy in an individual and family counseling clinic. Miller's approach to the ethnography of institutional discourse (Miller, 1997) is a form of narrative ethnography. His book is a powerful demonstration of how a comparative ethnographic approach provides insight into how lives, troubles, and their solutions are storied and how that changes through time. Darin Weinberg's (2005) book *Of Others Inside: Insanity, Addiction, and*

Belonging in America pursues a similar theme. While Miller discusses how therapeutic narratives changed over a decade in the same institution, Weinberg discusses how two purportedly identical treatment programs became dissimilar narrative environments to accommodate different residential circumstances.

Organizational differences are further highlighted in *Out of Control: Family Therapy and Domestic Disorder* (J. F. Gubrium, 1992), which describes narratives of family troubles in distinctly different therapeutic venues. Susan Chase's (1995) *Ambiguous Empowerment: The Work Narratives of Women School Superintendents* and Amir Marvasti's (2003) *Being Homeless: Textual and Narrative Constructions* offer nuanced examinations of the accounts of some of society's most and least successful members, accenting the context-sensitive narrative work that is done to construct vastly different stories of life and its challenges.

We should note that our use of the term *narrative ethnography*, and the perspective to which it refers, differs in important ways from another popular usage. Some social researchers have applied the term to the critical analysis of representational practices in ethnography. Their aim is to work against the objectifying practices of ethnographic description. Practitioners of this form of narrative ethnography use the term to highlight *researchers'* narrative practices as they craft ethnographic accounts. They feature the interplay between the ethnographer's own subjectivity and the subjectivities of those whose lives and worlds are in view. Their ethnographic texts are typically derived from participant observation, but are distinctive because they take special notice of the researcher's own participation, perspective, voice, and especially his or her emotional experience as these operate in relation to the field of experience in question. Anthropologists Barbara Tedlock (1991, 1992, 2004), Ruth Behar (1993, 1996), and Kirin Narayan (1989), and sociologists Carolyn Ellis (1991), Laurel Richardson (1990a, 1990b), and others (Ellis & Bochner, 1996; Ellis & Flaherty, 1992) are important proponents of this genre. The reflexive, representational engagements of field encounters are discussed at length in H. L. Goodall's (2000) book *Writing the New Ethnography*, while Carolyn Ellis (2004) offers a description of the autoethnographic approach to narratives.

The version of narrative ethnography we are formulating is less immediately self-conscious about researchers' representational practices. Accommodating naturalistic, ethnomethodological, and conversation analytic impulses, our approach focuses on the everyday narrative activity that unfolds within situated interaction. It entails an acute awareness of the myriad layers of social context that condition narrative production. While we are aware of the reporting and writing strategies and the tropes of ethnographers, we are more centrally concerned with the narrative practices of the people and circumstances ethnographers study.

As ethnographers of narrative practice, we have been in the habit of both listening to and taking systematic note of actual and possible stories in various settings. Our research procedures have varied from in-depth life history interviews in nursing homes (see J. F. Gubrium, 1993), to courtroom observations that completely eschewed interviewing (see Holstein, 1993), to studies that combined observation, interviewing, and discourse analysis (see J. F. Gubrium, 1992). As we have plied the traditional craft of ethnographic fieldwork, we have used a range of in situ modes of inquiry to discern the organization of narrative reality.

In systematically observing the construction, use, and reception of accounts and textual material, we have found that the internal organization of narratives, while important to understand in its own right, does not tell us much about how stories operate in society. This isn't a judgment about the explanatory value of text-based narrative analysis, but rather is meant to highlight what can be added to that approach if we attended to narrative production. While the themes and plot structures of stories such as accounts of jack rolling, sexual abuse, or childhood socialization might be identified and documented, discerning how these relate to particular social contexts requires an understanding of what people do with words to create and structure meaning. As Stanley teaches us, the same account might be appreciated in one setting or at a particular time, but be disparaged, ignored, or silenced in others. This, we believe, is a valuable partner in the project called "narrative analysis."

Conclusion

Herbert Blumer (1969) once argued that concepts are as much procedural as they are theoretical. They not only provide understanding but also sensitize us to ways of embracing the empirical world. Such is the case with the idea of narrative reality and the form of analysis presented here. The concept of narrative reality is both theoretical and empirical in specifying an analytic field and calling attention to an object of inquiry. It is procedural in that it recommends a method that is necessary to capture narrativity in its circumstantial complexity. Following Goffman, Hymes, Bauman, Briggs, and others, we aim to consider the social organization of the storying process. Narrative ethnography directs us to the talk, interaction, and going concerns that both inform and shape stories in society.

3

Into the Field

The empirical field of narrative reality centers on the reflexivity of narrative work and its environments. Given the operating components simultaneously at play, coming to grips with this field can be tricky. Stories are constructed and conveyed in myriad settings. In turn, the diverse understandings of these settings mediate the process of story construction. The trick is to approach this field in such a way as to avail oneself of the opportunity to document the complexity. Centered as text-based narrative analysis is on stories' internal organization, the conventional researcher enters a mostly transcribed narrative field. Our interest in the broader terrain of narrative reality requires a more nuanced conception of the field, one informed by an abiding sensitivity to the organization of communication and the situated features of accounts.

Getting Started

Having selected a narrative topic and interactional locale, fieldwork can move in two directions. Since one component of narrative reality is the everyday work done to assemble and communicate accounts, this might serve as a beginning. Given this choice, we would be drawn to the question of *how* stories are interactionally constructed for the purposes at hand. Alternatively, we might begin with the other operating component of narrative reality—narrative environments. Starting there, we would turn to questions of *what* meanings, understandings, and contingencies are storytellers up against in the circumstances. Given this choice, we initially would trace and document details of those circumstances and contingent meanings. Regardless of which starting point we choose, the interplay of the components oblige us to eventually shift analytic gears to bring into view how each component plays out in relation to the other. The key is to remember that narrative work and narrative environments are reflexively intertwined.

Precisely when a shift in analytic gears should be undertaken cannot be spelled out in advance. Some researchers instinctively move in one direction or the other to start, and then move on in the other direction (J. F. Gubrium & Holstein, 1997). More naturalistically oriented researchers would likely start with the narrative environment. Researchers with constructionist inclinations would likely begin by considering narrative work and subsequently take account of the local circumstances and challenges that condition that work. Some researchers would place more emphasis on one over the other throughout the research process, but nonetheless attend to both components in some fashion. Some prefer to continuously move back and forth, while others treat the shift in focus more as analytic steps in a formal research design. Circumstances themselves might determine which choice is most convenient. These are only a few of the factors that affect where one starts and when analytic shifts take place. That they do take place is at the reflexive heart of the approach presented here; this is more important than when the shifts should occur or what emphasis each should have.

Analytic Bracketing

Elsewhere, we have termed this process of shifting back and forth between the *hows* and the *whats* of narrative reality as *analytic bracketing* (J. F. Gubrium & Holstein, 1997, 2000; Holstein & Gubrium, 2000b, 2003, 2005). Analytic bracketing is related to a similar analytic strategy employed in phenomenological research, but it is not identical. The phenomenological version of bracketing begins analysis by setting aside all assumptions about the reality of personal and social forms in order to highlight the everyday assumptions that undergird the sense of the real, sustaining it over time (see Schutz, 1970). The phenomenological project starts from this initial bracketing move and continues within that framework. (See K. G. Young, 1986, for a useful discussion of the phenomenology of narrative.)

Analytic bracketing operates differently. It is applied throughout the research process, not just at the start. As analysis proceeds, the researcher intermittently orients to the different aspects of narrative reality. At one stage, for example, the researcher may be more or less indifferent to circumstances and available narrative resources in order to document features of narrative work. In the next analytic move, he or she might bracket narrative work in order to assess the local availability, distribution, and/or regulation of resources and circumstances that condition narrative production. The researcher may eventually revisit narrative work to describe how resources or circumstances are brought into play in working up accounts. The procedural goal is to shift the analytic focus to capture the interplay between narrative work and its environments.

It is important to emphasize that analytic bracketing is a methodological, not an ontological, move. It is a strategy for shifting analytic perspectives in order to capture complex empirical terrain. Bracketing has sometimes been wrongly construed by social researchers in ontological terms, leading to questions about the very nature of objects, being, and existence (see, e.g., Heidegger 1962, 1967; Husserl 1931, 1970a, 1970b). When philosophers of social science have raised ontological issues, considerable controversy and confusion about the constructionist project and its empirical concerns have ensued (see Holstein & Miller, 1993; Woolgar & Pawluch, 1985). Our approach to analytic bracketing takes an agnostic position vis-à-vis ontological matters, focusing instead on what is subjectively treated as real without needing to resolve philosophical issues. From our perspective, bracketing is a way of temporarily putting some matters of empirical interest aside in order to bring other matters into focus. The strategy is not designed to question the ultimate existence or the substance of reality, nor is it intended to minimize the everyday work of reality construction. Rather, it provides a procedural basis for considering narrative work without depicting it as purely artful and unconstrained by substantive resources and circumstances. At the same time, it provides justification for describing narrative environments without giving the impression that they determine narrative construction.

A key element of analytic bracketing is the refusal to grant analytic primacy to one operating component of narrative reality over the other operating component. The interplay between narrative work and environments is pivotal. The components are viewed as mutually constitutive; each reflexively depends upon and incorporates the other. Consequently, one can't argue that analysis should necessarily begin or end with any particular component. If we are indifferent regarding the question of which should come first or last, or which should be assigned priority at some point of the research process, we can designate a reasonable starting point from which to begin and proceed from there.

Still, there can be rhetorical value in emphasizing one component over the other (P. Atkinson, 1990, 1992; Clifford & Marcus, 1986; Geertz, 1988; J. F. Gubrium & Holstein, 2000; Van Maanen, 1988). For example, more naturalistically inclined researchers can aim to illustrate what is omitted from narrative reality when there is too great an emphasis placed on the process of storytelling. Highlighted, in contrast, are the scenes of narrative production, such as the institutional cultures and social structures that influence the work of storytelling. The rhetorical force of these studies capitalizes on what a procedural preference makes empirically available. Other researchers with decidedly constructionist leanings are more attuned to the organization of language use from the start. They, too, reap the rhetorical benefits of a procedural preference, such as the aim of showing how the realities of varied narrative environments, like indigenous codes of conduct, are actively and continuously constructed. (See Maynard, 1989, 2003, for alternate discussions of points of analytic departure and emphasis.)

The classic instance of a research report that teaches the empirical lessons of analytic bracketing is D. Lawrence Wieder's (1974) book *Language and Social Reality*. The book presents the results of an ethnographic study of language use in a halfway house for ex-convicts. We'll return to Wieder's study later in the book when we raise the question of what is a good story, but it's useful to mention here because it is exemplary. The first part of Wieder's report on life at the halfway house has naturalistic sensibilities. This perspective on the field led to observations of how the "convict code" presented itself as a normative device for informally regulating behavior on the premises. The second part of the book describes what Wieder found when he bracketed the code as a recognizable set of behavioral strictures. Bracketing allowed him to examine how the code was actually used in practice. He was able to show that the code was a variable and emergent narrative resource whose regulating function was continually constructed in ongoing interaction between the ex-cons and staff members. The rhetorical force of the results stemmed from the concerted application of analytic bracketing.

On Interactional Terrain

Analytic bracketing alternately provides access to different components of narrative reality. Bracketing the *whats* of narrative reality opens to view the everyday work or *hows* of storytelling. This is interactional terrain. Moving into the field from this perspective, analysis centers on the discursive give-and-take within which narratives are formulated (see Chase, 2005). Storytellers work at assembling their stories, artfully picking and choosing from what is experientially available to articulate inner lives and social worlds. Narratives are actively and inventively crafted. Stories don't simply emerge from within, as if they were stored there for the telling. As Polletta (2006) advises,

"We should flesh out the discursive and organizational mechanisms by which culture defines the bounds of strategic choices, rather than locating those mechanisms in people's heads" (p. 5). Nor are narratives mere reproductions of social worlds. As Harold Garfinkel (1967) might caution us, storytellers are neither automatic information transmitters nor cultural "dopes." Rather, they strategically construct their accounts, organizing experience in the process. Listening or recording carefully and documenting these actions are critical to data collection.

In this arena, ethnographic fieldwork centers on the myriad aspects of social interaction from which narratives are formulated. The analytic focus necessarily moves beyond the internal organization of narrative texts. Training our sights narrowly on texts might lead us to overlook the interactional work that prompts, precipitates, and contextualizes accounts. The analytic trick is to neither dissolve stories into pure artifice, nor sacrifice the artfulness of storytelling to the structure and themes of stories in their own right.

The interactional terrain of narrative reality includes the specific constructive methods used by storytellers and others to assemble their accounts. Artful as the construction process is, it is also systematic and makes use of various devices for putting together accounts. This applies at the very start of the narrative process, including the activation of accounts, which is commonly ignored, if not altogether unavailable, in textual analysis. Storytellers do not simply lie in wait to tell their stories. Nor do they simply break out, unprompted, into storytelling (see Chapter 4). Someone activates the process, and this may or may not be the storytellers themselves. Someone may ask someone else "What's happening?" which may prompt elaborate storytelling that would not otherwise have emerged. In such a case, it is clear that the start of someone's story begins somewhere other than within the storyteller. Such starting points are not necessarily found at the beginning of transcripts of accounts, especially if prompting mechanisms are viewed as the mere facilitators of narrativity and are not included in text. This is important, because narrative activation can move accounts in different directions. A request to "Tell me about what happened at the party," for example, is likely to generate a different story, beginning from a different starting point, than if the same narrator were asked to "Fill me in on what's happening between you and Denise." The point is that the interactional terrain of narrative reality is not just artful but artfully *methodical*, and includes the discernible procedures storytellers deploy to assemble accounts that align with alternative middles and endings.

Interactional terrain extends to processes of meaning making—how storytellers assemble stories that make sense to themselves and others. Once a narrative is activated, the researcher can consider how it is put together in a way that is meaningful to an audience. Of course, documenting the interactional terrain of narrative work invariably leads the researcher toward the situated character of interaction and, in particular, to local understandings. There is no such thing as a generally meaningful account, one that makes sense across all situations, even while we commonly orient to this as a matter of principle. Meaningful accounts are generated for the purposes at hand, which fieldwork on interactional terrain can document and analyze.

On Situational Terrain

The reflexive relation between the work of storytelling and the environments within which this work transpires also implicates the circumstances of narrativity. What a brief account or extended life story means on one occasion may be substantially transformed in other circumstances. An account may be formulated in a particular way for one audience, and notably altered for another. Practical purposes also come into play. Bracketing the *hows* of narrative work helps reveal the contingent understandings and communicative conditions of storytelling—or the *whats* of narrative reality. This is situational terrain.

The work of storytelling doesn't occur in a substantive vacuum. As skillful and active as storytellers and listeners might be methodically assembling and responding to accounts, their actions transpire in the here and now of narrative occasions. Narrative work takes place in real time, in concrete places, often in relation to specialized interpretive demands, utilizing distinctive vocabularies and knowledge (also see Chase, 2005; Loseke, 2007). A psychotherapy clinic, for example, provides a different situation for storytelling than a retirement party. The clinic furnishes a substantive agenda that shapes the meaning and organization of accounts on its own terms. The situational terrain of the clinic provides a preferred, often medicalized, vocabulary for assigning motives to experience (Mills, 1940), for characterizing troubles, and for projecting solutions. The narrative environment of the clinic is an accountable context of its own for storying experience. As a narrative environment, a retirement party is commonly light-years away from this, one that can humorously disparage what the clinical context privileges.

Stories are told in light of local understandings, in order to achieve particular outcomes. Situated demands may be formal or informal, compelling or contrived. Narratives are tacitly persuasive, since they always advocate a particular version of reality that is related to what is at stake for storytellers in the circumstances. Stories are formulated to address particular interpretive communities, both near and distant (Fish, 1980). They are not just assembled more or less skillfully, but with objectives that may have little connection with a storyteller's intentions. If stories are at all viewed as generalized accounts, their generality in practice is formulated out of the particulars of their consideration.

Situational terrain includes the specific audiences—both present and anticipated—to which a narrative is or might be addressed, or to whom it may be (or become) accountable. In this regard, the field is both prospective and retrospective. In practice, the interactional circumstances of storytelling are always the emerging situation at hand, with the storyteller (and the researcher) ongoingly glancing backward and forward in time. It is important to remember that narrative work does not simply unfold within the immediate spatial, temporal, or interpretive boundaries of particular interactional or organizational situations. While audiences may be tentatively specified, they have a way of contracting and expanding as occasions cast the net of narrative relevancies in various directions.

Situational terrain is a landscape of meaning-making preferences. On this front, the moral horizons of stories and storytelling are paramount. The shape and meaning of a narrative is subject to local understandings and expectations for how a story should be composed as well as for preferred outcomes. A tale of teenage troublemaking, for example, may be told in a particular fashion in the presence of adolescent peers, but reconfigured for presentation in a juvenile court or a child guidance clinic. Recall how Stanley closely monitored his circumstances and appropriately recast his own story of criminal exploits for local consumption. Such occasioned differences suggest that anyone's personal story may vary from telling to telling, based on the meaning-making relevancies and consequences of what is said. The result is a variegated field of preferred and dispreferred narrative meanings and story organization.

Some of the most important contingencies of narration are the material mediations of a social setting. The appearance of people's bodies, the location of rooms and objects such as doors and furniture, and lighting can prompt particular kinds of storytelling (Goffman, 1959). So-called mood lighting is far from being simply emotional; it is meant to fashion particular kinds of storytelling. The mood lighting of a tavern, for example, is meant to signal the emotionality of accounts in a different way than the mood lighting of a classroom or a clinic. Buildings, architecture, and other material conditions can relate to situated meaning in the broadest terms, coming in the form of discourses that give shape to buildings. Michel Foucault (1965, 1975, 1977) has argued that the discourses of particular sites and institutions establish not only conceptual but also visible limits for storytelling—"conditions of possibility" for plausible, accountable stories. Such preferences continually come into play as individuals fashion accounts.

Culture also plays out on situational terrain. The characterization of behavior as "charging around like a bull in a china shop," for example, draws upon a cultural cliché to supply a constellation of meanings, casting the behavior as recklessly out of control rather than as innocently impulsive, say. Clichés, cultural idioms, figures of speech, subcultural argots, professional jargon, organizational terminology, and institutional categories all provide locally preferred vocabularies and categories for storytelling. Increasingly, in today's world, on situational terrain we are witness to stories spoken through the voices and under the auspices of formal organizations. For example, the narratives of alcoholic demise and resurrection typical of Alcoholics Anonymous (AA) meetings are individuals' stories, to be sure. But they are spoken in the now familiar voice of an organization, lending personal stories a distinctive AA flavor and trajectory in this case, thanks to the AA vocabulary and schema for characterizing the alcoholic experience (see Holstein & Gubrium, 2000b). The personal account thus is both an individual's narrative and AA's story at the same time (see Narayan & George, 2002).

Data Collection

In situ data collection is essential to documenting the field of narrative reality. The researcher needs to collect detailed data in the actual settings where narrative work is undertaken. Data collection procedures differ from the methods applied in text-based narrative research. The aim in analyzing narrative reality is to capture details of both present-time interactions and the various contextual elements that influence those interactions, as each of these relates to accounts and storytelling. In some respects, this mandate resonates with the traditional ethnographic admonition to provide "thick description" (Geertz, 1973) of settings and interactions (see Emerson, Fretz, & Shaw, 1995). But in addition to capturing substantive circumstantial details pertinent to storytelling, the narrative ethnographer is especially concerned with documenting discursive actions and transformations.

Most ethnographic data collection methods are useful in this regard, but must be fine-tuned to capture sufficient conversational detail to support the form of narrative analysis under consideration here. Traditional field notes, for example, sometimes include discursive detail, but often they amount to more or less detailed paraphrases of what actually transpired. Field notes are never literal reproductions of field realities. As inscriptions (Emerson et al.,

1995; Geertz, 1973), they invariably alter actions, events, and social settings because these reports are filtered through the field-worker's note-taking limitations, preconceptions, conventions, framing, and other forms of subjective perception and reporting. Whereas traditional field-workers strive for rich portrayals of the field, which can then be used to describe social settings, narrative ethnography is especially concerned with a setting's communicative activity. Consequently, the field-worker interested in narrative reality aims to capture as much of the unfolding verbatim detail of interaction as possible. This makes it possible for the researcher to later provide in vivo illustrations of narrative practice.

Audio- or videotape recordings may be the best method of securing discursive data of this kind. They allow for a detailed consideration of what has been said. When conducting formal interviews, such recordings generally pose only minimal challenges for the field-worker and are usually worth whatever they might cost in terms of the informant's and interviewer's self-consciousness or willingness to be completely forthcoming about the parts they play in narrative production. Of course, tape-recorded interview material cannot be substituted for observed interaction, especially since this material offers little of the social organization of settings. It does, however, provide the opportunity to revisit the data to uncover patterns that might not have been apparent in earlier listenings.

Riessman (1993) offers an excellent discussion of recording and transcription techniques that is pertinent both to text-based narrative analysis and to narrative ethnography. As we will show in the following chapters, detailed notes or transcripts of conversation are most useful for analyzing the interactively unfolding narrative work that constructs accounts. In such instances, the fine-grained details of conversational sequencing and structure are necessary. Taking a cue from conversation analysis (Sacks, 1992a, 1992b; Sacks, Schegloff, & Jefferson, 1974), researchers can analyze the turn-by-turn production of matters such as narrative activation, production, and closure. This requires the notation of turn exchanges, pauses, overlaps, and silences (see Holstein, 1993).

In ethnographic fieldwork, it is often impossible to record all the talk, and sometimes even some of the talk, that transpires. Naturally occurring interaction may be too spontaneous, unstructured, sensitive, or private to allow for tape recording. Sometimes, tape recording is not permitted, such as in legal or therapeutic venues. In such instances, the field-worker must rely on note taking to capture the desired data, even while this can result in summary descriptions of some of the interaction. Close to verbatim notes on pertinent spates of talk should be jotted down as much in speakers' own words as possible. Field-workers should avoid the editorial "filtering" that sometimes goes on in the field because it may screen out communicative detail important to the analysis of narrative practice. Later, attempting to reconstruct accounts becomes difficult, if not impossible, if important detail hasn't been recorded in the first place.

Addressing the needs of discursively oriented researchers generally, Candace West (1996) suggests that there is good reason to produce highly detailed field notes that approximate verbatim records of talk. J. Maxwell Atkinson and Paul Drew (1979) refer to these as "do-it-yourself" transcripts. Because tape recording can be impractical, do-it-yourself transcripts may be the best available option and have often proved to be very useful. Taking such notes is challenging and may be successful only in highly formalized institutional settings such as court hearings because interactions there are extremely predictable and ritualized, and turns at talk are pre-allocated (see Holstein, 1993, Appendix; West, 1996).

Of course, this is easier said than done, since taking such detailed notes on talk is challenging and often tedious. West (1996) offers an enlightening discussion of both the practical and analytic limitations of do-it-yourself field transcripts, and instructs researchers about the occasions when such practices might be appropriate, and when they might be overly ambitious, if not impossible. In doing so, she makes two crucial points. First, it is essential to collect data at the level of detail necessary and appropriate to the goals of analysis. Second, the researcher should be careful not to make analytic claims that cannot be supported by the level of detail available in the recorded data. Researchers producing field transcripts of narrative practice should take heed of these admonitions.

But the situational terrain of narrative reality always beckons. If notes or transcriptions of talk and interaction are important for analyzing narrative work, detailed ethnographic field notes are required for capturing the richness of narrative environments. This is another important difference between the form of narrative analysis under consideration here and the form centered on textual material. Because the field is conceptualized more broadly than just the narrative text itself, conventional ethnographic fieldwork techniques are useful. They provide information that describes the circumstances that shape narratives, such as the audiences in place and the purposes for which they are addressed. Procedurally, this means that the field-researcher needs to be attuned not only to talk and interaction, but to the everyday contexts of narrative production.

Interviews have provided much, if not most, of the data examined in text-based forms of narrative analysis. While the analysis of narrative reality demands access to naturally occurring interactional and situational data, interview material nonetheless remains important. As some have argued, in a so-called interview society, interview encounters are prime settings for constructing accounts (P. Atkinson & Silverman, 1997). As Ken Plummer (1995, p. 4) puts it, we live increasingly in societies in which "tell, tell, tell" leads the way in social interaction. But, as far as research procedures are concerned, narrative researchers need to keep in mind several important features of interview dynamics as they conduct interviews and analyze transcripts.

Traditional approaches to interviewing tend to view the interview as a medium that transmits information (Holstein & Gubrium, 1995a; Kvale, 1996; Wooffitt & Widdlecome, 2006). The informant or respondent is treated as a repository of answers or stories about his or her inner life and social world. The interview is seen as a means of tapping into that repository. As will become clear in the following chapters, in narrative reality, interview results are as actively constructed, collaborative, and situationally mediated as other communicative ventures (Holstein & Gubrium, 1995a). As such, it is important to treat interviews as occasions for narrative work and not just information transfer, considering the dynamics of *how* interview narratives are constructed and *what* transpires under their auspices.

Interviewing in narrative ethnography might proceed much like traditional interviewing (see J. F. Gubrium & Holstein, 2002). Interviewers would observe many of the guidelines and strictures that conventionally inform the interview process. At the same time, however, the narrative ethnographer should be keenly aware of the unavoidably collaborative nature of the process (see Holstein & Gubrium, 1995a). As a consequence, researchers should take more explicit note than usual of their participation in the interview conversation, recording their contributions along with those of the informant.

Typically, in text-based studies, the interviewer's role is obscured in, if not eliminated from, the final transcribed narratives that are subjected to analysis. While an interview guide is occasionally appended to an analysis, narratives are commonly presented as unified productions, as single, coherent spates of talk produced by the informant. A concern for the interactional work involved would suggest that the give-and-take of the interview process be included in data sets. Again, Riessman's (1993) book provides important insights into how the questioning process should be analyzed as part of narrative production. Holstein and Gubrium's (1995a) book *The Active Interview* specifies how the interview can be conceptualized as an active, constructive narrative occasion and how interview data may be accordingly analyzed.

There has been considerable debate in social research about the advantages and disadvantages of using naturally occurring data versus the sort of contrived or prompted data that result from formal interviews (see P. Atkinson & Coffey, 2002; Becker & Geer, 1957; Lynch, 2002; Potter, 2002; Speer, 2002). In analyzing narrative reality, naturally occurring talk and interaction is preferred for at least two reasons. First, it offers accounts that are less apt to be formulated in the terms and constructs provided by researchers. And, second, it better reflects the indigenous language, constructs, orientations, and diverse circumstances that condition accounts. But there is no reason in principle to avoid structured interviews as a means of eliciting stories, so long as the narrative work that is done during the interviews and the environmental mediations of interview talk are taken into account.

Conclusion

The complexity of narrative reality prompts a word of analytic caution. Stories commonly connote extended accounts of something, such as a significant experience, a spectacular event, or an interesting dimension of inner life. The texts of stories that some narrative researchers analyze can run to 20 or 30 pages of transcription. Researchers often think that the longer the story, the better, especially if rich and compelling detail comes along with it. The note of caution is that such accounts rarely emerge spontaneously on narrative terrain. Narrative work and its environments have a way of shaping stories in their own terms, for their own purposes, and for the time available. We would guess that most narrative occasions do not yield the lengthy, coherent, and detailed accounts commonly desired in text-based narrative research. In everyday life, most narratives are shorter and far from the sole-authored entities that the texts of individual stories would suggest. It is helpful to be prepared to engage surprisingly abbreviated accounts, convoluted storying, remarkably repetitious narratives, and the less-than-unified commentaries that commonly inhabit this terrain—all of which have good practical reasons for taking the forms they do.

PART II

Narrative Work

Accounts that transpire in narrative reality are much more than what is simply set in print. The transcript of a life story appears in black and white, seemingly frozen in place and available for continuous inspection and analysis. In everyday life, the "same" account changes in meaning and in its consequences, depending on speakers' and listeners' purposes and the circumstances. If there is a text to a story, its plot, theme, and organization develop in relation to its many practical connections and the diverse contexts within which it is presented and heard. Researchers who limit their analysis to written texts out of context are faced with the challenge of either not knowing or having limited access to narrative production.

The chapters of Part II turn us to the everyday work that enters into the construction and elaboration of stories. The term *work* suggests that someone or other actively orients to a task; narrative work is purposeful effort. It isn't automatic or driven by outside forces. It's also craft-like in that it relies on the artful application of communicative skill. In practice, there are issues of when and how to provide accounts and there are problems of meaning to deal with. Solving such problems requires strategic effort.

Narrative work is not done self-consciously. Rather, the concrete challenges of living command people's practical attention. Narrative work goes mostly seen but unnoticed. The goal of Part II is to open this work to view, orient the researcher to its mechanics, and provide an analytic vocabulary that captures how it operates. We begin with a chapter on narrative activation, which deals with the mechanisms that spawn the production of stories. The chapters that follow turn to the mechanics of meaning making, the process of putting together meaningful accounts. This ranges from the linkages that are drawn between things said and done, and the elaboration of these linkages into meaningful wholes, to the performative contours of narrative presentation, the collaboration of participants, and the operating controls that constrain accounts.

Stanley's story continues to lead the way. The reflexivity of his account and its analytically telling moments echo throughout Shaw's book. As we discuss the many mechanisms of narrative work, references to or excerpts from Stanley's story serve as touchstones for the kind of narrative analysis being presented. From chapter to chapter, we find that even if stories are textual and even if their storytellers' performances seem scripted, the boundaries and organization of these texts and scripts are produced through the continuing work of storying everyday life.

4

Activation

Narratives are ubiquitous. Catherine Riessman (1993, p. 54) suggests that the "impulse to narrate is . . . natural, and apparently universal." Implying that stories are always there, just waiting to be told, she argues that they are readily available to researchers, if research procedures don't "get in the way." But do people just burst out with stories? Is the impulse to narrate an adequate springboard for storytelling? Recall that Stanley was quite circumspect about the matter, knowing in his fashion that if there was an impulse, it needed to be kept under control. This chapter turns to the interactional mechanisms that incite storytelling. The leading question is "How is storytelling activated in practice?" As we will show, this is far from being a matter of simply launching into storytelling.

Orienting to Activation

Narrative work envisions the subject behind the storyteller to be an agent who skillfully crafts stories in response to the communicative demands of everyday life. While this hardly sounds radical, it differs significantly from the storytelling subject presumed in much narrative analysis. When stories are viewed as "narratives waiting to happen," the storyteller is conceived, in broad strokes, as a repository of accounts that will emerge if only given the chance. The stories themselves are held to be the communicative property of the storytellers.

Narratives are thought to be especially revealing or informative because they are their subjects' personal accounts—"their own stories" (Shaw, 1930).

Their authenticity makes such stories special because they are thought to convey the actual circumstances and sentiments of the individual telling the story, as that individual (and only that individual) knows them to be. A kind of narrative humanism pervades this vision, casting individual accounts as genuine reflections of the lived experience retained within and recounted outwardly in relation to others, not produced in collaboration with them. The social contingencies of narration are assumed to be exogenous factors that might "get in the way" of the subject's already-formed expressions of experience.

In contrast and in practice, the narrating subject is enmeshed in a social world. If the narratives are personal, they are worked up and conveyed with others under discernible circumstances. To be sure, storytellers have access to unique storyable material, such as biographical particulars and recollections of specific life events. But such tellable material does not constitute narrative wholes. Narratives are not a mere collection of facts held within the subject and waiting to be tapped. As short or long, simple or complex as stories can be in practice, they are generated, put together, and communicated in some fashion (see Ochs & Capps, 2001). They need to be formed, told, and heard. As a result, the facts of experience are locally configured as storytellers and listeners actively take part in discursive exchanges. Storytellers and listeners respond to concrete exigencies, configuring accounts in the give-and-take of the process.

This view of the active (and situated) narrating agent has major implications for how stories and storytellers should be approached methodologically and analytically. Narratives emerge in context—interactionally, situationally, and organizationally. In practice, narrators are the architects and builders of their stories, but they accomplish their craft interacting with other storytellers and with listeners. The narrative process—from start to finish—yields an ever-emergent, pliant product that should be treated as something more dynamic than a more or less accurate, waiting-to-be-told text. Analysis needs to orient to the interactions and circumstances of narrative production as well as to the story that is produced. In practice, narratives are social to the core.

Harvey Sacks (1992b) provides a useful framework for approaching the sociability of narratives. Sacks tells us that stories in conversation are extended turns of talk. In describing stories this way, he suggests that studying narrativity requires us to look beyond the single spate of talk that is the traditional focus of text-based narrative analysis. It requires inspection of the conversational environment of accounts, especially the mechanisms that provide interactional space for an extended utterance. While we cannot do justice here to the entire analytic framework of what has come to be called "conversation analysis" or CA, a few rudiments will help us examine how storytelling is activated.

CA holds that "talk-in-interaction" is highly coordinated and methodically produced (see J. M. Atkinson & Heritage, 1984; Heritage, 1984; Sacks, 1992a, 1992b; Sacks, Schegloff, & Jefferson, 1974; Schegloff & Sacks, 1973; Silverman, 1998). Conversation analysts often use the metaphor of machinery to convey the systematic way that conversation is self-organized to produce orderly communication. The metaphor suggests that conversation proceeds in an orderly, methodic fashion, one person speaking at a time, in sequences of exchanges. Turns at talk do not merely follow one after another; instead, they work together as organizational units with methodic relationships between the different units. In conversation, mutual obligations are established by the structured relations of sequenced parts, with each conversational action projecting a next turn or preferred response (Sacks, 1992a, 1992b; Whalen, 1992). Changes between speakers occur at recognizable speakership transition points, preserving single-person speakership, with orderly mechanisms for designating who will speak next. While speakership exchange does not occur automatically, conversational participants are nonetheless accountable to this normative expectancy.

Speakers usually alternate turns at talk, with one person speaking at a time. A conversation may involve several speakers, however, so transitions from one speaker to the next must be orderly or conversational disorder arises. The challenge is to seamlessly transfer speakership from a first speaker to a single next speaker. Sacks, Schegloff, and Jefferson (1974) argue that coordinated, single-speaker turns are achieved with remarkable regularity, regardless of substantive variations in the conversation. This is even true when multiple potential speakers are involved. Turn taking is far from being extemporaneous or capricious. And it is also subject to cultural and institutional variation in turn-taking practices and normative expectations (see Drew & Heritage, 1992).

From the CA perspective, *adjacency pairs* are the building blocks of conversational organization. Schegloff and Sacks (1973) offer a simple description of how adjacency pairs operate: "Given the recognizable production of a first pair part, on its first possible completion, its speaker should stop and a next speaker should start and produce a second pair part from the pair type the first pair part is recognizably a member of" (p. 206). These sequences are normatively invariant, so that even when the second pair part is not forthcoming, the second speaker is required to show that he or she is oriented to the normative framework. When turn-taking "errors" or adjacency pair "violations" occur, participants exhibit their accountability by invoking "repair mechanisms." For example, when more than one speaker talks at a time, one of them may stop, recognizing the basic rule that only one person should be speaking. If speakership isn't shifted appropriately, the previous speaker may repair the sequence by speaking again, respecting the ongoing sequence-in-progress. The turn-taking system is preserved even when violations occur.

Fundamentally, CA views conversation as sequences of action. These sequences, and the exchange of turns within sequences, rather than individual utterances or sentences, are the units of analysis. Normative expectations regarding the turn-taking sequence virtually compel potential participants to pay attention to the ongoing conversation. Taking account of others means that speakers constantly orient both to what has gone before and what is likely to follow. Interactional accountability is thus achieved through the "recipient design" of one's contributions to the conversation (Sacks & Schegloff, 1979). That is, any particular turn at talk is crafted so that hearers are likely to understand what's being said and what's going on interactionally. Because speakers take one another into account, are prepared to show that they understand what is going on, and are ready to take their turns when appropriate, participants in conversation are truly partners. Conversation is a deeply collaborative enterprise.

Storytelling takes place in this sequential, collaborative, and interactional environment. As we shall see in the remainder of this chapter and in chapters to follow, narrative production requires constant orientation to both the emerging conversational context and the broader organizational matters that are themselves brought to bear in narrative production. This suggests the following guideline for orienting to the activation of storytelling:

Guideline

Be alert to the communicative machinery from which stories emerge. Consider how narratives are activated in the context of ongoing talk and interaction.

Into the Field

So how do narratives get started? How are they activated? Since, from a CA perspective, stories involve extended turns at talk, prospective storytellers are immediately obliged to secure the right to extend their turn in conversation (Schegloff, 1984). As Sacks (1992b, p. 18) puts it, a story is "an attempt to control the floor over an extended series of utterances." Contrary to the impulse-driven view of storytelling, the teller must be able to string together multiple sentences while holding the attention of listeners without having them intrude into the conversation with anything more than signals that they are paying attention. In other words, a space for storytelling must be established in the give-and-take of social interaction. The story must "fit in"; it must take account of both what previously has been said and what will likely follow in the conversation (Jefferson, 1978). This involves getting potential next speakers, who may themselves want to speak at the first opportunity, to allow the aspiring storyteller to speak. Then the narrator must hold the floor until the story is hearably complete. All of this activity can be construed as part of the work that goes into providing and securing narrative space.

Researchers might begin by scanning a spate of interaction for conversational actions that invite or incite a story. For example, a speaker may say something at a particular moment that reminds another participant of a story, which subsequently may or may not be told. Researchers should not presume a story's inevitable emergence. Following our guideline, they should examine the conversational environment for factors that incite or activate narrative production—or that curtail storytelling, as the case might be.

Gail Jefferson (1978) suggests a variety of mechanisms that are used to introduce or initiate a story. Most of them display a relationship between the emerging story and prior talk. They work to create a sequential environment that allows the story to emerge and establishes the appropriateness of the story's telling. Perhaps the most straightforward way a narrative enters a conversation is by way of a direct invitation or a question. Stories are often explicitly solicited; extended narratives can be openly invited. We find this, for example, in situations where one party requests information from another. This may take place in an informal setting such as the dinner table (e.g., "Tell me about your day, honey.") or in more formal information-gathering venues. Research interviews are a prime example, but media interviews and job interviews are similar. Indeed, interviews may be characterized in general as intentionally designed attempts to activate or incite narratives (Holstein & Gubrium, 1995a, 2000b).

Consider the following example from an interview project conducted in a nursing home. Jay, the interviewer, explicitly asks 82-year-old Rita Vandenberg to tell her life story, and the story quickly ensues.

Jay: Everyone has a life story. Why don't you tell me a little bit about your life?

Rita: Well, there's not much. I worked as a telephone operator before I was married. After I got married, I moved to New Jersey and had two boys. [The story continues uninterrupted, as Rita tells of her work life, her married life, her children, her extended family, her illnesses, and several other aspects of her life's experience.] (J. F. Gubrium, 1993, p. 29)

In the context of the research interview, this explicit request clearly opened space for storytelling and granted permission for the story to emerge in an extended turn at talk. The ways in which stories are invited or incited, of course, have implications for what sort of stories develop. Hence, the study of narrative activation should carefully document the different forms of incitement as part of the narrative process. Different forms produce different stories. Consider the implications of the following interview questions for the sorts of stories that ensue.

Example A: Miss Mary, why don't your tell me about your life? (J. F. Gubrium, 1993, p. 76)

Example B: A lot of people think of their lives as having a particular course, as having gone up and down. Some people think it hasn't gone down. Some people see it as having gone in a circle. How do you see your life? (Holstein & Gubrium, 1995a, p. 47)

Example C: As you look back over your life, what are some of the milestones that stand out? (Kimmel, 1974, p. 116)

Example D: Let me ask you this. If you were writing a story of your life, what chapters would you have in your book? Like what would the first chapter be about? (J. F. Gubrium, 1993, p. 158)

Each of these queries aimed to elicit a life story. All culminated in a direct question, an invitation to narrate the respondent's life. And each succeeded in eliciting a spate of storytelling. But consider how the form of incitement—the interview question itself—served as an activation resource as well as a prompt for assembling the story in a particular way. Example A, for instance, which followed a discussion of death and disease, elicited a story of the informant's recent illnesses, her husband's death, and the various jobs she had held (J. F. Gubrium, 1993). Example B produced a story of a complicated life, told in terms of the metaphor of a "tangle" (Holstein & Gubrium, 1995a). Not surprisingly, Example C generated a narrative of various professional milestones described as central to the informant's life (Kimmel, 1974). And Example D led to a series of accounts, each addressing a more or less discrete segment of the informant's overall life story (J. F. Gubrium, 1993).

The point to be gleaned from this is not that research questions "contaminate" informants' answers. Rather, it is a reminder to look outside the story itself for traces of the interactional environment that inform the narratives that emerge. Most interview studies fail to report, or generally gloss over, the interactional sequences within which narratives are produced. Our suggestion is to consider the conversational environment surrounding story-telling for the ways in which it activates particular kinds of accounts. Given this orientation, we wouldn't be so readily tempted to reach the conclusion that we had derived "a" life story. We would be less likely to overlook the dynamics of narrative production that contribute to the elasticity of accounts.

Storytellers themselves can pave the way for extended accounts, accomplished in the context of social interaction. Simple story "prefaces" (Sacks, 1992b), for example, are often used to set narratives into motion, securing the conversational rights and space for an extended turn at talk. Offering a preface signals that the speaker has a story to tell, thus announcing the reasonable expectation that the next speaker will allow the prospective story-teller to speak again and at length. From that point onward, the storyteller may expect that others will allow the story to proceed.

When looking for mechanisms of story activation, the researcher should be alert for the most recognizable of preliminaries of this kind, statements such as "Did you hear what happened to me last night?" or "I heard something interesting today." These prefaces virtually announce that there is a story in the offing and that other potential speakers should hold back until the nascent story is hearably complete (Sacks, 1992b). But even the simplest of story-opening gambits require cooperation, as in the following example:

Sally: The most fascinating thing happened to me today.

Pam: Oh, yeah?

Sally: Yeah, I ran into a teacher I had 35 years ago. [An extended story of the encounter follows.]

Note that Sally's claim to the opportunity to tell her a story proceeds because Pam encourages the storytelling in her turn at talk. In effect, after prefacing her story, Sally awaits Pam's tacit invitation for her to launch the narrative. The turn-taking sequence virtually demands it. Consider, for example, what might happen conversationally, if Pam had responded with "Yeah, I had a real exciting day today, too." Rather than continuing with her story in the next turn, Sally would have found herself vying with Pam for narrative space and opportunity.

The researcher should remember that opportunities and space for story-telling are never automatically achieved. These opportunities need to be artfully crafted within the ongoing flow of conversation. In the following example, an animated conversation is in progress, with mother and daughter discussing what the teenager will take for her school lunch. In the midst of the exchange, the daughter uses a type of story preface to clear the conversational space to tell her brief story. (Double slashes [//] indicate the onset of overlapping talk.)

1. *Mother:*   Whatter you takin' for lunch?

2. *Daughter:*   Peanut butter, there's nothin' else.

3. *Mother:*   What about yogurt?

4. *Daughter:*   I don't like yogurt.

5. *Mother:*   Wait a minute. You don't like yogurt?

6. *Daughter:*   Not // for lunch.

7. *Mother:*   // You won't eat yogurt? I ASKED you Tuesday what you'd eat and you specifically said yogurt. // Why do you think we bought it?

8. *Daughter:*   // No:::oo it's not that. I just I just I don't // want it.

9. *Mother:*   // That's it! You change your mind about what you'll eat twice a week. That's it. I'm makin' your lunch // from now on.

10. *Daughter:*   // No no::oo just lemme tell you // I wanna say something

11. *Mother:*   // What

12. *Daughter:*   I like yogurt, I know I said to buy it but I did NOT change my mind, I always eat it. I have always liked yogurt, but not for lunch. Not for lunch at school. I eat it at home. I am NOT changing my mind.

13. *Mother:*   Well how can I tell?

14. *Daughter:*   All right I'll EAT it. (Holstein & Gubrium, 2000b, p. 133)

In the exchange, both mother and daughter quickly claim turns at talk. They are in the midst of a disagreement and there is considerable contention over who is going to get to talk. Finally, at utterance 10, the daughter objects ("No no::oo") to her mother's prior declaration ("I'm makin' your lunch // from now on") and offers a preface that forcefully indicates that she has something to say that may involve an extended turn at talk ("just lemme tell you // I wanna say something"). This elicits an expression of interest and invitation to proceed from the mother ("What"), which in turn creates an opportunity and space for a story of the daughter's history of liking yogurt, which emerges at utterance 12. The prefacing move was instrumental in creating the opportunity to extend an utterance in a conversational environment previously marked by repeated contests for speakership. The story that eventually emerged was an artful, collaborative achievement. Here, again, taken out of narrative context, the story told in utterance 12 might easily have been read as the account of an obstinate child, without recognizing the interactional dynamics in which the utterance is embedded.

Issues relating to narrative rights, obligations, and power may come to the fore if the researcher takes seriously the fine-grained conversational work done to produce stories. (See Shuman, 1986, 2005, for extended discussions of narrative rights, obligations, and entitlements.) A social structural analysis would likely look to an individual's social status or roles, for example, as entitlements to storytelling, a topic to which we will return in Part III. We suggest that the researcher look closely at how narrative rights and control are actually enacted and achieved, rather than taking this for granted.

If status were the key to controlling speakership and narrative production, adults would likely do most of the talking and control the floor in adult–child conversations. But this is empirically far from the case. Sacks (1992a) tells us that, while adults often permit or encourage children to speak, children have many effective conversation-seizing devices at their disposal. Consider the following example from a dinnertime conversation where two parents and a grandmother were questioning three school-aged children about the standardized testing administered at school that day. In the midst of the conversation, a fourth child, 4-year-old Marticia, piped up:

Marticia: Guess what, Momma? Guess what?

Mother: What, baby?

Marticia: I got to take Coco [the neighbor's dog] for a walk today. [Marticia proceeds to tell a story of how she was invited to walk the dog and what happened on the walk.]

In a conversational environment where Marticia previously was nearly unable to get a word in edgewise, she used what arguably could be heard as a question of her own to secure the floor for telling her own story. This gambit trades on the normative convention that when asked a question, the next speaker is obliged to provide an answer or to indicate that an answer is not available, thus returning speakership to the person who asked the question. In this instance (as in most other instances of this gambit) there is no good answer to "Guess what?" By replying "What?" the mother explicitly invited Marticia to supply the answer to the original question that the mother herself could not supply. In so doing, she activated Marticia's story. (Alternatively, Marticia's utterance might be heard as a command, a riddle, or even an opening move in a childish game. In any case, the utterance was not designed to elicit an answer; regardless of how it is heard, it is more likely to provoke another question.)

Schegloff (1980) observed that it is common for prospective storytellers such as Marticia to gain access to extended turns at talk by asking questions themselves. "You know what?" or "You know something?" are common examples. Although such moves appear to prompt next speakers to answer the question, they are asked in such a way as to nearly ensure that an answer is not forthcoming. (Providing a substantive reply to "Guess what?" for example, would create the sort of normative "breech" that some of Harold Garfinkel's [1967] ethnomethodological demonstrations prompted. It would very likely lead to a breakdown in the conversation.) When no answer is available, another question—"What?"—is a warranted alternative. This, of course, provides the opportunity for the original questioner to supply an extended answer (see Schegloff, 1980).

Conversation analysis supplies myriad other insights into the methodic organization of talk-in-interaction that are pertinent to the study of narrative production. To be sure, we are not suggesting that the study of narrative be reduced to the mechanics of conversational sequencing. If the mechanics of turn taking provides space for storytelling, it does not construct the story. But attention to how narratives are incited and activated helps us to see how thoroughly interactional stories are, from the very start and throughout the storytelling process. In Marticia's case, for example, it helps us to take a more nuanced view of the idea that one's position in society determines one's storytelling rights.

Not all activating mechanisms are direct or explicit. Nor do they necessarily operate at the start of storytelling. By means of an unfolding series of exchanges, the overall flow of a conversation may itself be an activating mechanism. In the next example, we would be hard pressed to think of the life story that emerges as a continuously narrated whole because its activation unfolds throughout. We would be equally hard pressed to conclude that it was straightforwardly the respondent's own story, as ownership appears to be a diffuse artifact of participants' collaboration.

Recall our earlier discussion of how the following questions were used to activate a nursing home resident's life history narrative: "Let me ask you this. If you were writing a story of your life, what chapters would you have in your book? Like what would the first chapter be about?" (J. F. Gubrium, 1993, p. 158). We noted earlier that the emergent story portrayed the respondent's life in more or less discrete segments in response to the request for a chapter-like format. Here is how the life story eventually emerged. Carol is the interviewer and Opal is the resident.

Carol: Like what would the first chapter be about?

Opal: Fighting arthritis.

Carol: Fighting arthritis? That'd be the first chapter of your book? Okay. What would the next one be about?

Opal: How to handle it. [Opal provides a brief story of how she's managed her condition over the years.]

Carol: Other chapters?

Opal: Well the other chapters would be, as you realize it's getting worse, you have to see the limitations coming on . . . to accept them. [Opal continues a story of dealing with limitations and protecting her family from being overburdened by her health problems.]

Carol: What about the last chapter?

Opal: The last chapter? Well, I think it's not a terminal disease. [Opal continues with an extended narrative about persistence in the face of adversity, ending with an exhortation:] Don't give up. Whatever you do, don't give up.

Carol: I'm curious. I've asked some other people the questions, you know, about chapters, and most of them started out with things like their childhood. I noticed you went right away to arthritis. Why do you think you did that?

Opal: Because I've lived with it a long time and I'm so familiar with it . . .

Carol: So, it's been a huge thing in your life?

Opal: Oh, yes! [Opal talks again of disease and degeneration, and how she's suffered.] But I didn't let it win. That's my mission in life. (J. F. Gubrium, 1993, pp. 158–159)

As is clear in this interview conversation, narrative activation is an ongoing process. Opal's story is invited in the form of chapters, but they don't simply flow forth. Carol, the interviewer, maintains the chapter motif, repeatedly prompting Opal for another installment. By activating a series of small stories, Carol eventually gets Opal to assemble her "book-length" life story, which is thematized around disease, disability, and determination. If this is Opal's life history, formulated around her most salient and abiding concerns, it is not her story alone. Activated by Carol's repeated questions and enlivened by Carol's prompts, Opal narrates her life according to her own plans and preferences, but in collaboration with her conversational partner's proffered framework. To analyze this life story—as the book of Opal's life—without acknowledging Carol's contribution would shortchange its situated, collaborative character. This admonition applies not only to the analysis of interview talk, but also to those more "naturally occurring" contexts of narrative production.

Finally, it is impossible to discuss narrative activation without considering its absence. The flip side of story activation, of course, is narrative silencing. Just as stories need to be incited, opened up, and elaborated, they are also discouraged, preempted, ignored, and shut down. To fully appreciate the emergence of narratives, we must also empirically examine their failure to materialize. Silence is often attributed to macropolitical factors such as power, status, authority, and hegemony. To be sure, these are important considerations for appreciating narrative production. But it is crucial for our understanding of narrative reality to show how such forces are empirically manifested in the interactional circumstances from which narratives do or do not emerge.

Taken by itself, a transcribed narrative seldom demonstrates what is *not* said. The researcher might speculate regarding what was omitted, ignored, or could otherwise have been said, but ungrounded conjecture falls short of being an empirical explanation. The ethnography of narrative, however, affords the researcher the opportunity to focus outside the narrative itself, to consider narrative contexts and resources that may influence narrative production. But it is up to the researcher to demonstrate in explicit empirical detail how "external" factors shape how, when, and where particular narratives might emerge and flourish, or not emerge and flourish as the case might be. This is a mandate for the researcher to describe how phenomena such as narrative rights, power, obligation, authority, and entitlement are actually realized in socially situated interactional practice.

This amounts to showing explicitly in practice how narrative competition might emerge and be resolved, or how some narratives might come to be widely asserted or preferred, while other narrative possibilities remain dormant (see Vila, 2005, for a rich discussion of competition between discourses). As Pablo Vila (2005, p. 240) suggests, some narratives "have the upper hand in the struggle for the construction of hegemony. Consequently, they are much more locally available, have much more local prestige, and look much more locally genuine than others." It is the task of the narrative ethnographer to unpack the interactional, cultural, political, and organizational circumstances in which such hegemony is constructed. This may be accomplished, for example, by demonstrating ethnographically how cultural or organizational resources and preferences are brought to bear in the interactional production or preclusion of particular narratives.

It's one thing to claim that status, authority, or power "work behind people's backs" to control what they say or do. It's more compelling to actually demonstrate ethnographically how narrative resources, preferences, and entitlements are brought to bear interactionally to enact the narrative "power" of influential or privileged social actors such as doctors (Heritage & Maynard, 2006), judges and other officers of the court (J. M. Atkinson & Drew, 1979), teachers (Mehan, 1979), or therapists (Vandewater, 1983). One point of departure for such an analytic project is to show how different narrative strategies and resources are employed to activate or silence particular narratives. Alternatively, one might unpack the practices, circumstances, and resources brought to bear on other occasions of narrative collaboration, contest, and control (see Chapters 8 and 9).

Conclusion

The key analytic lesson of this chapter is to carefully consider the myriad interactional influences on narrative activation. Just as an interviewer helps shape an informant's responses, so does a partner such as a listener in ordinary conversation. A full understanding of storytelling (or narrative silence) requires attention to all participants in the process. While we can only surmise that storytellers impulsively narrate, we can empirically document the hearable mechanisms that prompt and sustain, or curb, the narrative process. We see this clearly as we step back to look at the talk and interaction that activate storytelling.

5

Linkage

The machinery that opens interactional space for storytelling does not generate meaning. In this chapter, we begin to consider the meaning-making process, viewed initially as a matter of narrative linkage (J. F. Gubrium, 1993; J. F. Gubrium & Holstein, 1997; Holstein & Gubrium, 2000b). In practice, no item of experience is meaningful in its own right. It is made meaningful through the particular ways it is linked to other items. Linkage creates a context for understanding. For example, we understand a choking incident linked with an illness differently than a choking incident linked with laughter. The first linkage forms a context of dire meanings with possibly morbid consequences. The second linkage forms a context in which the choking is likely to be "laughed off" as inconsequential in the immediate scheme of things. The chapter moves into the field by considering narrative linkage in two urban ethnographies, attending especially to how circumstance mediates the understandings that linkage puts into play. While linkage is part of the narrative work of everyday life, it reflexively responds to the purposes at hand.

Orienting to Meaning Making

In her book *The Ageless Self: Sources of Meaning in Late Life*, Sharon Kaufman (1986) argues that the meaning of growing old is not straightforwardly linked with chronological age. Nor, for that matter, is it directly linked with the specific era in which one came of age, such as the Great

Depression or World War II. Kaufman found, instead, that people in general, and the elders she studied in particular, make meaning on their own terms and in various ways. They actively participate in making their lives meaningful; they are not simply products of their age or of the times in which they came of age. To say, for example, that older people view themselves as aged because they have passed a certain chronological marker, or that the generation of the Great Depression has a particular identity, short-changes the complex linkages put into place by the aged themselves as they story their lives.

Kaufman's perspective resonates with the rallying cry of narrative researchers from Mayhew to McAdams, who encourage researchers and others to turn to the indigenous construction of accounts and not be taken in by popular understandings or monumental historical claims. In Kaufman's view, if old people take account of age and reference historical events, which indeed they do, these events do not operate as narrative tethers. Instead, they enter their accounts as narrative resources. Individuals *use* age and the events of their lives to make meaning on their own terms. Identifying her research aim to be old people's own accounts of their lives—how they view where they've been and have come to be what they are now—Kaufman explains:

> My method was to gather data on old people's view of their lives and to con-centrate on the ways in which they interpret their experience. My goal was to study aging through the *expression* of individual humanity. *The old Americans I studied do not perceive meaning in aging itself; rather, they perceive meaning in being themselves in old age.* (p. 6; italics in the original)

Kaufman comments on this as it bears on the interviewing process, in which she provides opportunities for indigenous meaning making to develop. Her sentiments resonate with the guideline we will offer for how to orient to meaning making in the formulation of accounts. The comment casts storytellers as purposeful narrative agents of their inner lives and social worlds.

> In my interviews with many old people who reflected on the course of their lives, I found that the ageless self maintains continuity through a symbolic, cre-ative process. The self draws meaning from the past, interpreting and recreat-ing it as a *resource* [italics added] for being in the present. It also draws meaning from the structural and ideational aspects of the cultural context. (p. 14)

The approach takes inspiration from the orientation to culture adopted by Clifford Geertz (1973), as the following epigraph from Kaufman's book indicates:

Believing, with Max Weber, that man is an animal suspended in webs of significance he himself has spun, I take culture to be those webs, and the analysis of it to be therefore not an experimental science in search of law but an interpretive one in search of meaning. (Kaufman, 1986, p. 5)

The sense of linkage and narrative agency described by Kaufman and culled from the short excerpts from Stanley's own story, discussed earlier, provide an opening to the work of meaning making. Meaning making is a practical activity that transpires in particular circumstances and puts into play the available resources for constructing stories. Meaning making cannot be reduced to accounts simply lurking within inner life, awaiting the opportunity to be expressed by storytellers. Nor can meaning making be reduced to the reproduction of shared understandings. Linkage and other meaning-making activities have their own everyday logic, for which the following analytic guideline is pertinent:

Guideline

Taking care not to presume that meaning is self-evident, be open to the linkages actively used to assemble meaning in particular circumstances. Focus on the occasioned work of meaning making, documenting its contextual parameters. Do not assume, reductively, that linkages will be drawn directly from inner formulations or automatically reproduce cultural or historical understandings.

Into the Field

Where does one go to observe narrative linkage in operation? How does linkage coalesce into constellations of meaning to produce contexts of understanding? Answers to these questions can be found both inside and outside of narrative texts. The internal organization of a story text does provide evidence of meaning-making activity. The resulting linkages can be analyzed by examining how a storyteller has assembled biographical, cultural, and historical particulars into a meaningful account. For example, transcripts can show how mothers and fathers with different cultural backgrounds and views of childrearing are able to link together bits and pieces of their relationships with children to construct similar accounts of good parenting. Conversely, similar subjective concerns and shared cultural understandings can, when drawn through differential linkages, lead to divergent meanings and contrasting accounts of what it means to be a good parent (see Kurz, 2006; Warner, 2006). The general point is that, while the meaning of things is formed from the linkages storytellers put into place, the particulars can be linked together in different ways.

But circumstances, purposes, and stakes in the matter also come into play, which can't be readily discerned in text-based material. We need ethnographic knowledge to sort out how linkages form meaning in practice. We initially illustrate how a set of linkages in a brief account can yield contrasting contexts for understanding when put to use for different purposes. The account is drawn from Elijah Anderson's (1999) discussion of the mating game in his book *Code of the Street,* part of his research on decency, violence, and moral life in the African American community. The discussion shows how an account of courtship can serve distinctly different purposes, whose identical textual linkages generate contrasting meanings when differential stakes in the matter are brought to our attention.

According to Anderson, male peer group standards in the community place a high premium on casual sex. "Getting some" is taken very seriously as a measure of a young man's worth. Young men continually "describe their successful campaigns as 'getting over' young women's sexual defenses" (pp. 150–151). In this context, females and their bodies are objects of a competitive "sexual game." Winning brings status to the conquering male, but simultaneously makes "a fool of the [conquered] young woman" (p. 150). At the same time, if young men work assiduously to develop their "game," young women have more complex stakes in the matter and are generally wary, fully cognizant that the game has varied meanings, not all of which are in their interests.

Anderson describes both male and female perspectives on the game, indicating many of the subtleties of sexual conquest, resistance, and the genuine romantic attachment that might be involved. Encounters and relationships are seldom narratively straightforward. Consider, for example, how a 23-year-old woman who became a single mother at age 17 describes the game as she knows it.

> Yeah, they'll [boys will] take you out. Walk you down to Center City, movies, window shops. [laughs] They point in the window, "Yeah, I'm going to get you this. Wouldn't you like this? Look at that nice livin' room set." Then they want to take you to his house, go to his room: "Let's go over to my house, watch some TV." Next thing you know, your clothes is off and you in bed havin' sex, you know. (p. 153)

This narrative is presented to show that the young woman conveys considerable skepticism regarding the young man's actions and intentions. In this case, according to Anderson, her purpose is to disparage the outcome. Linking together a set of what might otherwise be viewed as acts of courtship, the woman connects them in her own way to construct the boy's seduction plot. Anderson's ethnographic work provides background information—the sort of knowledge shared by the participants in the game—against which the narrative and its linkages are meant to be understood. The background information, not just the linkages alone, constructs a context for understanding. From information that Anderson provides, we can see how the woman constructs a negative scenario through the ways she links the particulars of the situation.

It is important to note that the seduction plot is not evident from the transcript alone. If the preceding reading of the extract's linkages are negative, different purposes and stakes can form a context that alters its meaning. Anderson points out that young women are not only wary, but also have romantic dreams of their own. According to Anderson, "This dream involved having a boyfriend, a fiancé, or a husband and the fairy-tale prospect of living happily ever after with one's children in a nice house in a good neighborhood—essentially the dream of the middle class American lifestyle, complete with nuclear family" (p. 151). In this context, with this purpose and stake in tow, the linkages supplied in the preceding extract (going out, walking to Center City, going to the movies, window shopping, promises of future gifts, expressions of interest in domestic life such as the living room set) provide a different understanding. Indeed, taken together, the linkages read like an inventory of qualities and actions a young woman might actually look for in a partner.

The ethnographic knowledge supplied by moving outside the young woman's account—outside the text—presents distinctive contexts and a resulting complex narrative terrain for understanding the linkages that are drawn. A young woman can completely transform the potentially positive meaning of these linkages by drawing them together as evidence of a pattern of deception aimed only at sexual conquest. Against the background knowledge Anderson provides, the linkages make the seduction gambit clear. But, as Anderson indicates, another reading is possible in the context of young women's romantic dreams. The "same" linkages can be used to construct the particulars of a much more desirable plot. Text-based narrative material would not readily show evidence of these alternative meanings. The lived and circumstantial dimensions of linkage are likely to be missing—unless the storyteller, like Stanley, steps outside of the account to contextualize it for us.

Some circumstances boldly problematize meaning making and the different ways linkages might be drawn. Victor Turner (1985, 1986) focuses on how rituals work to performatively produce and reproduce shared worlds of meaning from ambiguous situations (Turner, 1985, 1986, 1969/1995). He describes such situations as "liminal" phases in which meaning production is especially complex or unclear. Turner uses the term *liminal* to characterize circumstances where roles, relationships, and identities are particularly uncertain or problematic. In liminal phases, linkages may be drawn in several directions, producing varied contexts of understanding. Senior-level college students, for example, are no longer constructed as novice learners, but they haven't graduated either, and therefore continue to retain student characteristics. Their identities are betwixt and between, as it were, tenuously located in a life course that is otherwise highly ritualized in its progress. This can apply to the meaning of the body as well. A child who looks like an adult in size and stature, yet still resides with his parents and does not support himself, stands with one foot over the threshold of adulthood while the other foot remains behind in childhood. He looks like an adult, it might be said, but is still (a child) dependent on his parents.

We find Turner's concept of liminality to be quite useful in analyzing narrative practice, and as we will see shortly in discussing the narratives of so-called exotic dancers, ritual can be used strategically to manage what is otherwise unclear. The concept can be applied to highlight the complex narrative work that transpires in narratively fluid circumstances, where ritual figures more as a narrative resource than a storytelling template. The work of meaning making is foregrounded in liminal circumstances because the allocation of narrative linkages has little immediate direction. This works in tandem with ritual usage to sort ambiguity.

The classic organizational role of the shop foreman has been viewed as distinctly liminal. While foremen are commonly recruited from the ranks of workers, they are responsible to those higher up in the organizational hierarchy, even while an informal identity with and allegiance to former coworkers remains in place. The foreman's narrative challenges and purposes are neither firmly embedded in management nor in labor. Under the circumstances, we would expect foremen's work narratives to be continually subject to divergent linkages. The persistent need to choose between competing narrative options highlights the challenges and tensions of foremen's accounts of their work.

The job circumstances of "sex workers," including prostitutes, exotic dancers, and dancers for hire, are also highly liminal. The ambiguous narrative impulses of "the sex game," for example, has been of longstanding interest to social researchers (Cressey, 1932; Donovan, 1920, 1929; Gubrium, 2007). This game is somewhat different from the mating game that Anderson writes about. If liminality is present in what Anderson describes, it transpires in the competing contexts of "the game and the dream," one of sexual conquest and the other of romanticized domesticity. The narrative liminality of the sex game referenced by Donovan, Cressey, Egan, and others centers on the competing contexts of business and romance.

The betwixt and between of business and romance is omnipresent in Paul Cressey's (1932) classic study of the taxi-dance hall. The taxi-dance hall was a popular urban institution in the American recreational landscape of the 1920s and 1930s. Attractive young women were hired for a "dime a dance" by male customers, many of them unmarried immigrants. The term "taxi dancing" derived from the idea that, like taxis, the women could be hired for the intended purpose. While the purpose was formally recreational, a sex game tensely located at the border of love, sexuality, and economic exchange was always present—along with its competing narrative linkages.

The standard come-on line and lingo of these "working girls" applied the language and demeanor of commitment and sexual attraction for profit. Sometimes the girls actually "fell for," and became emotionally involved with, customers, which echoed love stories, not accounts of cash transactions and "making a bundle" on a particular customer. The latter accounts linked together fun and profit, not intimate relations and dedication. The love stories of these working girls could become desperate, as customers aimed to turn a recreational service into sexual servicing or prostitution. Meaning making in the liminal shadow of profit, pleasure, devotion, and love was a continuous narrative challenge.

Applying this chapter's analytic guideline in such circumstances turns the researcher to the shifting linkages within girls' stories about customers, dancing, and the social world of the dance hall. It would suggest taking note of, and field notes about, what the girls say to each other about their work, about themselves, and their customers and intimates. An important issue might be how accounts of the past, present, and future unfold in the circumstances, especially as the balance of narrative linkages shifts back and forth between the competing contexts of profit and love. The analytic aim in this case would center on how the girls sort the competing linkages and contrasting understandings, and in the process manage their complex relations with customers.

Danielle Egan's (2006) urban ethnography *Dancing for Dollars and Paying for Love* brings this up to date. Her study of the relationship between hired dancers and their patrons takes place in what are now called "dance clubs," where women dance "exotically" on stage for male customers. Egan participated in the exotic dance scene as both worker and ethnographic observer. Listening to dancers' stories and reflecting on her own experience, she takes note of the complex narrative linkages of the sex game. In the dance clubs, the sex game transpires in the context of "dancing for dollars," not for a dime a dance, and can extend to the sexual exchanges of lap dancing. Egan explains that "during a lap dance a seminude or nude woman grinds her genitals, buttocks, and/or breasts against a man's lap. . . . Men are required to keep their hands off women's breast and genitals (though they may touch a woman's back)" (p. 16).

The narrative tension apparent in the title of Egan's book is perennially present in the clubs. Much of the book deals with what Egan calls "leaky boundaries," with an explicit reference to liminality. This refers to the competing narrative options available to the dancer for formulating her identity in relation to customers. Also in focus are the narrative linkages constructed by regular customers, whose stories crisscross the border between customer and lover. Liminality is sometimes painfully in view, shadowing stories of intimacy and avoidance on the dancer's side and intimacy and desire on the patron's side.

Consider dancers' narratives of intimacy and avoidance. As dancers tell stories of their relations with regulars, it's evident that they work to keep purely economic or "customer" linkages in the foreground of their narratives. This is especially difficult when regulars become friends and confidants; as familiarity and trust develop, linkages that signify intimacy and desire easily come into play. Egan's dancers show a decided awareness of the ease with which intimacy can trump avoidance when emotions veer out of control. As the final comment below in dancer Serenity's conversation with Egan indicates, the work of keeping the border in place "isn't always easy"—because it's leaky. Egan uses her first name Danielle in the extract, initially lamenting the extra effort that goes nowhere when she "stupidly" spends too much time with customers.

Danielle: Yeah. I am stupid sometimes. I sit with a guy for an hour.

Serenity: Oh no. If they don't show interest in spending money quickly they aren't serious.

Danielle: So what do you think men want?

Serenity: Looks-wise or in general?

Danielle: In general, what type of woman do you think they want?

Serenity: Well, different men want different things. Some men like stupid women, some men like smart women, some men like artistic types, but at base they want women who are interested in them. You know it's fine if she's smart but she has to "want him," . . . she has to like to grind against him . . . and make him feel special. . . . Know what I mean?

Danielle: Yeah.

Serenity: That shit has to come across. . . . You have to be confident and be the slut. . . . It feels weird saying it . . . but it's true. If you're shy or hesitant or worried or pissed off or desperate for money, man . . . men pick that up.

Danielle: What about the regulars?

Serenity: They want a relationship. I'll tell you what, man, that shit isn't always easy. (p. 42)

Regulars are customers, of course, but their added friendship with the dancers encourages them to cross the border from intimacy and avoidance to intimacy and desire. The many stories the dancers hear from regulars—stories about their pasts, their present situations, and their future plans; stories rent with feelings, love, generosity, and hope—can lure dancers into offering heartfelt accounts of future, serious commitment in return. Dancers are well aware of this and, while expressly sympathetic, try not to indulge regulars' desires by embellishing the intimate meanings regulars repeatedly summon.

But if "that shit isn't always easy," shit nonetheless happens. As dancer Trena's following account illustrates, the liminality of the dancer role can readily let matters slip into a reversal of meaning, creating unwanted contexts. Trena indicates how painful this once was for her as she talked with Danielle about a "huge fight" that developed with her boyfriend John when they were out having a good time. The moral consequences of liminality and its slippery linkages are clearly at the forefront in her comments (cf. J. Emerson, 1970).

Trena: There was this one time when John and I were out at this bar and we were having a really good time. We were drinking and dancing. It was just really great.

Danielle: Mmm hmm.

Trena: And . . . this is embarrassing. [pauses]

Danielle: It's okay.

Trena: Well, I feel bad because I just, . . . because I started working the room like I was at work. I was flirting and walking like I was in the club. John got really hurt. We got in a huge fight. The fucked up thing was it just happened . . . I wasn't even conscious of it. It just happened. I was on automatic. (p. 60)

Such accounts are ethnographically telling. Trena's story boldly underscores the meaning-making function of narrative linkage, but also flags its complexity in liminal circumstances. The particulars were accountably different in their consequences on this occasion than they would have been if John hadn't been there. Like Stanley, Trena steps outside of her story to tell us as much. According to Trena, being "out at this bar" with John cast the same linkages differently than they would have been cast without him. The extract shows that linkage operates in relation to discernible contexts of meaning, which can unexpectedly overlap or work at cross-purposes in liminal circumstances. Such circumstances emphasize both the agency involved in sustaining tenuous narrative borders and the interpersonal risks tense borders generate. As Egan explains, "The line separating work and a date became fuzzy." Fuzziness, of course, is what liminality is all about. When fuzziness looms, as it did in the circumstance reported in the preceding extract, the work of meaning making is highlighted. The effort involved in keeping particular meanings in place is magnified, which again is something that is ethnographically discernible but often textually undistinguished.

Pointing to the narrative work that keeps customership and love, and their respective contexts, separated, Egan refers to the (ritualized) "script" she and others apply to deal with the accompanying meaning-making tension. References to scripts, tricks of the trade, well-known accounts, the usual stories, and other familiar narrative strategies are also ethnographically significant and should be carefully documented as part of the surrounding "ritual process." They indicate that narrative linkage is not a free-for-all nor uncontrollable, but relates to discernible horizons of meaning, the management of one's choices in the process, and its strategic resources.

Recounting a typical conversation with customer Marcus—and knowing full well that the typical is worked out in practice—Egan again takes up the meaning making at the leaky border of "dancing for dollars and paying for love," this time in context of actual talk and interaction. In the following extract, Marcus tries to establish himself as something more than a mere customer. Note Egan's strategic and otherwise ritualized use of accounts such as "I'm broke" and "It's just crazy now," as she then tries to maintain the illusion of intimacy while not actually crossing the contextual border of the relationship. She deflects but does not fully deny Marcus's narrative. She maintains her own "professional" position by being slightly vague or ambiguous about the prospect of her feelings being otherwise. All of this is part of the narrative work of managing a professional attitude while simultaneously playing upon the customer's "non-professional" desires. Marcus speaks first in the conversation, with Egan following in turn.

"I don't want to just be a customer."

"You aren't."

"Then why should I have to pay for time with you?"

"Because I am broke and trying to get through school, because I need to pay my bills."

"If you come home with me, I will pay all your bills. But we shouldn't have to pay to be affectionate. It's weird when I came here I was just looking for fun and some excitement and then I met you. I never thought I would meet someone like you. You know my colleague at work said that you guys [exotic dancers] just want me for my money, and that's all. But we're different. We have a great future together. I mean . . . I am more than your customer . . . right?"

"I have a wonderful time with you, it's great."

"Yeah it is . . . so when can I see you outside?"

"Soon . . . it's just crazy right now."

"Yeah of course."

"Why do you have to keep doing this [dancing]?"

"Rent. Bills. You know . . ."

"Yes."

"This is what I am doing to make it through."

"You shouldn't have to."

"I know."

"Those other guys are such assholes."

"I know."

"Yeah." (pp. 64–65)

In the end, Egan has sustained a customer–client understanding without destroying Marcus's more romantic inclinations. The narrative tension palpably relates to vagueness in meaning making.

Regulars do acknowledge the customer relationship, but other linkages point to a persistent agonizing desire. The latter is as much situational as it is realized in expressions of feeling. Regulars' accounts of hope for authentic love and of caring intimacy can be heartbreaking, as we see in the preceding extract. On the one side, regulars speak sympathetically of the dancers' need to "make money" and "earn a living." Regulars understand the direction this can take in terms of cultivating talk and interaction with dancers. On the other side, their status as regulars, not just customers, rides the coattails of "something special," separating them from being "just a customer." Egan notes that regular customer Marcus "wanted an authentic relationship and wanted to make invisible the fact that our relationship was a commodified one." At the same time, Egan reports, it was "one of the hardest parts of my job; trying to handle the challenge of having feelings of friendship, but having to feign feelings of romance and love" (p. 64).

Regular customers tell their own stories, of course. Their narratives also are mediated by liminality, but in their case relate as much to life with the dancers outside the clubs as within them. Regulars' desires, hopes, and their feelings about the dancers and other customers understandably orient more to the future than do the dancers' accounts. Dancers aim to keep the present in narrative focus, while regulars have a hopeful eye on things to come. Henry, for example, is a regular who sees Trena several times a week. Just as dancer Trena found herself at a hazardous crossroads while on a date with her boyfriend, we now hear Henry speak with Egan of the difficulties of his desires for Trena. This continues to transpire at the intersection of fantasy love and the local marketplace of desire. The linkages drawn are complex, ranging from what Henry wants, to his feelings of being special in the circumstances, and to his disdain for other customers. If dancer Serenity found that it wasn't easy to toe the line between money, friendship, and love, Henry recognizes a parallel "hard" world of meaning in what he conveys as the love between dancer Trena and himself on the one hand, and her need to work and ultimately treat him as a customer on the other.

Henry: It's hard because I love Trena and she loves me.

Danielle: Yeah.

Henry: And we like have something special.

Danielle: That's great.

Henry: It's like I never thought I could have these feelings again and here they are . . . it's wild. But unfortunately you know she's busy. . . . She goes to school and so the only time we spend together is here.

Danielle: Um hum.

Henry: Which is fine, but I want to take her out and make her feel great. I want to go to dinner and the movies, . . . have something like other couples . . . And I hate having to watch her with other men . . . I know she has to work, but I wish I could just support her so she wouldn't have to deal with these guys. Some of them are such assholes. That's why we go to the back [to the lap dance room] so much so we can have alone time together. (p. 67)

Conclusion

Fieldwork oriented to the meaning-making process informs us that narrative work entails constructing linkages between bits and pieces of experience.

Fieldwork especially opens to view the added circumstances of meaning making, not just particular narrative results. It points to the alternative linkages available for constructing stories, and how the stories that do form, do so in relation to distinguishable contexts. Following the guideline to orient to how accounts are actively put together, especially in circumstances that foreground alternative meaning making, we learn that narrative work not only establishes space for storytelling, but also fills the space with distinctive and, at times, decidedly complex accounts.

6

Composition

Matters linked together to make meaning can be elaborated into accounts with distinctive plots and themes. One individual, for example, may link a physical disability to the downsides of life, while another links it to life's challenges or even rewards. But meaning making doesn't stop there. As linkages create contexts, they can be expanded into more comprehensive narratives. Asked "What do you mean?" "Why do you think that?" or simply a questioning "Oh?" in response to a linkage establishes space for an elaborated story with a content and shape of its own. We refer to the process of elaboration as *narrative composition* and, as usual, consider how circumstances relate to the elaboration process.

Orienting to Composition

Textually focused narrative researchers have shown that diverse plot structures and themes are discernable in transcripts of accounts. But unless the researcher is aware of compositional options at the start, circumstantial influences on meaning making or even counterplots are likely to go unnoticed. As we saw from snippets of Stanley's narrative, the plot and themes of his story varied depending on the circumstances. Stanley took into consideration what was at stake for him in various situations in assembling and thematizing details of experience. Shaw's book understandably homogenized Stanley's story by ignoring the occasioned work of storytelling and how that shaped the results.

As in the last chapter, narrative composition is tenuously related to circumstances. Storytellers take circumstances into account in linking experiences together to make meaning, but circumstances do not determine the by-products. Narrative composition is an active process of elaboration, not a regurgitation of local themes or received plotlines. At the same time, as we continue to orient to the agency of storytellers, we are not suggesting that narrative composition is haphazard. Not just anything goes in the work of composing a story. If there is improvisation in narrative composition, there also are discernible patterns, formats, and circumstantial constraints on story formation. Ethnographic knowledge of the circumstances of storytelling, which also can point to untold stories, can show us as much.

Kaufman (1986) makes overtures to these concerns in *The Ageless Self*. She presents the ways elderly individuals compose their accounts when asked to tell their life stories, but she listens carefully for diverse, even unexpected elaborations. Certainly, the circumstances of aging and the historical events of respondents' lifetimes are taken into consideration. But, as Kaufman emphasizes, these do not determine life stories. At the same time, the stories she analyzes share compositional characteristics. They are not homogeneous, but neither are they idiosyncratic. There are regular or familiar configurations in the way they are put together, especially in the way personal values, in her material, function in assembling lifetimes of experience. In Kaufman's view, values function constructively in narrative composition, drawing together in distinctive ways the influences of history and biography.

> Values are highly abstract constructs drawn from the experiences of living in a particular society during a certain historical period. Values emerge from, and in turn are shaped by, the interactions among individuals and institutions in a social system. . . . Values emphasize the individual's conformity to shared and fairly explicit indices of social worth. As such, values clearly fix the individual in a historical–cultural cohort, that is, in a group with common ideals derived from common experiences. (pp. 114–115)

If values are shared ideals, they also are resources for heterogeneous composition. One of Kaufman's respondents, 72-year-old Mary, for example, composes her story of "being herself in old age" in terms of a wasteful–productive dichotomy. The theme dominates her life story as she elaborates by drawing linkages with the wasteful things in which she engaged, which contrasts with the self-confidence she expresses in speaking of her achievements. History and age play into her account, but they are not the leading themes. Another respondent, 76-year-old Harold, composes his life in relation to the theme and value of personal success. The value of being successful in life, in his case of being a successful businessman, is palpable throughout his story. A third respondent, 81-year-old Alice, composes a story thematized by spiritual understanding, picking up on major and minor events of her life along the way. As Kaufman writes, "[Alice] explains that her whole life has been oriented toward 'probing,' 'seeking,' and 'finding' spiritual insight" (p. 142).

The use of personal values to compose a life is both particular and general to the stories. If being successful is used to compose the links Harold makes with various events of growing up and coming of age, it provides broader meaning as well, related in Kaufman's analysis to the similar value he shares with others. Likewise, while spiritual understanding provides a thematic touchstone for the links Alice makes with aspects of her own experience, she is more or less like others who similarly bring values on board.

Because individuals use values or other resources such as generational characteristics and significant historical events, among a variety of "coherence systems" (see Josselson & Lieblich, 1993; Kleinman, 1988; Linde, 1993; Rosenwald & Ochsberg, 1992) to elaborate their life stories, it behooves the researcher to consider the ways they are compositionally similar and different from each other. Another concern is how similarities and differences relate to circumstances. The researcher should figure that similarities and differences may derive in various ways from the circumstances of their production (see Briggs & Mantini-Briggs, 2003; Ochs & Capps, 2001). We offer the following procedural guideline for orienting to this:

Guideline

Orient to storytelling with a view to how participants in particular circumstances actively compose their stories. Document how circumstances enter into the process. Look for distinctive patterns of composition, comparing and contrasting types of themes and plotlines across and within circumstances.

Into the Field

How can researchers position themselves to capture the work of narrative composition? The guideline suggests that the risk is to homogenize what might otherwise vary. We saw elements of this in Shaw's (1930) account of Stanley's story. Shaw listened to Stanley tell his story in several sessions spread over a longer period of time. He conducted a series of interviews with Stanley, took notes, and reproduced the story from that. But it was done with an analytic eye to describe a particular social world. "The" jack-roller story is about a role and status in "the" world of social marginality and disadvantage. It's not especially about Stanley or even the type of delinquent he represents. The story's significance derives from the social environment that is portrayed. In not following Stanley into the field, into the varied nooks and crannies of his social world, Shaw homogenized Stanley's account into "the" delinquent boy's own story.

Consider two strategies for avoiding homogenization and discerning compositional variety. One is more ethnographic and the other is more interview based. Applying the first strategy to Shaw's study would have meant following Stanley around his world in and out of the reformatory. As the guideline recommends, the researcher would orient to the work of narrative composition, documenting how Stanley took events, objectives, and circumstances into consideration in composing accounts. This would have provided the opportunity to present Stanley's story in more variegated form, making visible the narrative agency and compositional diversity underpinning what was otherwise labeled "the" delinquent life. Participating and observing in various situations, as Anderson (1999) did in the African American community and as Egan (2006) does in the dance clubs she studied, helped them to identify the various ways a life or a social world might be composed, or remain tenuously articulated at the border of possible compositions.

A second strategy for resisting homogenization, which we'll focus on in this chapter, is interview based and was applied by Jaber Gubrium (1993) in his study of how nursing home residents composed the quality of their lives. Gubrium conducted multiple open-ended interviews with residents, with a concerted eye to their pasts as well as to the quality of their present lives in the nursing home. Had Shaw chosen this strategy, he would have been more attuned to the ways Stanley and other boys he interviewed incorporated lifetimes of experience into their stories of the delinquent life. Gubrium saw his interviews as a way of identifying the varied horizons of meaning the residents brought with them to compose their stories of nursing home living. The aim was to resist homogenizing "the" nursing home story by encouraging residents to talk about life as a whole—drawing upon diverse lifetimes of experience—in commenting on what life was like now living in a nursing home.

The broader background of the study related to the persistent public image of the nursing home and nursing home residents' lives. The public image is one that is almost wholly negative, even while varied efforts continue to be made to make nursing homes more "home-like" and to draw residents and families into decision making about cares and daily living. The public image deploys a homogeneous story of final homes for the aged, whose denizens look back with longing on their earlier lives, are enormously depressed about their current circumstances, and look ahead with despair.

To provide the opportunity for greater balance, Gubrium began his research by orienting to the narrative activeness of nursing home residents, which he viewed as extending to the way they characterized lifetimes of experience. This was informed by earlier ethnographic fieldwork dealing with everyday life in nursing homes (J. F. Gubrium, 1975/1997). In the interview study, Gubrium raised the question of how individuals in a common circumstance would meaningfully story their lives. Would they all be the same and uniformly negative, or would they vary in discernible ways? He was especially interested in residents' accounts of the current quality of their lives as well as the quality of the care they received.

In order to draw the longer term directly into the interviews, each resident was initially asked to tell his or her life story. The strategy was a deliberate attempt to prevent the public image's homogenizing story from being the exclusive context for composing meaning. As one might expect, the life stories varied in detail. Some were lengthy and others were rather short; some were told vividly and others conveyed in hum-drum fashion. In subsequent interviews, the life stories were used both to probe further into, and to contextualize, accounts of the quality of the resident's life in the nursing home. Respondents were encouraged to relate their current circumstances to earlier experiences and to themes culled from their life stories. The overall goal was to avoid organizing the interview process in relation to "the" nursing home resident, but rather to encourage the composition of biographically sensitive accounts, foregrounding life as a whole. Gubrium was especially interested in long-stayers, residents for whom the nursing facility had putatively become home. Such residents are denizens of their worlds. If anything, it was long-stayers whose stories might be homogenized by their circumstances. Short-stayers are passersby in the nursing home scene, typically being in residence for physical and occupational therapy or for post-surgical recovery.

Now consider how two residents link together elements of their past and their current circumstances to compose stories of the quality of life in their nursing homes. First is resident Myrtle Johnson, a 94-year-old widowed African American woman who has lived in her nursing home for a year. She suffers from Parkinson's disease, arthritis, and has difficulty maintaining her balance. According to Johnson, falls have been the bane of old age for her and the main reason she was placed in a nursing home. Her comments on the present quality of her life and her care in the home contrast starkly with the quality of her life in her earlier years. Like some others, her story resonates loudly with narratives of the hopelessness of life under the circumstances.

Residents such as Johnson "look back on their lives—filled with hard work, enjoyment, and kindness toward others—and grimly wonder how God could have planned this for them" (J. F. Gubrium, 1993, p. 53). Some shake their heads tellingly as they relate their story, lamenting how "it's come to this." Gubrium used this phrase to identify a type of narrative composition, one with plots and themes that construct accounts of being useful before and fatefully useless now. In these accounts, the current quality of nursing home life seems to envelop the life story. Gubrium describes the type of composition this way.

> The stories' horizons extend well beyond the local and interpersonal. If it is understood that there are things a nursing home cannot offer, this is overridden by the broader question of life's meaning. If there are complaints about, or an appreciation of, staff members' efforts, these pale against the issue of what people [like them] have come to be [useless]. In this narrative context, the quality of care, while a concern, hardly bears on the quality of life. (p. 53)

As Johnson compares an earlier useful life with a life now hardly worth living, she refers to suicide. But she then links that with those who don't have the faith to sustain themselves in the circumstances. If it had not been for her faith in God, Johnson explains, hers would be the story of those who take their own lives because life is no longer worth living. This happens to them because, as she points out, "it's come to this." The following extract from one of Johnson's interviews is illuminating. It flags the plot constructed in terms of before-and-after and the theme of tragic destiny that permeates both her own and others' similar stories.

> But I worked hard all my life. And I enjoyed life. I'll say that what I enjoyed the most was when I lived on a farm in Missouri. Now that's where I enjoyed myself the most because I was able to get and do things, you know, help others. If there's one thing I don't like, it's just sittin'. That's what I have to do now. But then I try to make the best of it. But I would say that when I was able to be up and around and work is when I enjoyed myself the most. . . .
>
> Of course I'm not happy sitting here this way. But then it's part of life and you've got to . . . I say. I've often thought about it, just since I've been passing between the chair and the bed. What use is it?
>
> You know, I can realize why some people commit suicide. They don't have faith. People that have faith in God don't commit suicide. But I can see why when people are in my position and don't have faith in the Lord, they commit suicide. I've thought about that so much. You know, you often say, "Well, why did so-and-so do so-and-so?" Well, if you sit down and study about it, you can figure that out . . . there's nothing. . . . But as long as you have faith in the Lord, you are going to go ahead and take what He sends you. But there's times you really wonder. (pp. 54–55)

Across the interviews Gubrium conducted with her, Johnson broaches an understanding that gives overall meaning to her thoughts and feelings. This is the work of composition, in which certain linkages recur or are highlighted in a story, providing narrative direction. This operates over and above particular acts of linkage. If the storyteller, say, discerns what something meant at one time and distinguishes that from what it means now, what is proffered over and above this, especially in its recurrence or emphasis, serves to fashion linkages into a meaningful whole to make a point. Johnson's life is plotted as a trajectory from being useful to being useless. It is thematized as puzzling in the first instance, tragic in the second. And it is cast as an exception to the suicidal rule because of her faith in the Lord in the third instance.

Before moving on to the other resident's story, a few comments about research procedure are in order. First, it is important to take note of and code the recurrence of narrative material, such as Gubrium found in Johnson's interviews. Recurrences not only signal compositional work, but work that conveys patterns of meaning. In some instances, a respondent may step outside of her account and comment directly on its overall meaning or importance. However this is done, indirectly or directly, it serves to inform the listener that the storyteller is not only making meaning by linking experiential material and pulling this together in a particular way, but is also sharing an understanding of the whole.

Overall meaning is sometimes prompted by someone other than the storyteller. The listener who asks what this means to the speaker is inquiring into something beyond the linkages of a plotline. This can extend further, brought forth, for example, by an actual request for the point of an account or the request to consider what something means in the broader scheme of things. In Johnson's case, this was provided both by Gubrium's life-oriented prompts and by Johnson herself. Noting time and again that "it's come to this," Johnson meaningfully underscored the overall course of her life in terms of what her life had come to, namely, something repeatedly referred to as "this"—an unfortunate end.

At times, we can observe compositional work taking paralinguistic form. The audible crescendos that can accompany repetition—"That's what it *really* means to me"—serve to emphasize a theme or the point of a story. Significant pauses, emotional expressions such as cries and whimpers, or physical gestures such as upturned or downturned hands and rolled eyes can add recognizable meaning over and above what is actually said. These forms of compositional work are often absent from interview transcripts. But they can be noted by means of conventional conversation analytic transcription notations (see Jefferson, 1978) or in accompanying field notes. The analytic lesson of this is that, whether compositional work takes the form of thematization, recurrence, or emphasis, or is conveyed paralinguistically, it is noteworthy for the way it elaborates meaning beyond the particular linkages in tow.

The "scenic presence" of accounts is especially important in this regard and is ethnographically, but often not textually, available for analysis (Holstein & Gubrium, 2000b, pp. 190–197). By this, we refer to the added understanding provided a text when it is accompanied by extended knowledge of the setting in which it is presented. The ethnographer knows that transcribed accounts, including interview material and paralinguistic expressions, transpired in a particular circumstance, in this case a nursing home, not a reformatory for juvenile delinquents. While this knowledge doesn't automatically translate into full understanding, it does help to rule out other interpretations. In Johnson's case, her cries and whimpers flagged the meaning of her earlier life as it related to nursing home living. Their scenic presence communicated meaning not apparent in her utterances and expressions alone.

Johnson grieves for a lost life, not for the opportunity to get back to delinquent activities—even while the emotional expressions accompanying their respective accounts might be the same. We can imagine Stanley crying and whimpering with identical longing all alone in his cell. But their scenic presence composes this in strikingly different ways. The videotaping of their respective actions might bring forth both scenic and text-based knowledge and help to sort the differences (see Luff, Hindmarsh, & Heath, 2000). But this would still fall short of being ethnographically informed, which brings on board institutional and cultural knowledge of the circumstances in relation to the specific actions and biographical facts, all of which play into compositional understanding.

The scenic presence of Johnson's accounts became poignantly evident on more than one occasion. Following the familiar recollection of her earlier useful life and her current useless existence, one time Johnson haltingly raised her eyes and very gradually turned her head to her left and then to her right as she commented on "this life." This transpired as if in slow motion. As she shrugged her shoulders and then shook her head in an equally familiar way in a recognizable gesture of despair, Gubrium and Johnson's shared knowledge of the meaning of such actions in the circumstance collaboratively composed the linkages being made well beyond what each gesture and comment could tell on its own. In the subsequently unfolding seconds, what she had referred to as "this life" was taken by both of them to relate to previous exchanges and discussions, extending to a horizon of meaning not audible or visible at the moment but extending to what each knew about lives that come to an end in this way. It made what transpired from that point on a painfully meaningful narrative whole. Their shared knowledge and familiarity was the basis for Gubrium's sympathetic responses, hers in turn, and the chain of emotional interactions that followed. "I know and I understand," Gubrium whispered. Johnson quietly added, "I know."

The sensibilities of the exchanges surrounding accounts can draw as much from the broad contours of their scenic presence as from what is conveyed in so many words in talk and interaction. This is a form of knowledge and, equally important, understanding that text-based material leaves untold. But they are data that are ethnographically available. The researcher should take analytic direction from this, along with empirical notes that reflect the particulars. We should add that, while controversial, such scenic, especially locally immediate features of composition have led some narrative researchers to reenact material viewed as in need of dramatic realization in order to bring their full force into view (see Ellis & Bochner, 1996).

Now compare the composition of Johnson's account with that of a second resident, Peter Rinehart. Peter's story centers on lifelong equanimity, and its scenic presence is dramatically different, even while he also is a nursing home resident. He doesn't use the word "equanimity," but the term suits the purpose of distinguishing this theme from that of Myrtle Johnson's and others' "it's come to this." A 77-year-old widowed white male, Rinehart is paralyzed from the waist down, the result of a fall from a roof, leaving him in chronic pain. The fall figures prominently in his story. But if it divides biographical matters chronologically into before and after, it does not thematize the quality of his life in the nursing home.

Regularly referring to particulars conveyed in Rinehart's life story, Gubrium encourages him to compare life now with what it was like in the past. Rinehart responds accordingly, retrospectively elaborating on the linkages he makes in describing life in the nursing home. But there is a striking contrast with Johnson's account of the quality of her life. Rinehart's accounts broadly differ from the depressing public image of nursing home life. When Rinehart looks back, then and now are not evaluated in terms of better or worse. Rather, then and now are compartmentalized and constructed as different facets of a lifetime. If similar linkages are made in terms of before and after, such as being able bodied before and incapacitated now, the compositional spin given to the difference is remarkable. Rinehart's story is at once less dour and more accepting of his current circumstances than Johnson's is, even while they both reside in nursing homes. Nursing home living is more benign in Rinehart's narrative. There is no overarching evaluative framework that serves as a basis for figuring that things now are better or worse than they were before. The value of then and the value of now are not attributed to God, destiny, or any other general sense of the relative worth of things in life. If despair provides moral scaffolding for Johnson's evaluation of the quality of her life in the nursing home, Rinehart speaks of the facets of his life with an equanimity unrelated to a broader scheme of evaluation.

Rinehart was one of two male residents interviewed who had been itinerant salesmen. He worked in sales for the Oster Company and, according to Rinehart, he was constantly on the move. The compositional tone of the two men's stories was organized against this background, in which coming and going was viewed as the normal state of daily affairs. Home was not so much a headquarters or base of operations as it was one more stop along the way. If anything, home was time-out from the routine matters of Rinehart's life. Gubrium summarizes.

> To paraphrase one of them, they did a "lot of livin'" on the road and have stories to tell about it. For them, home was a place experienced as a break from life on the road. Home was time out from the usual and customary. These men *went home* for vacation; they didn't leave it. (p. 103)

For residents like Rinehart, the overall meaning of life isn't puzzling because life's meaning is found in its parts and occasions. Their narratives show that if life has a plotline, it doesn't move in any particular direction. It unfolds along a winding pathway. If life has a moral horizon, it's constructed in fits and starts, each of life's facets having its own evaluative purview. If these stories centered on anything, it was incidents along the road of experience, the nursing home being a kind of stopover along the way. Again, the distinctive vocabulary, repetitions, and related gestures and expressions are a telling part of the compositional work that makes their accounts meaningful in their own ways, Gubrium explains.

> Destiny isn't so much puzzling or decried as it is something that, like life on the road, one follows. [These men] refer to fate in phrases such as "c'est la vie," "things just happen," "goin' where the road takes you," "so be it," and "easy come, easy go." While the men describe the many paths their lives took, the so-called ups and downs of the years, and the good and poor choices they made at various turns, they recognize that such matters are part of the design of living. They don't lament fate; it's just there, the essential "road" ahead. (p. 103)

Such is the compositional context within which Rinehart relays his accounts of the quality of life in the nursing home. For Rinehart, his current circumstance matters, but it doesn't overwhelm his story as it does for Johnson and others. He accepts the nursing home as a place offering care, security, and shelter for the weary, who might not otherwise be able to carry on. Rinehart adds at various points in his interviews that the facility isn't home, but under the circumstances it's the next best thing to it. Care paraphernalia and sickness aside, for traveling men like Rinehart, the nursing home offers respite; it's a kind of hotel, having both the best and the worst features of such establishments. Residents more or less are fed, have a bed to sleep in, and have their cares attended, but understandably not to everyone's satisfaction. Rinehart takes pride in the quality of his life and what he has accomplished, but his accomplishments are storied independently from his accident or his present circumstances. The following interview extract is instructive.

> I see people that are worse off than I am. I feel sorry for them, but I'm not looking back with remorse. It's something I can't help. It happened [the disabling fall] and I have to live with it. Life's been happy and pretty good to me otherwise. I made a good living. You take the good with the bad.
>
> When it first happened, I hoped that I would be able to get back to normal. Then I hoped to get . . . they got me in a wheelchair. I hoped to be able to stay in a wheelchair, maybe graduate to crutches and that. It never happened that way though. But it didn't make me despondent.
>
> Gradually, I began to know that I would probably never walk again and I've been about the way I have been now for the last couple of years. They brought a specialist in from the University of Pittsburgh and he put a brain tap in the nerve center of my brain. But that didn't work.
>
> I'm hoping to clear up the pain in my back so I can, if nothing else, sit up. But I read a lot and that takes time and they treat me good here. The aides come in and I kid with them and that. The rest of the time is about the same as an average day when you aren't working. Only instead of working now, I read. It's a long weekend, you might say. (p. 113)

The emotional tone of Rinehart's accounts is distinctive. Unlike Johnson, Reinhart's emotional expression is muted. He emphasizes lessons learned along the path of life rather than lamenting what has happened in the course of living. Rinehart's is a story composed with little crescendo. Its horizons rise and fall in close proximity to the facets of life he describes. This is notable because it works against popular understandings of the sustained despair of nursing home living.

Conclusion

In orienting to composition, our guideline turned us to the way narrative linkages are put together to give accounts overall meaning. Featuring the agency of the storyteller, the guideline encourages the researcher to identify similarities and differences in story composition, the analytic goal of which is to specify types of accounts in particular circumstances. The comparison of nursing home residents Myrtle Johnson and Peter Rinehart's stories suggests that circumstances are indeed taken into consideration in accounts, but they do not determine plotlines, themes, or moral contours. Rather, the work of narrative production, while sensitive to its environment, moves ahead according to its own logic.

7

Performance

If stories are actively composed, storytelling is staged. It is animated and transpires somewhere, in relation to some audience, for some purpose. Stories are designed accordingly, with their linkages and composition shaped for, and by, listeners. This again takes us outside story texts, to their performative circumstances. Once more, we're in Stanley's territory, where swagger and bravado, for example, suit the purpose of addressing some audiences and measured description the purpose of addressing others.

Orienting to Performance

Performances have casts of characters and separate scenes, which relate to accounts in different ways. Narrators present their stories for particular effect. Listeners respond to a speaker's story with diverse embellishments of their own, which, in turn, give accounts distinctive experiential and emotional resonances. The pace and tone of scenes can change, highlighting alternative sentiments and consequences. The following anecdote from the experiences of the chairperson of a university academic department is instructive in bringing this together in the context of storytelling. It orients us to story's performativity.

University departments are full of academic war stories. Such is part of the informal banter of any workplace. On one occasion, during hiring season, faculty members, graduate students, and interested outsiders attended the job talk of a candidate for an entry-level assistant professor position. The candidate had not been happy with the usual hotel accommodations and had been openly grumbling about them. The candidate also was perturbed that the interview was taking place during his spring break. Making matters even worse, he was dissatisfied with the food served at each of his meals. News of these complaints spread quickly, as the candidate was uncommonly vocal with his opinions.

During the job talk, when it apparently became obvious to the candidate and to the audience that he was doing poorly, he grew visibly agitated and claimed that he was not receiving the enthusiastic response he'd expected. He continued with long awkward pauses, repeatedly turning away from his notes, and in audible asides complained about the lack of respect in the room. Finally, he stopped and started to yell at the audience. "I have better things to do with my time," he shouted. He then insinuated that he was smarter than anyone in the room and finished by blurting, "So take your job and shove it."

Needless to say, this caused quite a stir and there were plenty of stories about it in the days ahead. The stories were composed similarly, although with some variation in narrative linkages. Responses from the audience for these stories clearly showed that something lamentable, if not academically tragic, had transpired. The stories were conveyed in terms of the unfortunate events surrounding the talk. They were embellished in the language of disgust and disbelief. Some worried that the vetting process had not been conducted more carefully, even while most agreed that "you can't win them all," that "things slip through," and, referring to applications in general, "you can't always tell from what a person looks like on paper." There was general dismay regarding the candidate's conduct, who, after all, could have acted with greater civility, even if he weren't interested in the job or felt he was underappreciated. Some accounts highlighted the candidate's immaturity, while others focused on the unreasonable expectations he brought with him.

As time passed and the shock of the event wore off, the ongoing narratives' dramatic realization changed. Earlier stories were repeated but now with a different audience and purpose. This could be discerned from both their presentational style and responses to the accounts. If early on storytellers soberly presented stories as tales of professional woe, later tellings related to how ludicrous academic life can be at times. Storytelling was prefaced differently and directed to eager listeners of another kind. Earlier stories were started and embellished with disgusted headshaking and comments such as "I'm really appalled," and "This is really unfortunate." Later stories—both their prefaces and audience responses—were distinctly comedic. They began with broad smiles, incipient laughter, and promises of hilarity, such as "Wait till you hear this" and "Remember the time that crazy guy gave his job talk?" Storytellers and listeners now related to each other with accompanying guffaws of incredulity. The earlier and later performances of accounts were remarkable for differences in dramatic effect. The meaning of the accounts contrasted accordingly.

How are we to judge differences in dramatic realization? Is there any basis for comparing the relative truth value of variably performed accounts? If we assume that the work of storytelling is an integral feature of the story, we have no choice but to treat matters of presentation as integral aspects of narrative production. This adds an important criterion besides correspondence to the real world for evaluating the truthfulness of accounts, an issue to which we will return in Part IV of the book. It refers to the importance of considering the everyday purposes and expectations of articulation and the need for an ethnography of performance.

Anthropologist Lila Abu-Lughod (1993) makes two points related to these concerns at the start of her book on Bedouin women's stories. Inspired by feminist theorists (see Butler, 1990; Haraway, 1988; Smith, 1987), she generalizes her observations to the performativity of all stories. The first point is that the positions and purposes of storytellers and listeners—the cast of characters—figure prominently in the everyday validity of an account. Stories are shaped with this in mind, which bears on a practical truthfulness.

> [Regarding the inevitability of positionality] A story is always situated; it has both a teller and an audience. Its perspective is partial (in both senses of the word), and its telling is motivated. The Bedouin women's tales presented here are no exception. (p. 15)

As we will see shortly in discussing material from Abu-Lughod's fieldwork, if a mother and a son on separate occasions recount similar details of an event that could have had tragic outcomes, their accounts are always partial renditions. In practice, as lamentable as tragedy is in principle, its performative contours matter in how it operates in everyday life. Mothers and sons are often differently positioned in their relationships with others, especially in this case within the patriarchy of Bedouin society. Their roles, relationships, and related expectations invariably result in conditional truths. Accounts are always "incomplete" and "partisan" in practice. From one storytelling occasion to another, events are communicatively shaped to accord with the distinctive roles played in telling about them, the roles taken in responding to them, and storytelling's purpose.

Abu-Lughod's second point is that since audience and purpose are always in play, there is no sense in pretending that one can obtain and convey objective stories. The text of a story bereft of context is no story at all as far as society is concerned. Rather, in Abu-Lughod's view, we must orient to the meaning of stories as meaning is worked out on the occasions when stories are told. Abu-Lughod's mission in authoring her book *Writing Women's Worlds* is to trace the presentation and organization of stories in social context. As she writes, "Only a false belief in the possibility of a nonsituated story (or 'objectivity') could make one ask that stories reflect the way things, over there, 'really' are" (p. 17).

Similarly, in his book *Story, Performance, and Event*, Richard Bauman's (1986) goal is to unpack the situated groundings of narrative diversity. As he would argue, narrative truths are tied to their dramatic realization. Tellingly, the book is subtitled "contextual studies of oral narrative." The book provides a performative framework and vocabulary for orienting to the dramatic realization of accounts. Bauman introduces his approach this way:

> The investigations on which this book is based were motivated by my long-standing interest in the ethnography of oral performance. The ethnographic perspective that has guided my work centers around a basic reorientation from a conception of folklore as things—texts, items, mentifacts—to verbal art as a way of speaking, a mode of verbal communication. (p. 2)

Just as *Analyzing Narrative Reality* considers the reflexive relation between what is told and the telling, Bauman calls attention to the long-standing importance of keeping their "radical interdependence" in view.

> Narratives are keyed both to the events in which they are told and to the events that they recount, toward narrative events and narrated events (Jakobson, 1971). . . . The radical interdependence of narrated events and narrative events is no new discovery. [Philosopher] Walter Benjamin [1969, p. 87] stated it well: "The storyteller takes what he tells from experience—his own and that reported by others. And he in turn makes it the experience of those who are listening to his tale." (p. 2)

Bauman provides concrete direction for the researcher. Orienting to occasions of storytelling brings with it terms of reference that not only inform us of how to view the field but also cue us as to what to expect.

> The first task in the study of performance events is to identify the events themselves in ways consistent with local understandings and relevant to the analytical problems at hand. Events may be locally defined in terms of setting (e.g., Bauman, 1972), institutional context (e.g., Bloch, 1975; Brenneis, 1978), scheduling or occasioning principles (e.g., Abrahams, 1977), and so on. The

structure of performance events is a product of the systemic interplay of numerous situational factors, prominently including the following:

1. Participants' identities and roles (e.g., Bauman, 1972; Stoeltje, 1981, pp. 136–139)
2. The expressive means employed in performance (e.g., Cosentino, 1982, pp. 88–143)
3. Social interactional ground rules, norms, and strategies for performance and criteria for its interpretation and evaluation (e.g., Burns, 1983, pp. 19–24; Darnell, 1974)
4. The sequence of actions that make up the scenario of the event (e.g., Falassi, 1980, pp. 3–4)

The dramaturgical language is clear, flagging events, scenarios, roles, expressions, performance strategies, theatrical purpose, and criteria for interpretation. We will draw upon the approach in moving into the field with Abu-Lughod to consider Bedouin storytelling. The following analytic guideline leads the way:

Guideline

In considering the compositional activity of storytellers, orient to the scenic mediations of accounts. Document how performative particulars, such as roles, purposes, audiences, modes of expression, and emphases, reflexively shape stories over and above their texts.

Into the Field

Abu-Lughod spent years doing fieldwork in the Awlad 'Ali Bedouin community on the northwest coast of Egypt. She had always been interested in gender relations and, specifically, in the women of a small Egyptian hamlet where she herself resided for the first time in the 1970s. Being an anthropologist, she brought along with her the concept of culture, which, as she explains in the book from which we take exemplary material, became increasingly difficult to apply. According to Abu-Lughod, the remarkable facility of the women to performatively shape cultural particulars in the everyday stories they told was too vivid to ignore. By the 1980s, when she took her second trip to the community, Abu-Lughod also had been influenced by the sea change in anthropology and especially in feminist studies that led many to turn away from the traditional view of culture. In the old view, culture was a more or less coherent configuration of shared meanings. The newer thinking was that culture was narratively fluid, formed and reshaped in its practical realizations.

The Bedouin women's stories Abu-Lughod heard resonated with the newer view of culture. The women combined cultural details in different ways, accenting them for varied purposes in relation to listeners. Stories told for one purpose produced a particular response in listeners. When they were told for a different purpose they would strike listeners differently. In this way, the women staged culture in contrasting fashions. They used it distinctively, depending on the circumstances. Culture was a living thing, at once growing out of, turning back on, and mediated by its narrative and scenic practices. The Bedouin women (and men) were always *doing* culture, in other words. This stood in remarkable contrast to the tenor of culture echoed by the term "traditional society." Related to this and drawing from ongoing debates in feminist theory was Abu-Lughod's discomfort with the idea of a specifically female voice. While her informants often spoke "as women," multivocality also was evident in her material. The Bedouin women cast gender in diverse fashion, depending on the performative needs of storytelling occasions. If Bedouin society was patriarchal, it was a narratively pliable form of it.

Focusing on the women's narratives, Abu-Lughod initially set out to record life stories, assuming that cultural understanding could be documented in and through the transcripts. She assumed that the stories would be a transparent lens for viewing Bedouin society. Through distinctive themes and plotlines, the compositional by-products of individual storytellers could be used to trace the form culture took in the community. Key informant, Migdim, the eldest woman (the old mother) of four generations of men and women, is introduced for this purpose. Abu-Lughod initially explains that she simply requested that Migdim tell her life story. Migdim's response, surprising at the time, hints at this chapter's guideline. It quickly became evident that Migdim was unwilling or unable to provide a straightforward account. Rather, the story was reflexive. It selectively cast culture in particular ways for the purposes at hand. In turn, cultural details took on practical relevance in the telling.

The mode of activation—"tell me your life story"—was especially troublesome because it followed from the assumption that cultural meaning could be laid out in parallel fashion to the experience and events Migdim shared with others over four generations of living in the area. Abu-Lughod describes an early encounter with the issue.

> On a quiet day toward the end of 1979, the second year I had been living in the community, I asked Migdim whether she would tell me her life story. She said, "When you get old you think only of God, of prayer, and of the oneness of God. What happened has passed, you don't think about it. You don't think about anything but God." And she refused to say any more. (p. 45)

On Abu-Lughod's second field trip in 1986, she tried again to elicit Migdim's life story. This time she was better equipped to take ethnographic notice of narrative work and the performativity of accounts. She was armed with a more nuanced understanding of cultural practice. She became interested in, rather than frustrated by, Migdim's repeated evasions. Abu-Lughod would orient to the idea that the contrasting stories that Migdim would tell were the meaning-making work of culture, even if they were not the stories Abu-Lughod initially wanted to hear. There was no need for Migdim to lay out cultural details in linear fashion and with substantive coherence. In hindsight, Abu-Lughod found that to be asked to do so would understandably be seen as odd, if the request were not altogether ignored. Abu-Lughod describes how Migdim's response shed light on the need for ethnographic fieldwork that could capture the importance of experience on its own—often timeless—terms.

> By the time I returned in 1986, seven years later, she [Migdim] could hardly stand and walked only to go outside to the bathroom or to do her ablutions for prayer. An eye operation had been unsuccessful, and she squinted to see people. She rubbed her red eyes and often kept them closed. Sitting hunched over all day, a blanket over her lap, she had more time for me. When I asked her to tell me her life story, she said, "I've forgotten all of that. I've got no mind to remember with any more." But then she went on, "We used to milk the sheep. We used to pack up and leave here and set up camp out west. And there we would milk the goats and milk the sheep and churn butter, and we'd melt it and we'd put the clarified butter in the goatskin bag and we'd cook wheat until it was done and we'd make dried barley cheese." (p. 46)

Such was the ordinary eventfulness of Migdim's life, organized in terms of the seasonal migrations and mundane acts of sustenance shared with others. If temporal at all, her life was cyclical. Then again, if it was perennially cyclical, why take notice of the cycle in its own right? What would be the practical need for such realization, unless, of course, one were repeatedly requested to do so for some acceptable reason by someone one cared about? Migdim's life was made up of the collective activity in which her life was unremarkably immersed. It was not organized according to an individualized time frame from birth to death. Migdim laughed at how performatively canned her response was.

> She laughed, knowing how formulaic this "story of her life" was. That was all I got, though, from my direct questions. For her, like the other women I knew in this community, the conventional form of "a life" as a self-centered passage through time was not familiar. Instead there were memorable events, fixed into dramatic stories with fine details. (p. 46)

Consider in this context one of the most vivid stories Abu-Lughod heard from Migdim. We won't repeat it in its entirety, since it's quite long. For our purposes, the length and detail are not as important as its dramatic realization. The story takes its shape from the drama of the telling as well as from the events recounted. Abu-Lughod introduces the account this way. An important performative factor is that the story is being told to an audience composed of future generations of women.

> One of the most vivid I heard from Migdim was the tale of how she had resisted marriages her father had tried to arrange for her. I even heard more than once, nearly word for word, the same tale of how she had ended up marrying Jawwad, the father of her children. I heard it for the first time one evening that winter; she told it for the benefit of her sons' wives, Gateefa and Fayga, and some of her granddaughters.
>
> She explained that the first person whom she was to have married was a paternal first cousin. His relatives came to her household and conducted the negotiations and even went as far as to slaughter some sheep, the practice that seals the marriage agreement. But things did not work out. The time was over fifty years ago, just after the death of her mother.
>
> "He was a first cousin, and I didn't want him. He was old and he lived with us. We ate out of one bowl. His relatives came and slaughtered a sheep and I started screaming, I started crying. My father had bought a new gun, a cartridge gun. He said, 'If you don't shut up I'll send you flying with this gun.'"
> (pp. 46–47)

As Migdim elaborates, she vividly presents the strategies she used to escape the marriage. The patriarchy of Bedouin society notwithstanding, Migdim recounts a tale of personal artifice and resistance. This transpires even in the face of a sealed marriage agreement and its associated expenses. Her father and relatives eventually do come to an agreement based on another arrangement ostensibly made between them, not between them and Migdim. The theme of the telling is that Migdim actively worked to form the agreement her father and relatives made among themselves, but on her terms. The story is a vivid lesson for its listeners. Episodes highlight Migdim—a woman—as the "actual" determining force behind the events. The telling is a momentarily useful cultural model for the women listening to the practice, not the rule, of patriarchy. It informs them all that cultural events are as much the effects of their actions, as their lives are regulated by the events.

Abu-Lughod provides some of the amusing ethnographic detail of the telling. It is noteworthy how daughter-in-law Gateefa in particular cleverly responds to various episodes. The humor involved in the undoing of patriarchy is significant, as is the sarcasm surrounding the comparison of then and now. Those gathered even make light of Abu-Lughod's tape recorder (a male), whose lack of narrative agency is contrastingly spoofed, prompting everyone to laugh at the thought.

> They laughed at themselves and then went quiet. Suddenly Grandma Migdim referred to my tape recorder with its red light glowing in the kerosene-lit room. "Your friend there, doesn't he talk?"
> The girls laughed and said knowledgeably, "No, this one just listens to the talk, grandmother. It doesn't speak." (p. 50)

Two points about data collection bear mentioning here. First, details of performativity should be reflected in field notes, which should document the way purpose and audience figure into narrative composition. It is important to trace what speakers do with words to produce particular effects and, in turn, take note of how listeners respond to what is said. The researcher should detail how everyone involved in storytelling contributes to the outcome. Second, the researcher should keep in view not only what is said and how listeners respond to accounts, but also facets of added meaning over and above specific linkages and composition. For example, in the preceding description of a concluding and very brief exchange, Abu-Lughod highlights participants' layered understanding of the story, one that wouldn't readily be obvious in a transcript of Migdim's account. The humorous inflections point to narrative agency, sarcasm, materiality (the agency of the tape recorder), vocalization, and the recognition of the reflexive relation between speaking and the control of experience.

Abu-Lughod continues to draw our attention to alternative ways of presenting events from the perspective of different roles, this time in relation to the thrilling and dangerous drama of "rubbishing." The term refers to scavenging in the desert for saleable items from abandoned World War II ordnance. If the composition of stories is shaped for recipients, the differential roles storytellers take in conveying stories shape them as well, revealing the different representational purposes that inform varied experiential scripts. Rubbishing's performativity alters the meaning of something that might otherwise be taken to have a singular reality. Abu-Lughod compares two accounts of the dangers involved in scavenging for metal from unexploded bombs. One is Migdim's account and the other is told by her son, Haj Sagr. The dramatic realization of danger relates to their respective roles in the action. As a preface to these accounts, the son provides some historical background.

> After they drove the Germans out, the English left. Then the Arabs could return to their territory. They went back as soon as they could. But they found

that the armies had left the area covered with mines and bombs and big guns that had not gone off. We found hand grenades, some that had been tossed but had not exploded, some that were untouched. . . . Dealers from Alexandria and Cairo came to buy the copper, one kind yellow and another red, and the gunpowder. People would go into the desert in cars and on foot, any way they could. One time someone would pick up a mine and it would explode in his hands. Another time someone would touch a bomb and it would explode. Another time someone would try to undo a detonator, to get out its cartridges or gunpowder, and it would blow up. (p. 59)

Abu-Lughod then compares Migdim's and her son Sagr's accounts of a close call with danger. From this and other comparisons, she demonstrates how roles and related performative concerns give shape to the "same" story. Ever the mother and caregiver, Migdim's first tells of her son's close call. According to Abu-Lughod, her purpose in relating this story is to describe a parent's continuing worry over rubbishing activity and the despair at possible outcomes. Through her vivid show of concern, Migdim emphasizes what only a mother knows.

Migdim tells of her son's close call with these mines, before the tragedies of her brother-in-law's death and then her husband's. As she told it, Sagr had gone off scavenging with his older brother. They took a long time getting back, and she became quite worried. When she finally saw them returning she ran out to greet them. Her older son arrived, walking with his arms folded. "Show me your hands!" she demanded. "Are you all right?" He showed her his hands and there was nothing wrong. She was relieved but then they said, "Get Sagr down from the donkey." She cried out, "What wrong, what's wrong?" They lifted his robe and it was all bloody. It was bandaged. He had stepped on a mine. (p. 59)

Sagr later tells Abu-Lughod this story. The drama is less centered on concerns about bodily harm than it is on elements of the hunt. There is considerable talk about war materiel and how the scavengers deal with it. At the forefront of the narrative is a description of the kinds of materiel available in the desert and the work and tactics surrounding salvaging operations. There also is an animated description of what happens during an explosion. Sagr highlights camaraderie, especially the warm wartime relations between the English and the Arabs.

Sagr's story is meant to impress, not to encourage lament. It isn't a narrative of worry, care, and despair. It is an adventurer's account, composed as a tale of bodily hazards, daring escapades, Herculean efforts at obtaining saleable items, market savvy, even intercultural honor. It is a masculine story with a male cast of characters. Eventually, it features his father's dutiful patriarchal hospitality in the circumstances, appropriately extended to guests and others outside the family.

> Haj Sagr himself told me the story in much more detail and with a different emphasis. Migdim, who remembers staying up all night to nurse him and massage his foot, barely figures in this account; his story has become fixed instead as an illustration of the mutual generosity of the English and the Arabs. His father, Jawwad, not his mother, is the central character. [Sagr describes how an English man encountered in the desert helped bandage his injured foot.] "Then he [the English man] looked at me and saw the blood. He took off his backpack and took out a box with three pills—one small pill, one grey one, and a third capsule with each half a different color. He opened my mouth and put the medicine in it. [Sagr describes at length the medical care offered by the English man.] When we got home my father came out and met us. When he first saw me he asked where I had been hit. When he found out where the wounds were, he said it wasn't serious. [Sagr then details how his father found the English man and gave him water and shelter.] My father really was kind and compassionate." (pp. 62–63)

Conclusion

In his writing, Erving Goffman (1959) repeatedly reminds us of the performativity of everyday life. How we present ourselves to others and how they, in turn, present themselves to us are dramaturgically realized. This is the ordinary choreography of who and what we and our social worlds are to one another. Storytelling is an integral part of this activity, communicatively mediated by gesture, movement, selective detail, emphasis, call, and response. Orienting to the situated performance of storytelling brings this to the fore. It is eminently discernible through ethnographic attention to the staging of accounts and audience responses to narrative actions—yet another dimension of the narrative work that, in this case, constructs stories as scenic entities.

8

Collaboration

It should be increasingly clear that the idea of "one's own story" is problematic. Close examination of the substance and machinery of everyday communication shows that the work of storytelling is far from an individual matter. Instead, it's a full-blown, interactional accomplishment. As Neal Norrick (2000) observes, "Sometimes two or more participants collaborate in producing a story, so that it becomes impossible to say just who is the teller or even the primary teller" (p. 189). This raises two compelling questions: How do those involved in storytelling relate to each other in narrative production, and whose story is being told?

Orienting to Collaboration

The interactional demands on storytelling don't cease just because the storyteller has the floor. Following activation, for an extended utterance to continue, the storyteller must secure tacit (if not explicit) permission to speak past possible turn completion points. Such permission typically comes in the form of signs that the story in progress is being understood and appreciated as an extended account. Such "response tokens" (Sacks, 1992b) commonly emerge as a story is told. Statements such as "Go on" or "Tell me about it" indicate that the listener is following the story, encouraging the storyteller to continue. Even minimal displays of attentiveness or understanding, like "Mm-hm" or Uh-huh," are important response tokens, and serve as encouragement. According to Sacks (1992b), they are even ways for a listener to indicate something like, "The story is not yet over. I know that" (p. 9). Indeed, response tokens almost require the storyteller to continue until a story is hearably complete.

Sometimes one story will literally spread into another. Listeners frequently indicate attentiveness and appreciation by incorporating the actual vocabulary, topic, characters, or other aspects of an emerging story into their own turns at talk. This "co-selection" (Sacks, 1992b) can turn into a subsequent and related story. The apparent relatedness of such "second stories" not only shows that the recipient understood the first story, but it also allows the story recipient to then tell his or her own story. This implies that stories are not merely reflections or accounts of individual experience.

Actions that keep the story going do more than merely lubricate conversational storytelling. Conversational collaboration may also influence where the story is going and what the story is about. As we saw earlier in examples from research interviews, interviewers often provide consequential incitements for particular storylines (see Holstein & Gubrium, 1995a). Recall from Chapter 4 that when an interviewer activated life story narratives oriented to "milestones," the ensuing stories were notably different from life stories prompted by the request to talk about "chapters of your life." While this may be an integral feature of formal interviewing, listeners in casual conversation can activate and encourage particular storylines through similar story-facilitating actions. Listeners, as much as tellers, are implicated in the narrative work of storytelling.

Recognizing the collaborative character of storytelling, we offer the following guideline for orienting to how stories unfold in social interaction:

Guideline

Be alert to how conversational partners collaborate in the production of accounts. Consider the ways this is accomplished as well as how meaning within narratives is collaboratively shaped.

Whether analyzing the various kinds of interview data that narrative analysis often considers, or examining naturally occurring conversational material, the researcher should approach stories as interactional projects. This involves partners—storytellers, listeners, and bystanders—who can each contribute, in some measure, to the emerging narrative detail. As we noted earlier, analysis might emphasize *how* stories are collaboratively told, drawing upon conversation analytic insights and techniques in the process. Or it might concentrate on *what* is accomplished through collaborative storytelling. In this case, the focus would be on the content or meaning of the emergent story, and the kinds of linkages and contexts deployed. In either case, the researcher should attend to the full course of interaction surrounding a story's development.

As we noted in Chapter 4, narrative authority, rights, obligations, and entitlement may all be implicated in how stories are collaboratively produced. Accordingly, the researcher should attempt to document their empirical traces and not simply assume that they are operating to shape narrative production and leave it at that. Researchers should be alert for the ways in which power and influence are manifestly asserted in the process of narrative collaboration.

Into the Field

Consider the myriad interactional contingencies that affect the emergence of an extended narrative in the following spontaneous conversation. The ostensible storyteller—April—offers an account of her first job, which she and her conversational partner then transform into a story about April's most embarrassing moment. (Square brackets [ ] are used to indicate overlapping talk in this extract.)

Ellen: What was your first job?

April: First job, um oh, that was the Halsted Burger King in Halstead Minnesota.

Ellen: That near your house?

April: About six miles away.

Ellen: m-hm

April: and they—they built it brand new, and I was one of the first employees, and because of that we ah—um we had a head honcho woman from International Burger King come and train everybody in, because there was like thirty of us.

Ellen: Wow. Yeah?

April: And uh we had about a week of training and I remember the most embarrassing moment of my life happened then. {laughs}

Ellen: {laughing} What does that *mean*? {laughing}

April: {laughing} Um no this is just—I can't believe I did this but—um I was really nerv—well it was my first job, and I was nervous and there's so much to learn. I mean y'know there's so many things at Burger King you have to [make and uh—]

Ellen: [how old were you?]

April: I was like a sophomore in high school.

Ellen: Okay.

April: Yeah, [the summer after my sophomore year.]

Ellen: [You were young,] okay.

April: And um we were learning the drive-through and just the thought of speaking on—into that microphone and y'know into outside—

Ellen: Yes.

April: And you have to pretend to take orders and, and I was so embarrassed and the first time I had to do it, I said "Welcome to McDonald's [may I take your order?"]

Ellen: [Oh, no.
            {laughing}]

April: And everybody just laughed at me. {laughing}

Ellen: {laughing} Did you try to pull it off like a joke, like you meant to say that?

April: No. {laughing}

Ellen: No. {laughing} Good job.

April: Yeah, that was my very first job. (Norrick, 2000, pp. 30–31)

Note in this exchange how April and Ellen work together to move into and complete the narrative. Ellen activates the storyline by asking about April's first job, and April begins with a factual description. Ellen encourages the nascent story, signalling her attentiveness and interest by asking a clarifying question at the first opportunity. In effect, Ellen has both prompted the story and authorized April to continue in detail when the first line of talk (the first job) might have been exhausted.

For an extended utterance to continue across possible speakership transition points, a storyteller must both secure permission to continue at possible turn completion points and detect signs that the ongoing story is being understood and appreciated. Response tokens can be key mechanisms in this process. In the exchange above, Ellen encourages April's story with a brief mark of attention ("m-hm") and even more explicit encouragement ("Wow. Yeah?"). The utterances are especially noteworthy because they come at places where April's narrative might have been treated as complete. April had hearably informed Ellen about her first job, but Ellen's strong expression of interest clearly encouraged the story to continue.

But the *hows* of the matter are not all there is to the collaboration. Next, April turns the narrative in the direction of her most embarrassing moment, which is a topic change that veers partially away from the invited report of her first job. Ellen, however, encourages this line of talk (a new *what*) with a direct inquiry into the "embarrassing" topic. This juncture in the conversation is rich in alternate possibilities; Ellen could use her turn at talk to reassert the focus on the first job, or she could terminate the line of talk altogether. Instead, she explicitly invites continuation and embellishment, nearly demanding that April proceed to describe her most embarrassing moment. As the story progresses at length, Ellen again shows attention and interest by inquiring about details of the scenario ("How old were you?") and encouraging further talk through agreement ("Yes"). At the end, Ellen steps up her collaboration, posing a promising and face-saving finale to the story by asking if April tried to pass off her gaffe as a joke, a gambit that April declines. Working exclusively from the transcript, the last two utterances in the extract are ambiguous; it's unclear to what Ellen is referring when she says "good job." Nevertheless, the final exchange provides a note of closure with April's punctuating statement "that was my very first job," a direct response to Ellen's initial question. Together, April and Ellen have brought the conversation full circle, back to the opening inquiry.

Whereas Ellen's participation in April's story seems minimal, we can indicate several ways in which this narrative would not have developed without Ellen's collaboration.

- The story would not have started without Ellen's prompting inquiry.
- The story would have ended at several possible turn completion points had Ellen chosen to use her turns at talk differently.
- The initial topic of "first job" was Ellen's suggestion.
- The emergent allied topic—"most embarrassing moment"—was April's suggestion, but it would not have emerged as a full-blown part of the story had Ellen not authorized it.

Thus, both the storytelling itself, and the content of the narrative, depended upon Ellen as well as April. While this might ostensibly be considered April's story, it would not have come to fruition without Ellen's involvement. The story, then, can be analyzed as the product of conversational partnership, not purely April's doing.

No matter how minimal, collaboration should not be discounted. Indeed, sometimes declining to participate in conversational give-and-take can put an end to a storyline; an apparent lack of attention or interest can put a damper on any story. Conversely, measured participation may also facilitate storytelling, essentially allowing the narrator to command the floor in order to produce the extended turn at talk needed to formulate a story. At minimum, a conversational partner must refrain from speaking and pass on opportunities to speak at possible speakership transition points for an extended story to emerge. While Ellen had several conversational opportunities to alter or truncate April's narrative, both her conversational actions and *inactions* (i.e., silences) facilitated the emerging story.

The researcher also needs to be sensitive to how collaboration influences a story's content. For example, on occasion, complicity in actions that "keep the story going" also contributes consequentially to where the story is going. As we saw earlier in examples from research interviews, "prompts" can serve as narrative incitements for particular storylines. Similarly, listeners to informal stories can induce the elaboration of particular dimensions of narrative content and meaning through their own story-facilitating actions.

Consider the following narrative that emerged over the course of a nursing home interview. Grace Wheeler is a 70-year-old nursing home resident who is confined to a wheelchair due to a form of cerebral palsy with which she's been afflicted since birth. She shares a room with her 93-year-old mother, Lucy, who is present throughout the interview. While Grace is the designated respondent, we can see in the following extract how her life story is guided, if not directed, by Lucy's contributions to the conversation. As Lucy conscientiously attends to Grace's life story, she adds to its developing linkages and composition. Jay is the interviewer.

1. *Jay:* Why don't we start by your telling me about your life?

2. *Grace:* Well that was quite a many years ago. I was born in Brinton Station, Ohio.

3. *Lucy:* She was a seven-month baby.

4. *Grace:* I was a seven-month baby. That's what I was. (Elaborates story of growing up with her sisters and brother.) They've all been wonderful.

5. *Lucy:* They taught her . . .

6. *Grace:* And they taught me as well as my mom and dad. And then when radio and television came to the farm, why I learned from them. I love the quiz shows.

7. *Lucy:* She types with a stick in her mouth.

8. *Grace:* I type with a stick in my mouth. I paint with a brush in my mouth. (Grace elaborates a story of travelling with her sisters and the exchange between Jay and Grace continues.)

9. *Jay:* So you're a real sports fan.

10. *Grace:* Yes.

11. *Lucy:* Yes, she is. That television's on . . .

12. *Grace:*   I love it!

13. *Lucy:*   That television's all sports to her.

14. *Grace:*   Well, sports and shows. (Giggling) I love animal shows, too. I love animals.

15. *Lucy:*   Game shows.

16. *Grace:*   Game shows, animal shows, detective stories. I like to read detective stories. My favourite author is John D. McDonald. (J. F. Gubrium, 1993, pp. 152–153)

Whereas we might reasonably figure that this is the story of Grace's life, her mother Lucy clearly directs the content of the plot line. Lucy's role is at least formally that of a peripheral listener—part of the audience for Grace's story—but, as a participant in the unfolding account, that role changes. It is not uncommon for story recipients to display appreciation and understanding of a story by co-selecting words used by the storyteller to build and sustain topical continuity (Sacks, 1992b). Something like this happens here, but with broader implications. Lucy begins in utterance 3 to encourage a line of talk by picking up on Grace's mention of where Grace was born (utterance 2), and elaborating in terms of what kind of a "baby" Grace was. In her next turn at talk (utterance 4), Grace, the ostensible storyteller, appropriates Lucy's term "seven-month baby" to her account and elaborates the story of her (Grace's) childhood. At a possible completion of this utterance, Lucy once again offers her own elaboration on how the siblings related to one another (utterance 5), and in the next utterance (utterance 6), Grace once again appropriates Lucy's phrase ("They taught her . . .") to begin a new storyline. As the discussion progresses, we continue to hear Grace using Lucy's own words to tell her (Grace's) own story. This might prompt the individualistically focused researcher to ask, "Whose story is this?" But it's clear that Grace and Lucy own the account together. It is definitely not Grace's "own story."

While it might be tempting to say that Lucy had commandeered Grace's narrative (asserting narrative authority or status as Grace's mother), this is not precisely the case. Generally, Grace is brief in responding to the initial story activation and the interviewer's subsequent prompting. Lucy, however, keeps the story from lagging at possible turn completion points. At each juncture, where a next speaker may take a turn at talk, Lucy speaks. One might expect this slot in the conversation to be filled by the interviewer (Jay), since this is supposed to be a conversation between Jay and Grace, but in the absence of a specific designation of the next speaker, Lucy seizes the turn and extends Grace's story by providing an appropriately topical extension of Grace's prior utterance. For her part, Grace links her elaborations to Lucy's utterances. By repeating Lucy's phrasing, she establishes topical continuity. While not telling Grace's story, Lucy provides both reasonable topical options and conversational flow. Lucy doesn't so much commandeer the narrative as she provides substantive material and interactional support for the story's linkages and composition. If she asserts her influence, it is within the context of the emerging, three-way conversational give-and-take.

Let us expand on the ways in which narrative linkages and their developing contexts can be collaboratively accomplished. To illustrate, consider the linkages and contexts that are constructed in another life story interview (Holstein & Gubrium, 1995a). The following extracts are taken from a research interview completed with Helen Cody (HC), who lived at Frampton Place, an adult congregate living facility consisting of several houses and small blocks of apartment buildings located in a park-like setting. Helen was 88 years old at the time. The interview begins with Helen talking of the distant past and moving her story almost immediately into the present. JG is the interviewer.

JG: Everyone has a life story. I wonder if you can tell me a bit about your life.

HC: Well, I was born in Providence, Rhode Island and my uncle was the first figure skater in the country and he taught me figure skating. And I skated in the Boston area five opening nights and so there's that era. And then, of course, I just was married and had my son and not much else. I don't know what else to talk about. And then I, then after my husband died, I came on here to be near my son. So that's about it.

JG: If you could divide your life up into chapters, let's say you were writing your life story and you had chapters, what would the different chapters be about? What would, for example, chapter 1 be about?

HC: Well, my youth was very interesting. I did figure skating and dancing and things like that. That was a happy time, with my uncle. . . . I can't think of anything else. I haven't done too much, just living and doing my health work and what have you and having friends come in and things like that. That's about all. I've lived a quiet life outside of my youth when I was skating and was in the limelight. . . .

JG: What would the last chapter of your life (story) be about, if you were writing it?

HC: Well, I don't know. Just that I'm here.

JG: Where?

HC: Right here in (pause)

JG: In Frampton, you mean?

HC: No, not Frampton. (Pause) Well, of course. I'm not too happy with all the old folks. They're really old and I'm not in that class at all. I stand out because, well, I have my senses you know, and everything. I'm more interested in everything and so it isn't very interesting to me, the old folks. And they're old crabs, most of them. And the women. If they don't like you or think you're just wrong, they shun you and everything. Women are something, really they are. Especially with their own. And they're crabby and probably always very crabby. . . . So I sort of lived alone here. There's one or two people I can converse with, but they don't, you know, they're too old or something, you know. And they don't take that interest in visiting.

JG: That's important to you?

HC: Yes, it's important to me. So I have to sort of live alone, whether I like it or not. (Elaborates) I think if you have had an interesting life, you'd be more talkative when you're older, or interesting, but they never had that. So, of course, I kind of expect it. They just go their own way, so it isn't very happy here for me because I don't feel old, you see. So that's what's hard. I never would be old. I'm old now, but I never feel it, you know, so that's tough. (Holstein & Gubrium, 1995a, pp. 60–61)

To this point in the interview, Helen's life story was on a distinct trajectory toward a rather unhappy ending. Her interesting life before coming to Frampton Place had seemingly descended into an isolated and lonely existence, surrounded by inhospitable "old crabs." The commanding narrative linkage of the story so far was the stark contrast between Helen's interesting past and drab present, somewhat along the lines of Myrtle Johnson's story in Chapter 6. As the interview proceeded, Helen drew other distinguishable and contrasting narrative linkages with her interesting past.

Eventually the interviewer began to inquire into the current quality of Helen's life. Helen said that there was no one she felt especially close to at Frampton Place, that there was nobody there she might consider to be like family, and that she was sorely disappointed that so many around her acted and thought like old people. The interviewer then asked Helen what the word "home" meant to her. She returned to linkages that produced the developing narrative context of her story.

Well, home means everything I think, because it is home. If you make it a home, but you have to make it a home. And enjoy it. I'd like a lot of people coming in and visiting. Being normal, you know, instead of the woman next door who doesn't even speak to me. I don't even know her. See how ignorant it is here? When I came here, I saw there was a woman next door and I went over to see her and I said, "I thought I'd say hello to you." And she says, "I don't want anything to do with you." She didn't even know me! And she talks against me and everything and she doesn't even know me. Ignorant! (Holstein & Gubrium, 1995a, pp. 61–62)

The interviewer's prompt to talk about "home" occasioned the continuation of meaning making centered on Helen's life at Frampton. It became apparent that in the context of Frampton Place and its residents, Helen did not feel at home and the quality of her life was decidedly negative; the linkages between Frampton Place, and its occupants, and the quality of her life coalesced into this less than satisfying existence.

In time, the discussion casually shifted to what Helen called her "things," as we will see in the following extract. By this she meant her long-standing and meaningful possessions, particularly her furniture. Interestingly enough, at this juncture, the linkages with "things" began to compose a new context for judgments about her present circumstances, one that made Helen feel quite at home at Frampton Place. "Things" flagged a new set of meanings for understanding the quality of her life. As Helen pointed to various possessions as she showed the interviewer around her apartment, she created a new sense of what had been evidently there all along but unnoticed. The scenic presence of the talk and interaction and her things now supported a new story, one centered on pride of ownership and of place. Helen's narrative orientation to her things made all the difference.

JG: Now that you've lived here (Frampton Place) for about three years, I think, do you feel it's home now?

HC: No, because of the people. This is my home (points to her things), just this house here.

JG: But you feel this (points to surroundings) is home?

HC: Yes, it has to because some of my furniture is here, but my son took the rest of my stuff to put in storage. So this just (pause) There's two bedrooms here.

JG: Are there? (Helen shows the interviewer around) Oh, yeah, I see. What would it have to be like to be more like home here? You (said) you feel like home here in this place?

HC: Well, just because it's my furniture. (Holstein & Gubrium, 1995a, p. 62)

As the interviewer explored the linkages between place, possessions, and home, the quality of Helen's life changed dramatically from what she had portrayed earlier. Until now, the quality of her life was constructed from linkages with Frampton Place and its aged residents, which contrasted with

Helen's interesting early life. The newly emerging linkages of home and personal possessions provided the interviewer with the opportunity to explore an alternative set of meanings, namely, the more intimate setting of Helen's room at Frampton. This might lead us to wonder if Helen's story would have turned out differently if this setting had been the exclusive focus of an interview with her about the quality of her life. Would the story have been more sanguine if the interview focused directly on Helen's little world of her room and things, rather than dealing at the outset with her apparently more satisfying early life? Note how, in the following extract, this new context encourages Helen to speak rather fondly about her life, with which the interviewer collaborates.

JG: Do you feel this place (pointing to the surroundings), living here, is part of your life or is it separate from your life?

HC: No, it's part of my life, on account of the furniture. It feels like home, because it's my furniture, because if I don't have my furniture, I don't feel very much at home.

JG: Is that right?

HC: Yeah, I think if you had it all your life, you would. And had to give it up, you wouldn't. (Points to various objects in the room) My little details and everything. (Helen picks up a picture she painted and talks about her paintings) . . .

JG: Are these (things) very important to have around you, these things?

HC: Oh, yes, well because they were something I did, you know. No, I think it was wonderful that I could do it, you know. It's been good that I could do something that I could enjoy. So I've enjoyed those things.

JG: What would it be like if you lived here without all these things?

HC: Well, I wouldn't have those memories. They've been good memories, of my life, happy times. So, anyway, it's no fun to get old because you are lonesome, especially when people aren't friendly. That's doubly hard. That's the hardest thing I think I can put up with. People's actions, they speak louder than words. The old saying: actions speak louder than words. (Holstein & Gubrium, 1995a, pp. 63–64)

As Helen describes the paintings and other objects in the room, her experience comes alive in a story of a person who took great satisfaction from life. Asked later what meaning the things had for her, Helen answers in relation to the people who had shared her rich and interesting life, "Oh, everything, everything. They're my life, my folks. They were good people, very good." The quality of that life is now narratively connected with her things, as she called them, forming a context for constructing further detailed linkages by both Helen and the interviewer.

Nevertheless, the earlier context intrudes at the end of the extract. As Helen turns away from the pictures, other objects, and her immediate surroundings, her negative outlook resurfaces. She again speaks of the quality of her life in terms used in the first part of the interview. The transition appears to have been prompted by the question about what it would mean not to have her things surrounding her. The question apparently resurrected earlier concerns and once again linked Helen's evaluation of her life to her current state of loneliness and having to live in the midst of the "old crabs."

What was the quality of Helen's life in the nursing home? What narrative linkages and contexts drew her account into a meaningful story? It's difficult to know, other than to say that the extended account's narrative organization composed several possible stories of the quality of her life. The quality of Helen's life and the tenor of her life story ebbed and flowed in light of varying ways of composing it that were built up in the exchange. As the *whats* of the exchange came to the fore, were abandoned, and reinstituted in the course of the give-and-take with the interviewer, so did the meanings of her story. Collaboration fueled the shifts in composition as much as the putative circumstances of Helen's life.

Finally, let's turn directly to the question of narrative ownership, an issue we initially encountered in relation to Stanley's "own story." Narrative collaboration bears significantly on the issue. To empirically highlight the matter, consider various aspects of the following multiparty conversation—a "bad hair day" story told in the company of four friends. In orienting to its collaborative dimensions, the researcher is compelled to abandon the individual ownership view of stories. (Square brackets [ ] are used to indicate overlapping talk in this extract. Italics are used to indicate heavy emphasis on a word or phrase.)

Jean: Annie gave me a permanent once, too.

Louise: Annie did?

Jean: Once and only once. {general laughter} I would never allow her to touch my hair again.

Louise: Well, remember the time—

Jean: *Yoooh.* Talk about Afro, when Afro wasn't even in *style.* My God.

Annie: Well, see I *started* [something.]

Jean: [Frizz ball.] I was a frizz ball. It wasn't even Afro. I was just *frizz*

Louise: Remember [when—]

Jean: [It was] *terrible.*

Louise: Jennifer, the first time Jennifer had a perm when she came home, it was the funniest thing.

Jean: She put something on her head, a bag or something?

Louise: She wore her—

Annie: {laughs}

Louise: Well she wore her—

Helen: Hair ball, hair ball. Yeah because she—

Annie: She just always had this *hood* on, and she ran upstairs.

Louise: *No.* First she *threw* her bag up the stairs, almost *hit* me.

Annie: Oh, yeah.

Louise: Then, *bang,* the door slams and I'm like—I was on the *phone.* I was like "Ah I don't know. My sister just walked in. I think something's wrong." And [then she ran up the stairs.]

Annie: [Oh that's it.] "I look like a damn *poodle.*" {general laughter}

Louise: Like *sobbing,* "I look like a poodle."

Helen: Aw {laughing}

Annie: Then she came down to eat and she'd *wrapped* a towel about her head.

Helen: Aw {Laughing}

Louise: She barricaded herself for a while in her room.

Jean: *My* hair takes like *this.* I mean.

Annie: Yeah. (Norrick, 2000, pp. 154–156)

Arguably the main narrative told here is Louise's story about Jennifer's disastrous perm, but let's look at how this story ultimately takes shape. Louise's story grows out of the ongoing conversation that touched upon a bad perm that Annie had given Jean. The story appears to be activated by Jean's first mention of a bad perm experience. Even before Jean's story develops in detail, Louise makes a conversational bid to tell her own competing account, using the story preface "Well, remember the time—" to shift the focus from Jean's experience. Jean, however, does not immediately cede speakership, and forges on enthusiastically ("*Yoooh.* Talk about Afro.") to tell of her "frizz ball" hairdo.

Louise persists in trying to assume speakership, even after Jean again declines to let Louise start a new line of talk by overlapping Louise's second attempt at the "Remember" story preface. Louise, however, perseveres through the overlap, allowing Jean to finish her utterance but quickly moving on to the new, but related, topic of Jennifer's bad perm. Note here that Louise is not precisely trying to change the subject, as it were. Rather, Louise's "Well remember the time—" is an attempt to generalize the story from Jean's "bad perm" and link it to bad perms collectively. By eventually asserting this linkage, Louise is able to become part of the ongoing narrative, both as a teller and, eventually, as a subject.

Collaboration persists throughout the story's telling. As Louise launches her own nascent account, Jean stays involved, contributing detailed information about Jennifer's perm at the first possible speaker transition point ("she put something on her head . . ."). From the outset, it would be difficult to construe this as simply Louise's story. Annie and Helen, for example, quickly join in. While Helen's contributions are minimal, adding little to the story line or content, her brief comments and intonations indicate her attentiveness, tacitly encouraging Louise to continue with the story. Her laughter further promotes the story's telling. Annie offers several contributions, mainly providing additional detail to the ongoing account and offering tacit encouragement at several junctures.

But the collaboration is not purely cooperative or without glitches. Most notably, Louise corrects or contradicts Annie on nearly every occasion when Annie adds to the story. Louise allows Annie's description, "She just always had this hood on" to stand, but Annie's subsequent comment that "she ran right upstairs" elicits an immediate "No" from Louise. Louise changes both the facts and the tenor of the scenario, upgrading the seriousness of Jennifer's flight upstairs by adding that Jennifer "threw her bag up the stairs." Importantly, Louise also notes that Jennifer almost hit Louise with the bag. This statement underscores the gravity of the situation, making it clear that Jennifer was genuinely upset and acting out in distress. It also inserts Louise as a central character in the story as well as its teller, putting her at the heart of the action and lending authenticity to Louise's version of the account.

Later, when Annie adds to the story by quoting Jennifer as saying "I look like a damn poodle," Louise objects to the tone of Annie's characterization, saying it was "like sobbing." This transforms the possible meaning of Jennifer's outburst from annoyed or possibly even humorous to sad, again accenting the gravity of the situation—at least from Jennifer's point of view. Louise's reiteration of "I look like a poodle" omits "damn," further transforming the tone of Jennifer's lament. Analytically, we might note that there is a semblance of competition in this spate of storytelling, with Louise and Annie competing to be the authoritative voice in the narrative. In a sense, narrative ownership runs the gamut of the competition.

Matters of competition and ownership may implicate competing perspectives, as well as power and control. We encourage researchers to explore these dimensions of interactional storytelling, but again caution them to document how power and influence are interactionally asserted, and not take them to be exogenous characteristics exerting some sort of unseen, yet irresistible, social force.

Conclusion

The collaborative work of storytelling draws the contours of accounts quite differently than a simplified or distilled story text might suggest. Once more, we see that beginnings, middles, and endings are fluidly located in ongoing talk and interaction. The theme and content of a story cannot be divorced from its interactional development and the ongoing construction of meaningful contexts. If storytelling is a collaborative activity, how do we know who owns a story? Perhaps a text does, or the interaction or situation from which a story emerges.

9

Control

Narrative collaboration is not without disagreements and conflict. The issue of narrative control looms with these challenges; it is a common feature of all talk and interaction. Just as multiple parties may contribute to an ongoing story line, multiple speakers may vie for control over who might speak, the direction a story might take, and what it will contain. Consensus and agreement—or even disagreement—are never automatic in the work of storytelling. Sometimes they involve negotiation. Sometimes they need to be asserted or imposed. This chapter takes up the mechanics of narrative control.

Orienting to Control

Narrative control is the sterner side of narrative collaboration. But just like other forms of interaction, it is fundamentally collaborative; control can seldom be unilaterally asserted, even as matters of status, hierarchy, and entitlement may lurk in the background. Participants in talk and interaction have objectives and strategic preferences to which each will tend to adhere (see Goodwin, 1989; Mumby, 1993; Ochs & Taylor, 1992). Circumstances also come into play with their own normative expectations. Individuals, however, are not compelled to capitulate to them, but merely take them into account. Narrative control is therefore one further upshot of the complex work that constitutes narrative reality. Narrative rights, obligations, and power must all be interactionally accomplished; they are not simply manifest as narrative control.

Attempts at control may be more or less overt, more or less formal. Many of the examples we discussed in relation to narrative activation (Chapter 4) and narrative collaboration (Chapter 8) evince traces of informal control that are barely noticed within the flow of everyday communication. Recall, for example, that most of our illustrations of narrative activation imply some degree of control. Even the simplest of story prefaces may be strategically used to clear the way and set the stage for a story to be told. Prefaces play upon the normative expectancies of sequentially structured conversation to establish the space and opportunity to launch an extended narrative. The child imploring her mother to "Guess what!" is skillfully controlling the sequential environment of conversation to have her mother ask her to tell her story. And recall how even the most casual inquiry ("What was your first job?"), or an interviewer's prompt for a respondent to "tell me about the chapters of your life," subtly controls the ways that the person responding might construct his or her story. In each instance, activation itself is implicitly a mode of control. The same might be said of the myriad conversational maneuvers that constitute narrative collaboration.

Control can also be more formal. This is most evident when narrative preferences are shaped by institutional influences including rules, guidelines, roles, and the like that are explicitly designed to shape and constrain interaction. As "going concerns" (Hughes, 1984), institutions shape talk and interaction—and storytelling—in particular ways. There is, in effect, an external dimension to the collaborative influence over the way a narrative unfolds. If there are preferences in informal talk and interaction, the formal dimensions of what is "going" in institutional concerns move things along in discernible ways. This, of course, adumbrates the theme of Part III of the book—narrative environments. For now, however, we will touch on the less formal aspects of narrative work as control is articulated in talk and interaction.

During earlier discussions, the question of "Whose story is this?" repeatedly arose. As we extend our discussion from collaboration to control, the question is even more pressing. When narrative analysis documents the ways in which several parties contribute to, or resist, accounts, the researcher is forced to carefully consider how narrative content is affected by the multiple sources of narrative production. To fully understand what is conveyed in a narrative, the researcher should key into the circumstances under which the narrative emerged in terms of both how control is exerted and what effect circumstances have on the results.

Institutions ubiquitously mediate narrative collaboration. The research interview is a prime example. As we have already seen, expectations about interview interaction allow the interviewer to exert considerable (although not complete) control over the direction in which interview narratives develop. Courtroom talk is another form of highly regulated interaction. Special rules and procedures govern how talk in court cases proceeds. While courtrooms have much in common with other multiparty settings involving a variety of speakers, official rules set the boundaries of the proceedings, specify the parties who may legitimately participate, and predetermine the forms of participation. Transfer of speakership is strictly governed; turns at talk are procedurally preallocated (see J. M. Atkinson & Drew, 1979). Classrooms can be similarly regulated, with speakership limited to those who are given permission to speak in the context of lessons following a "(teacher) initiation-(student) reply-(teacher) evaluation" format (see Mehan, 1979).

Of course, rules and formal procedures do not, by themselves, control talk. They need to be articulated. It is rule *use*, not rules themselves, that is consequential in narrative work. Anyone familiar with courtroom interaction— or its television facsimile—is generally acquainted with the procedural preallocation of speaking rights. Turn order is fixed and the type of turn at talk is predetermined. In articulating the rules, attorneys ask questions, witnesses provide answers. Any variation from this can be sanctioned, but this is an interactional—not automatic—matter. When a line of questioning or a developing answer strays from what might be deemed appropriate, attorneys may object or judges may intercede. But control, in this instance, remains within the interaction, not simply in the institutional background. It is the way institutional rules are applied that has an effect on the sort of talk that eventually emerges.

Narratives are certainly part of legal proceedings, but their emergence is closely monitored and strictly controlled. In court, there is a time and place for everything, so to speak. If extended talk emerges at inauspicious junctures, it is immediately quelled. If it strays from the ostensible matters of concern, it will be drawn back on track or terminated through "objections" and orders from a judge. If parties other than the designated speaker attempt to contribute to a narrative in progress, their participation will be squelched. The upshot of the active management of the rules of procedure in formal, court-like settings is that narrative production is significantly different from storytelling in casual conversation. Indeed, in some types of hearings, the requisite question–answer format severely restrains extended witness testimony, and may even eliminate narrative production altogether (see Miller & Holstein, 1996).

Considerations of how the institutionalization of talk shapes narratives lead us to the verge of institutional mediations. Part III of the book turns explicitly to how socially organized settings provide discursive environments for narrative production. Such environments will be the point of departure for analyzing narrative control in those chapters. But at this juncture, we remain on interactional terrain and will defer such discussion, confining our attention to control's communicative dimensions. We offer the following guideline for analyzing how narrative form and content are interactionally controlled:

Guideline

Be sensitive to the ways in which narrative production is strategically shaped within distinctive circumstances. Move beyond narrative texts to consider how stories do or do not emerge interactionally and, if so, which ones ultimately get told.

The guideline serves to remind the researcher to scan interactional horizons beyond the actual narrative in question in order to fully understand its production, substance, and implications. A view confined to narrative texts doesn't help us to understand when stories are not permitted to be told. In narrative reality, the absence of stories—that is, silence or stories silenced—does not mean that there are no stories to tell. Within this broader field, researchers should approach narratives not as the sole property of a single speaker. Again, narration is interactional and, beyond that, related to surrounding going concerns. Narrative control resides in the way conversational partners cooperate during turn-taking exchanges that yield particular storied outcomes. The researcher needs to be equally alert to how particular narratives are advanced, or not advanced, as the case might be. This extends narrativity to untold stories, which is beyond the purview of text-based analysis. And, as we will see in the context of courtroom proceedings, untold stories may be as much in the interests of speakers and listeners as stories told.

Into the Field

Informal interactional control is often a subtle feature of narrative production. We can see this by briefly revisiting the "bad perm" story from Chapter 8. Recall that when Louise tried to launch a second story from the first "perm" story that Jean had started, Jean squelched Louise's first bid for an extended turn at talk. Jean continued talking over Louise's utterance, in effect, maintaining control of the conversational floor. From that point on, there was an implicit contest over which speaker would, in fact, control the story being told. Let's take another brief look at a portion of that conversation.

Louise: Remember [when—]

Jean: [It was] *terrible.*

Louise: Jennifer, the first time Jennifer had a perm when she came home, it was the funniest thing.

Jean: She put something on her head, a bag or something?

Louise: She wore her—

Annie: {laughs}

Louise: Well she wore her—

Helen: Hair ball, hair ball. Yeah because she—

Annie: She just always had this *hood* on, and she ran upstairs.

Louise: *No.* First she *threw* her bag up the stairs, almost *hit* me.

Annie: Oh, yeah.

Louise: Then, *bang,* the door slams and I'm like—I was on the *phone.* I was like "Ah I don't know. My sister just walked in. I think something's wrong." And [then she ran up the stairs.] (Norrick, 2000, pp. 154–155)

After her initial bid to assume speakership—which failed—Louise persisted by introducing a new storyline about Jennifer's perm at the first opportunity, latching this new storyline to Jean's previous story topic. This time, Jean tacitly endorsed Louise's story by contributing some additional detail ("She put something on her head, a bag or something?"). Significantly, this contribution came in the form of a question, thus inviting Louise to continue her story in the next turn at talk. Louise tried to proceed, but Annie and Helen chimed in with details of their own, not allowing Louise to proceed at length. Finally, Louise directly contradicted Annie ("*No.* First she *threw* her bag up the stairs, almost *hit* me") and, in the process, added emphasis and information that accomplished three things. First, it forcefully discredited Annie's contribution to the story with the strong "*No.*" Second, adding additional detail helped reestablish Louise as the authoritative storyteller. Finally, adding that the thrown bag "almost hit me" placed Louise at the heart of the incident in question, making her an actual participant in the scenario. Louise set a claim of firsthand, authentic knowledge that others were obliged to respect.

Analytically, the researcher can view each of these conversational gambits as subtle forms of informal control. The story that eventually emerged took form through Louise's adroit command of the sequential environment of this extended exchange—and the others' tacit cooperation. We might argue that informal control was exercised at nearly every turn-taking juncture, and that this control ultimately shaped the story conveyed. Indeed, if Louise had not asserted control within this conversation, the story of Jennifer's perm may not have been told at all, or the details of it might have been substantially different.

Formal control is also interactionally asserted. In considering narrative control in relation to going concerns, researchers should be alert to conversational practices and not assume that just because institutional preferences are in place, things will automatically move along as expected. If formal, institutionalized circumstances have preferred narratives, they must be interactionally and strategically set in motion. There is narrative work involved, the careful inspection of which can show that things are not so automatic after all. Even when institutional circumstances virtually prescribe interactional patterns, the formal organization of talk is subject to interactional variation. Borrowing a crude phrase, this is where "shit happens."

Courtrooms, for instance, seemingly have rules governing every aspect of court proceedings. Nevertheless, participants work strategically within the formal tenets of courtroom procedure and decorum to shape courtroom interactions to their preferences (also see Patterson, 2002). Take, for example, the way nascent narratives are short-circuited in involuntary commitment hearings (see Holstein, 1993). In the following extract, candidate patient Katie Maxwell (KM) has been hospitalized under charges of "grave disability" and is being questioned by her public defender (PD4). At issue is her ability to provide for her own food, clothing, and shelter. (Double slashes [//] indicate the onset of overlapping talk.)

1. *PD4:*   If they let you go today, Katie, do you have a place to live?

2. *KM:*   Uh huh my mother's (place).

3. *PD4:*   Where is your mother's place?

4. *KM:*   In Bellwood.

5. *PD4:*   What's the address?

6. *KM:*   One twenty Acton Street. I can come // and go as I please.

7. *PD4:*   ((breaking in)) That's fine Katie.

8.   Does your mother say you can live with her?

9. *KM:*   Yeah it's OK with her.

10. *PD4:*   Can you eat your meals there?

11. *KM:*   Yeah there's no one there // always watching me.

12. *PD4:*   ((breaking in)) You can just answer yes or
no. OK?

13. *KM:*   OK. . . . (Holstein, 1993, p. 97)

The PD's questions focused on formal grave disability criteria that relate to issues of residence, food, and other basic necessities. At the same time, we can see a set of conversational practices that promote the sort of brief, to-the-point answers the PD was seeking. Note, for example, how the PD's questions were formulated to elicit direct—often one-word—answers. The PD accepted Ms. Maxwell's brief answers as complete in each instance, and moved to a subsequent question. When Ms. Maxwell attempted to elaborate her answers, however, the PD broke into her talk. For example, at lines 6 and 11, Ms. Maxwell tried to embellish or qualify her minimal answer, suggesting an impending narrative response. Each time, the PD moved quickly to terminate the embellishments, stifling any potential story that might emerge. The content of each overlapping utterance indicated that the candidate patient's answer was adequately completed (e.g., line 7: "That's fine Katie.") and discouraged continuation. The PD thus controlled the candidate patient's talk at the first possible turn completion point (see Sacks et al., 1974), keeping the testimony brief and curtailing accounts that may have been in the offing.

We can see variations of this strategy of narrative curtailment in other cases involving candidate patients Fred Smitz (FS) and Roger Madison (RM).

1. *PD1:*   Where would you live?

2. *FS:*   I think I'd go to a new board and care home not populated by

3.   rapists // and Iranian agents

4. *PD1:*   ((breaking in)) Fine, Mr. Smitz. Now would you take your medication?

5. *FS:*   I would if it didn't pass // through the hands of too many Russians.

6. *PD1:*   ((breaking in)) Do you get an SSI check, Mr. Smitz?
(Holstein, 1993, p. 98)

1. *PD6:*   Will you go to the Mental Health Center for your medicine?

2. *RM:*   I'll try unless unless // unless the voices get too loud

3. *PD6:*   ((breaking in)) And you'll take it like the doctor says?
(Holstein, 1993, p. 98)

In each instance, the public defenders headed off the possibility of extended accounts by claiming their turns at talk before the accounts could emerge. In effect they were reining in spates of "crazy talk" (Holstein, 1993) that might be heard as evidence for commitment, the significance of which also relates to the PDs' stakes in the matter.

Particular narratives also may be encouraged through other turn-taking practices. Recall that story prefaces typically lead to storytelling when listeners respond to the initial preface with some facilitating utterance in their turn at talk. Sometimes this amounts to an invitation to expand a story. Other story instigators are more passive, even as they control storytelling just the same. In this regard, consider another example from involuntary commitment hearings. Here, an exchange between a district attorney (DA) and a candidate patient in an involuntary commitment hearing helps extend, not curtail, a nascent story within the context of a courtroom cross-examination.

In the next extract, the DA is cross-examining candidate patient Henry Johnson (HJ). Defense attorneys such as public defenders in commitment cases want their clients to provide succinct answers that are directly to the point. Typically, their concern is to keep clients from being committed, and, generally, the less said, the better. In contrast, district attorneys in commitment cases often encourage candidate patients to speak expansively, expecting that they will produce the "crazy talk" that confirms that hospitalization is needed. Sometimes the emerging talk is incipiently florid, demonstrating the candidate patient's psychiatric symptoms as in the three prior examples. Other times, the talk's form rather than explicit content can be heard as symptomatic.

Such was the case with Henry Johnson. During the direct examination in his case, the DA asked several questions that prompted responses from Mr. Johnson that hardly seemed noteworthy. Then the DA initiated the following dialogue:

1. *DA4:*   How you been feeling lately?

2. *HJ:*   OK

3.   ((Silence))

4. *HJ:*   I been feeling pretty good.

5.   ((Silence))

6. *DA4:*   Uh huh

7.   ((Silence))

8. *HJ:*   Pretty good, ummm all right

9.   ((Silence))

10. *HJ:*   Got a job with (several words inaudible)

11.   ((Silence))

12. *HJ:*   Pays OK, not bad.

13.   ((Silence 4 seconds))

14. *HJ:*   My car got hit, an accident, really messed it up

15.   ((Silence))

16. *HJ:*   Got to get it on the street

17.   ((Silence 5 seconds))

18. *HJ:*   They gonna let us go to the truck out front?

19. *DA:*   When you're all done here they might. (Holstein, 1993, p. 108)

After hearing this testimony, the judge ordered Mr. Johnson's hospitalization by reason of "grave disability," noting that Johnson's testimony was "confused and jumbled." As the judge put it, "He didn't know what to say. He was stopping and starting, jumping from one thing to another. You can see that he can't focus on one thing at a time" (Holstein, 1993, p. 108). But how, interactionally, did this seemingly disjointed, non-coherent talk materialize? Close examination reveals the DA's complicity in Johnson's apparent ramblings.

Commonsensically, the spate of talk that emerges from lines 2 through 16 is hearable as Mr. Johnson's narrative of what he's been up to lately. While Johnson was only minimally responsive to the DA's initial question, what follows can be heard as a halting account of recent events in Johnson's life. Note, however, that the narrative is spread across several possible speakership transition points. Having asked the initial question, the DA places himself in the conversational position of signaling at possible utterance completion points whether or not the question has been adequately answered. The first of these occurs at the end of Johnson's response at line 2. Here, Johnson has ostensibly completed his turn at talk by providing an answer to the initial question. At this point, the DA might be expected to take another turn in the question–answer sequence, but he remains silent, refusing his turn and signaling that the preceding utterance was insufficient as an answer to his prior question. Johnson responds in a conversationally accountable fashion, terminating the emerging silence with an elaboration of his prior utterance, offering a more complete answer to the initial question. Once again, at the end of the utterance, a possible speaker transition point emerges, but, rather than taking this opportunity, at line 6 the DA offers a minimal response ("Uh huh") that demonstrates his attentiveness and invites continuation (Maynard, 1980).

Mr. Johnson continues to elaborate, but when he tries to end his next utterance (line 8), he again encounters the DA's silence. Such silences may be heard as conversational difficulties attributable to the prior speaker, in this case, Mr. Johnson. A common solution to emerging silence is for the prior speaker to resume talking, in effect continuing his or her turn when a next speaker declines to speak, as Johnson does several times in this extract. Mr. Johnson's attempt to hold the conversation together in the face of his partner's reluctance to take a turn at talk resulted in a series of utterances that was broken up by silences but that nonetheless constitute a brief story. The DA passively controlled the construction of this story by declining to talk at points where his speakership might be anticipated. This provoked Johnson's elaborations and continuations, resulting in the story we eventually hear. (See Holstein [1993] for a more technically detailed analysis.) Even though Mr. Johnson did all the talking, we can see that he was adroitly led to produce the extended, yet discontinuous narrative that the judge cited as evidence of grave disability. The *form* of the narrative—full of stops, starts, and changes in direction—was the joint responsibility of the DA and Mr. Johnson, but the judge attributed it solely to Mr. Johnson for the practical purpose at hand. The DA's narrative control went unnoticed. We should point out, however, that the *whats* of narrativity—what story will or will not be told in this case—can't be fully anticipated from the manipulation of conversational machinery alone. While the DA hoped to extract the sort of crazy talk that would help his case, his conversational maneuvering could not ensure the content of what Mr. Johnson said.

Sometimes narrative control is difficult or costly to achieve. This is apparent when speakers overtly compete for the right to tell a story in "their own way." Such occasions may reveal that a storyteller's control over narrative particulars is not especially tight, as we saw in our earlier example of the bad perm story. We see more of this in the following example of how details of a narrative are conversationally claimed and challenged. Donna Eder (1995) reports hearing the exchange in a school. It is a setting in which, when certain topics such as athletic prowess emerge, male egos become sensitive. The story quickly shifts from jovial banter about a football injury to serious challenges to masculinity and toughness among adolescent boys. One of the boys, Sam, begins the story, presenting himself as tough and stoic in the face of a broken finger. The other boys, however, add details and nuance to Sam's self-presentation, leaving his toughness more equivocal than Sam might have portrayed. (Double slashes [//] indicate the onset of overlapping talk.)

1. *Sam:*   Hey Joe, remember when I told ya, I go, "My finger hurt so bad I can't even feel it?" He goes, "Good, you won't feel 'em hit it." [Laughter] He

didn't know I'd broke it, man. You remember in the Edgewood game, I broke my finger? //

2. *Hank:*   // I called him a big pussy when he told me that. "Hey, you big pussy, get out there 'n' play."

3. *Sam:*   He [referring to the coach] goes, "Don't worry, you won't feel it when they hit it."

4. *Hank:*   Sam goes, Sam goes, "Look at my finger." [In a high voice] I said, "Oh you pussy cat, you can't play."

5. *Sam:*   You liar.

6. *Hank:*   I did too //

7. *Sam:*   // Well I did, I played the whole game.

8. *Tom:*   [To Sam] You was cryin' too.

9. *Sam:*   Yes I did man. (Eder, 1995, pp. 65–66)

Sam's initial story and Hank's subsequent embellishment are built up through many of the conversational moves we have previously discussed. What is noteworthy about this extract is that full consensus never develops. There are several points of disagreement about what actually happened, as well as what to make of that. While there are institutional imperatives to encourage Sam, for one, to defend his prowess, things seem to drift along. There is an important lesson to be gleaned from such contested narratives and the conversation surrounding them. On the terrain of narrative work, things don't always work out smoothly. There is slippage between what we might expect, knowing the going concern in place, and the control dynamics at play. Narrative contests and accompanying attempts at control over the content and meaning of emerging stories tell us as much about narrative work as they do about the experiences that are recounted in the contested narratives. An ethnographic approach to narrative analysis helps researchers sort this out and capture both phenomena.

Sometimes, of course, narrative contests are more conclusively resolved. We find an example in Alan Young's (1995) study of a psychiatric unit in a Veteran's Administration center providing inpatient treatment for victims of post-traumatic stress disorder (PTSD). In this facility, individual and group psychotherapy addresses the etiology and symptoms of PTSD. The psychotherapeutic philosophy guiding the PTSD program is fundamentally psychoanalytic, so the keys to recovery are said to be located in the victim's past. Problems must be uncovered before they can be fixed.

The approach relies upon two assumptions about PTSD. One assumption is that the psychodynamic core of PTSD is a repetitive compulsion. The victim is psychologically compelled to reenact the behavior that precipitated the disorder in a futile attempt to gain mastery over the circumstances that originally overwhelmed him. The second assumption is that in order to recover, the patient must recall his traumatic memory, disclose it to the therapist and fellow patients during group psychotherapy, and subject the memory and its narrative to therapeutic scrutiny. The facility thus has a well-articulated "model" of the disease, providing staff and patients with a way of characterizing PTSD and related experiences. This offers a firm background of narrative preferences.

The therapeutic staff makes the center's model obvious to participants and its use develops quite naturally. Nevertheless, the policy of strict adherence to the model is sometimes tested, and narrative control can become quite explicit. When narratives emerge in ways that do not resonate with the model, group participants may be reminded to "use the model," to rethink or re-story experience more precisely in terms of the center's therapeutic discourse. In such instances, we literally hear the model being imposed in the ongoing conversation.

Consider the following exchange in a group psychotherapy session involving Carol, the therapist, and a set of patients. One of the patients, Jack, has related to the group some experiences, but has failed to formulate the narrative in the recognizable terms of the model. Carol intervenes:

Carol: Say to yourself, I've been punishing myself and people around me for twenty years. Say Jack, you *can* choose to stop.

Jack: Listen, Carol. On some nights, I feel anxiety going through my body like electricity. It started in Vietnam. It wasn't just a feeling. It was anxiety together with terrible chest pains and difficulty breathing. . . . And I'm still getting them.

Carol: What would you call it?

Jack: Well, I know that it's called a "panic attack." But I didn't know it then.

Carol: No, I mean what would you call it using the terms of the model—the model that you learned about during orientation phase?

Jack: I don't really know, Carol. My mind is confused right now.

Carol: The model says that we're dominated by two drives, aggression and sex, and that—

Jack: Listen, Carol. When I got these attacks, I sure didn't want to get fucked, and I can't believe it was my aggression.

Carol: We've got to think of these events, your difficulty breathing, we've got to think of them in terms of *guilt*, of your wanting to *punish* yourself. We need to get in touch with your conflict . . . (A. Young, 1995, p. 245, italics in the original)

Jack's developing account in this extract formulates his troubles with a commonplace clinical vocabulary. His use of "panic attack" to portray his experience is neither clinically incorrect, nor commonsensically unfamiliar. The account, however, fails to resonate with the model. Carol quickly moves to reconstruct the situation, asking Jack to think back to how he had originally been taught to conceptualize his problem "using the terms of the model." She continues to specify just what the model might imply in relation to Jack's problems, but Jack resists, asserting that the model doesn't seem to apply in this case. Insisting that neither his libidinal drives nor his instinct toward aggression were fostering his condition, Jack denies the applicability of the model. Carol, however, perseveres, insisting that problems be specified in terms of the model. While resistance is always possible, in the context of the therapy group, narratives are accountable to the model, and Carol, the group leader, is committed to enforcing the model's tenets. She stands firm against Jack's alternative accounts, openly seeking to control the way he thinks about and, more importantly, talks about his troubles. According to her, narratives offered in alternate terms are simply illegitimate. In the group, particular ways of framing troubles are formally specified and authorized. But this official authorization alone does not ensure the hegemony of particular kinds of narrative. Nor does it necessarily prevent competing, unauthorized narratives. Preferred narratives need to be locally, interactionally, and accountably asserted.

Conclusion

Strategic preferences were either directly or indirectly apparent throughout the extracts that appeared in this chapter. This went beyond the kind of control that is an artifact of the operating machinery of narrative work. Something else was in place that brought concrete preferences into play. As talk and interaction, conversational gambits can move in any direction. They do the operational work of narrative production. But talk and interaction in the extracts were transpiring in distinctive settings whose moral underpinnings differed from each other. Their going concerns set the background for preferred accounts. This is a fitting way to conclude this part of the book, as subsequent chapters move us full tilt to consider the way such preferences operate to give narrative control particular direction.

PART III

Narrative Environments

The chapters of Part III turn to the settings in which narrative work transpires. These narrative environments may be as informal as the sequential context of a casual conversation or as formal as a court hearing. Regardless of the setting, if the work of story construction deals with the *hows* of narrative reality, its environments offer preferences that propose the *whats* of the matter. While narrative work is an important operating component of storytelling, it tells us little by itself about the way local relevancies mediate outcomes. What a story means in the substantive scheme of things and the way circumstances shape accounts are central. These could be minor concerns or matters of life and death.

The settings and related substantive matters of storytelling are endless. Here, we limit the chapters to several conventional research concerns that bear on narratives. Some researchers study intimate relationships or family life in order to trace what, say, domestic narratives tell us about household relations or individual identity. They ask questions such as, does the familial environment bear on storytelling, and, in turn, do differences in accounts have varied consequences for growing up and coming of age? This is the subject matter of Chapter 10. Other researchers take a less intimate view. Chapters 11 through 14 consider the question of how local culture, status, jobs, and organizations, respectively, mediate the production of accounts. Chapter 15, on intertextuality, illustrates the usefulness of comparing the meaning-making preferences of various environments. In considering discursive matters that cross settings, the researcher is able to figure how participants in particular settings shape and respond to accounts pertinent to other settings. How, for example, is a life story, assembled in one narrative environment with its communicative relevancies, construed in the context of a different environment with its own relevancies? The substantive concerns and consequences for participants of the "same" story may contrast dramatically. This compels the researcher to be analytically attuned to the differences.

As before, we offer analytic guidelines and procedural suggestions. The aim in this part of the book is to draw attention to the way the conditions of narrative reality can be documented as they affect stories and storytelling. We will ask, for instance, how the leading "big stories" of various settings relate to the individual "little stories" that participants communicate within them. While we emphasize that narrative environments do not determine storytelling, we encourage researchers to describe ethnographically and empirically how these environments condition what is told in their purview. As always, if substantive matters are in focus, the combined operating logics at the core of narrative reality are still in place, centered on the reflexive relationship between narrative environments and narrative work.

10

Close Relationships

The term "close relationships" has traditionally referred to marriages and families (see Hendrick & Hendrick, 2000). There are narratives about types of marriages and families as well as stories about matters within them. Accounts of dysfunctional families, for example, present the shape and sentiments of troubled domestic life. Families also are settings for stories about kinship and identity, such as the character of children, parenthood, filial loyalty, and intergenerational solidarity. When we move into the field in this chapter, we consider how storytelling about marriage constructs the social form, as well as how narratives about particular families relate to how members view themselves and their world.

Orienting to Close Relationships

Metaphors implicating family are legion. As symbolic as they may seem, however, they affect our understanding of family life and lead researchers to view related aspects of domesticity in distinctive ways (see Lakoff & Johnson, 1980; Rosenblatt, 1994). The characterization of the family as a "shelter from the storm," for example, signals different narrative terrain than does the characterization of the "Manson family." Compositionally and performatively, each not only deploys distinctive contexts for storying family life, but also differentially orients those concerned to domestic matters.

Consider how the use of a particular metaphor can lead researchers to focus in a specific way on family stories. (See Rosenblatt, 1994, for a more comprehensive view of the use of family metaphors.) Using the "family dance" metaphor, William Marsiglio and Ramon Hinojosa (2006) point to the importance of choreographic adaptation to routine patterns of interaction for the adjustment of new members in "blended families," stepfathers in particular. They ask, how do new stepfathers relate to familial routines that are not their own? What can their accounts tell us about this? The stepfathers interviewed for Marsiglio and Hinojosa's study feature diverse issues related to what, in some instances, is actually called "stepping in," "keeping in step," and other rhythmic terms for describing stepfathers' adaptation to new circumstances. For stepfathers, the families they are entering are made up of girlfriends, new wives, and others' children. Issues of how to adjust and be accepted unfold choreographically, which is apparent in stepfathers' stories.

Rather than addressing the stepfather's relation to a new family environment in terms of stressors, role strain, or similar research contrivances, Marsiglio and Hinojosa call attention to everyday narrative articulations of "getting in step." Their concern is with how stepfathers frame adjustment issues in their own terms, the accounts of which are signally metaphorical.

> The metaphor [family dance] calls attention to timing and the choreographic dimensions of the stepfather's relationship with other family members, who commonly dance to different tunes as each adjusts to their life together. [Referring to stepfathers' accounts] Some stepfathers seem to have two left feet, figuratively speaking, as they join in and adapt or fail to adapt to domestic routines. Others get right into the swing of things. The family dance initially turns the stepfather's actions and other family members' responses into improvisations, the timing and paces of which may or may not settle into a mutually satisfying routine. Initially, the stepfather's dance is especially ad hoc since he is new on the scene and has to figure out how to get in step with all the others. (pp. 178–179)

The stepfather's story shapes the issues for him. In turn, such stories fuel the emerging experiential understanding of domestic life. In narrative practice, stories reflexively mediate close relationships. Equally significant is that, by calling attention to families as storied environments, the authors inform us that even the smallest or most intimate social context is narratively framed and understood (see Rosenblatt, 2006). Stepfathers' stories are not all organizationally sanctioned nor are they likely to become broadly emulated discourses. But they do figure in constructing who one is as a stepfather, one's developing status in the unfolding narratives of stepfathering, and why one is or is not becoming part of family life. Stories not only give meaning to close relationships, but provide explanation and direction for action—in this most intimate of social spaces. This suggests the first guideline:

Guideline

Figure that even the smallest and most fleeting of relationships can be viewed as narrative environments. Orient to and take note of the ways these relationships are characterized in accounts of their organization, paying attention to the linkages drawn between their overall characterization and particular elements within and outside of them.

Narrative environments are discernible social forces in their own right in shaping participants' identities, courses of action, and relationships with outsiders. This does not mean that they determine identity or action. Rather, their varied presence in people's lives prompts them to take the environments into account in some way in conveying who and what they are, and explain why they act the way they do. Narrative environments, in other words, are not just storied, providing grist for entertainment or cultural analysis. Rather, they are properly viewed as going concerns, useful mechanisms of conduct, and sources of moral invocation. They offer distinguishable stocks of accounts for experience (Hewitt & Stokes, 1975; Scott & Lyman, 1968). Families are narrative resources as much as they condition behavior and actions that are contemplated for the future (J. F. Gubrium & Holstein, 1990).

This is Elizabeth Stone's (1988) point in discussing "how our family stories shape us," which is the subtitle of her book *Black Sheep and Kissing Cousins*. The book relates to Bauman's concern with the performativity of storytelling (see Chapter 7), the lesson of which is that what is communicated simultaneously shapes us behaviorally. If stories about marriages and families are told for various purposes, these stories take on lives of their own, so to speak. Narratives return to storytellers as part of the ever-changing context for continuing talk and interaction. In relation to the many stories surrounding her own extended family life, Stone explains, "These stories seemed at once to sponsor and mirror our aspirations as a family" (p. 6). The accounts mirrored or reflected her family's sense of who they were and the meaning of events in their lives over several generations.

Stone describes different ways family stories function as narrative environments, many of them metaphorically. One is in terms of what psychiatrist Antonio Ferreira (1963) calls "family myths," which he defines as "beliefs shared by all family members, concerning each other and their mutual position in the family life" (quoted in Stone, p. 102). For example, the belief and continuing assertion that a particular member of the family is "the bad one," another member is "the sickly one," and still another "the smart one" has moral horizons for all concerned, both those so labeled and the others who interact with them. One parent or a particular sibling may be the one "you can count on" or, on the other hand, the one "you can never trust to follow through," which affects both their views of themselves and views of them. These are also the basis of explanations for why they act as they do and how they are treated. Related stories are recounted widely in the family circle, shaping assigned responsibilities, expectations about behavior, and the overall division of labor inside and outside the household.

Other myths are embedded in stories about whole families or even types of families. They, too, shape attitudes and behavior. Widely circulating stories about particular immigrant, rich or poor, celebrity, or criminal families, for example, construct environments in which both members and nonmembers organize their thoughts and sentiments about lifestyles, identity, and moral worth. This provides a second guideline:

Guideline

Treat stories of close relationships as narratives of explanation and causality for domestic talk and interaction. Consider the ways that members and outsiders use these accounts to construct environments that explain, justify, or otherwise offer understandings of their own and others' conduct.

As we cautioned in Chapter 6, it is important not to overemphasize the homogeneity of narratives for any social form. While there may be black sheep and kissing cousins, family members do not necessarily all figure accounts in the same way, as the terms "family myth" or "family dance" might imply. In this regard, it is useful analytically to orient as well to the social distribution of metaphors and accounts. If we approach family stories in terms of how they accountably shape lives, we also can ask how widespread and varied they are in their application.

Susan Walzer's (2006) research on family differences regarding divorcing couples is instructive and leads to a third guideline. Walzer is especially interested in how children make sense of divorce, arguing that they are far from being narrative wallflowers in the divorce process. They do, indeed, have thoughts of their own about the whys and wherefores of the matter. They develop stories of their own that account for why their parents' marriages are less than ideal, why they eventually failed, and what might have been done to make things better. Walzer's narrative material shows that children's accounts do not simply reflect their parents' or other adult opinion. In William Corsaro's (1997, p. 18) words, children do "not simply internalize society and culture, but are actively contributing to cultural production and change," in this case as they make sense of divorce.

This subverts the idea that there is "a" family story, or "a" shared view of a particular family member, or "a" legendary rendering of a momentous family event. If there are family myths, the pertinent questions are how widely and successfully are they applied? This also works against the assumption that every close relationship has its unique story. The question instead is how is uniqueness invoked in everyday talk and interaction? There actually may be a set of accounts that praise an event such as a marriage or even a divorce, and this is passed on for generations. There also may be another set of accounts that, alongside this, denigrate the event, likewise being passed on for generations.

In researching children's stories of divorce, Walzer found that the children she interviewed composed their accounts from various sources. They took on board what they knew from experience, from parents' and others' accounts, and combined these into stories of their own. They were active storytellers to be sure, but they did not fully invent the linkages they made, the plotlines they formed, or the themes they stressed. In short, they were "interpretively reproductive" as accountable members of their environments (Corsaro, 1997), composing stories of their own while borrowing from others' accounts. According to Walzer, "This reflects their ability to engage in active interpretation of their experiences in ways that both embrace and diverge from adult accounts" (p. 174). This leads to our third guideline:

Guideline

Do not assume that the smallness or intimacy of close relationships generates homogenous or all-consuming narratives. Whether stories are communicated by insiders or outsiders, consider the accountable positions and the stakes of storytelling that can foster narrative differences.

Into the Field

We enter the field of close relationships by raising two analytic questions. First, how shall we think about close relationships as narrative environments? We discuss Peter Berger and Hansfried Kellner's (1970) classic essay on the social construction of marriage to address this question. In the process and following the third guideline, we reflect critically on its homogenizing tendencies. Second, what comes into view when we turn to conditions that diversify storytelling? Here, we discuss Annette Lareau's (2003) work on childhood socialization, and examine the narrative distinctions that play out in family talk and interaction when differences in class and race are taken into account.

Berger and Kellner's essay on marriage followed on the heels of the publication of Berger and Thomas Luckmann's (1966) seminal book on the social construction of reality. While the essay does not take us into an actual empirical field, it does provide analytic leverage for how to view what transpires narratively in marital relationships. (See J. F. Gubrium & Holstein, 1990; J. F. Gubrium & Lynott, 1985; and Harris, 2006, for a related framing of family discourse.) The process Berger and Kellner call "*nomos*-building"—the construction of a distinctive reality—is presented as general to the narrative formation of close relationships. Berger and Kellner describe reality-constructing processes that shape relationships well beyond the domestic sphere. As they note, "Marriage is obviously only *one* social relationship in which this process of *nomos*-building takes place. It is therefore necessary to look first in more general terms at the character of this process" (pp. 50–51).

Following a general discussion, they ask how *nomos*-building plays out in marriage. First, the *nomos*—the social form that is built up in the construction process—is referenced and experienced as a reality standing over and above the individuals that make it up. The *nomos* of marriage is the phenomenological object that partners reference when they speak of who "we" or "they" are as a married couple. This is separate and distinct from who each partner is, was, or will be as an individual. When partners refer to who "we" are as a married couple, they draw upon narrative resources for elaborating a story over and above their individual experiences of the relationship, producing a narrative of a distinctive kind of marriage. When a recently married couple, for example, refers to themselves as "newlyweds," it places the relationship into a distinct category of narratives of experience separate from other types of relationships and marriages.

None of this is automatic. Berger and Kellner view *nomos*-building as a practical matter, developing out of the ongoing conversation between marital partners. The *nomos* is a narratively constructed entity. The marital partners might eventually typify who they are as a couple in terms of the kind of marriage they hope to have, or the kind of married couple they expect not to be. They might make use of more or less well-known exemplars of good and bad marriages in the process. But until such narrative resources are put to use in constructing their marriage, the marital relationship is simply a relationship (you and me, say) without a meaningful and moral horizon of its own (the sort of couple we are; the kind of marriage we have). Regardless of where the process is at a particular moment in time, the *nomos* continues to unfold in the ongoing marital conversation. Once formed, it is a referential and narrative entity that occupies a distinct space, separate from the biographies and identities of individual partners, other marriages, and other close relationships. Still, once the *nomos* is formed, it does not necessarily mean that the story has been completed. To apply a cliché, marriage and other close relationships are a continuing story, distinctive as they might be as social forms at any point in time.

Berger and Kellner use the metaphor of a "little world" to describe what is built up through the marital conversation. Emphasis is on the plenitude of the *nomos*. It is not just a categorically distinct entity, but something that provides a complete narrative context—a world—for the partners to orient to as a marriage. The *nomos* offers a broad understanding of the partners' ongoing sense of their relationship and defines who and what they are together as husband and wife. The *nomos* is a living story, of course, not just "the" story. It is not only communicated, but acts back, as it were, to shape attitudes, sentiments, and courses of action. Just as Stone (1988) writes of "how our family stories shape us," Berger and Kellner view the reality constructed as part and parcel of the unfolding experience of marriage, echoing McAdams's (1993) view that close relationships in this case *are* their developing stories.

Berger and Kellner do not provide empirical grounding in actual storytelling, but they do offer narrative perspective. So how does the researcher proceed empirically? Our guidelines recommend that the researcher listen and record the accounts couples, for example, communicate about their marriage through time, whether they are articulated in multiple interviews, in focus groups, in therapy sessions for troubled marriages, or in the ordinary banter of family life that fieldwork in households would provide. The researcher might listen in particular for narratives surrounding categorical distinctions, such as the respective accounts that follow references to "I" or "you," as opposed to "we," "us," and "them." Temporal references are equally telling, such as "us then" as opposed to "us now." (See Ricoeur, 1984, for philosophical bearing and Riessman, 1990; Harris, 2006; and Hopper, 1993, 2001, for empirical examples.)

It is important not to dismiss such talk as simply references in speech that cover or hide a more basic reality. As we discussed in Part I, talk and interaction, linkage, composition, and other meaning-making processes are part of the narrative work of *nomos*-building, not communicative conduits to a *nomos*. One might hypothesize, for example, that, as a couple speaks about themselves, if there are a great number of stories about "I" and "you," the narrative and experiential distinctiveness of the marriage might differ from the *nomos* constructed out of stories about "us." We are not suggesting that one or the other is preferable, as one might in a therapeutic vein, but only that one should take note of such differences in analyzing the narrative status of the *nomos* or, in this case, the close relationship in question.

More than two decades after the publication of Berger and Kellner's essay, Norbert Wiley (1985) revisited its thesis and found its view of the *nomos* overly homogenized. Marriages, he argued, were disintegrating and the times were not as partial to single-story views of any relationship, let alone marriage. Wiley heeds our third guideline, resisting the tendency in Berger and Kellner's analysis to see the marital story as a developing whole, unchallenged from within or from without. To be sure, Berger and Kellner consider the marital conversation in relation to the broader context of conversations about marriage. But, in their view, the narrative input from the varied sources constructively combine to form "a" marriage or "the" marriage the couple come to be. Their focus on how to think about the formation of "a" phenomenological object such as marriage understandably orients them to "the" entity under consideration.

On the contrary, Wiley suggests that, while extremely insightful, Berger and Kellner's view is grounded in middle-class sensibilities and is a product of its era. Its metaphorical status as a narrative resource has been supplanted by a struggle that relates less to a "little world" than to the shifting domestic winds of the world at large. Wiley points out that the current narrative environment of marriage and family life is more complicated and contested, even while its shared narrativity remains. In other words, a different metaphorical structure is now in order.

> Berger and Kellner's world is long gone, and the tacit assumptions of their [essay] are now the wrong ones. People are still hammering out that main reality in primary group settings. Lovers, couples and married still face each other and stitch together some kind of world. But the larger world has changed and family worlds have changed with it. The marital conversation is more struggle and less chitchat than in Berger and Kellner's base period. (p. 23)

Wiley's critique is worth quoting at length, because it not only provides analytic direction for entertaining a more complex view of this environment, but leads us to the second question we raised in moving into the field. That question points to the conditions that diversify the storytelling of close relationships.

> [Berger and Kellner's essay] is extremely insightful, opening up the inner world of the family and its symbolic culture as few others have done. This is the middle class family to be sure: highly verbal, possessed of a rich vocabulary of emotion-talk, and mobilized to make use of every social opportunity. Making sense of everyday, socio-emotional life is especially important for these couples, for they live off the world of interaction and symbolism. Meanings are particularly important for the white collar group, both in work and in family life. But even if the Berger-Kellner family is unusually talkative and sharp-eyed, their stance is merely intensification of what goes on in all modern families. (p. 22)

This observation brings us to Annette Lareau's (2003) work on the narratives of "unequal childhoods." Her interviews with working-class and middle-class families and her research team's fieldwork in their homes indicate that inequality plays out in contrasting narrative repertoires that cut across race. The focus of Lareau's study was the communicative organization of childhood socialization. Regarding homogenization, it is clear from Lareau's interview material that class makes a difference in how parents speak about their children's upbringing as well as in how children story their world. The difference also appears in parents' conversations with their children outside of the interview context. Lareau describes the mediations of class in summarizing her study (our annotation in brackets).

> This book identifies the largely invisible [not inaudible] but powerful ways that parents' social class impacts children's life experiences. It shows, using in-depth observations and interviews with middle-class (including members from the upper-middle-class), working-class, and poor families, that inequality permeates the fabric of the culture. In the chapters that lie ahead, I report the results of intensive observational research for a total of twelve families when their children were nine and ten years old. I argue that key elements of family cohere to form a cultural [and narrative] logic of child rearing. In other words, the differences among families seem to cluster together in meaningful patterns. (p. 3)

Family relations and class-based sensibilities permeate the very fabric of everyday talk and interaction. As Lareau puts it, they can be heard at the narrative interstices of ordinary activities such as doing schoolwork and getting ready for basketball practice. Family background and class are not just a matter of advantage and disadvantage, but provide impetus for storying everyday life, in this case as it relates to the challenges of children coming of age and being a parent dealing with growing sons and daughters. In listening to parent–child communication, Lareau and her team take notice of distinctive patterns of meaning making that vary by class. In so doing, they literally hear the narrative work of linkage, composition, and performance play out in the process. The "key elements that cohere" are not so much visible in behavior, as they are present in the heard but unremarkable accounts that articulate and frame talk and interaction in these close relationships.

Family and class differences cohere around distinctive ways of speaking and making meaning. If class reflects differences in terms of socioeconomic background, neighborhood location, available monetary resources, and material advantage, it works at a narrative level to speak the terminology and categorical preferences of daily life. Differences in family composition and history operate similarly. The accounts and accountability of children and adults across narrative environments diversify the family *nomos*. Middle-class and working-class families contrast in myriad ways, in understandings of children's lives especially in relation to recreation and schooling, ambition, and achievement.

Lareau identifies two repertoires of upbringing, whose metaphorical resonances are loud and clear. One informs the performative style of the middle-class family. In these households, parents orient to their children's upbringing in terms of what Lareau calls "concerted cultivation." The words signal active participation in children's lives. Stories feature parents as virtually planting the seeds for childhood development and, following that, providing extensive stage directions. Parents are the active interlocutors of their children's lives, and, if they are not, they unwittingly script the children's inner lives and social worlds. At the very least, parents provide supervised opportunities for children to organize activities on their own.

Children's identities in such families are amazingly audible. From accounts of children's intelligence and athletic skill, to the continuous articulation of children's motives and purposes, narratives of concerted cultivation produce detailed renditions of children's hopes and desires, attitudes and achievements. Lareau found that, day in and day out in middle-class households, parents were part and parcel of nearly all accounts of their children's conduct. Listen for select features of this repertoire in the following extracts from the middle-class family accounts presented in Lareau's book. In the first extract, Don Tallinger describes one of his sons, fourth-grader Garrett, who is "a tall, thin, serious boy with blond hair."

> He's shy and quiet, not very outgoing when you first meet him. But he's got a fierce desire to please, so he's very compliant. But he is also still very competitive. He likes to win, but he's still easy to manage. (p. 41)

Like other middle-class parents, the sheer volume of activities the Tallingers schedule for their three sons means that concerted cultivation must be coordinated and scheduled. This turns daily narratives of accommodation into a matter of time management. Four-year-old Sam, the youngest, "is already aware of the importance of the family calendar." He knows that his older brothers' commitments may preempt an invitation to a birthday party. The concerted workings of the calendar are evident in the following exchange between Sam and his mother Louise. It's early May at the time.

> [Louise] says, "I know we have to be somewhere on the eleventh. If we are home in the morning, you can go to this." . . . Louise walks over to the calendar and

flips ahead to June. She looks at the calendar for a moment. Sam asks hopefully, with a trace of concern, "Can I go to it?" Louise says, "You're in luck; we're home in the morning." (p. 44)

The next extract is an exchange between Don and a field-worker. In this case, it points to the concerted rationalization of his sons' athletic skills. As a narrative environment centered on the detailed scheduling of leisure time, the children within it have been precisely located in the daily scheme of things, which, by the way, also figure their identities. A family myth seems to be written all over the conversation. The myth hints at narrative control, the everyday elements of which provide preferences and direction, clueing us to the constructive power of accounts.

Don: We struggle with Spencer 'cause he doesn't like sports. We decided he's average. Louise and I decided. But when they [the sons] ask, "What can we do?" I say go out and play catch. I usually don't think of going and collecting spiders or doing something that Spencer would like. He's interested in science. I usually don't think about that.

Fieldworker: That's hard.

Don: Sports just comes naturally to us.

Fieldworker: Does Spencer try to compete with Garrett?

Don: He knows he couldn't compete with him. Garrett is so much better. (p. 55)

The second repertoire for upbringing is associated with working-class families and constructs the cast of characters differently. Parents are not as center stage in these family's accounts as parents are in the middle-class family environment. Storytelling about children's upbringing is told with parents situated at a distance from children's activities. Parents are not as concertedly involved in the children's lives, but they do take pride when the children deal with life's hurdles on their own. This is true of both the white and black working-class families. Here is how Lareau introduces the upbringing of 9-year-old Tyrec Taylor.

For nine-year-old Tyrec Taylor, organized activities were an interruption. In contrast to Garrett Taylor, Tyrec centered his life on informal play with a group of boys from this Black, working-class neighborhood. Aside from going to school and to summer day camp, Tyrec took part in only two organized activities: he went to Sunday school periodically throughout the year and to Vacation Bible School in the summer. In fourth grade, he pleaded with his

mother for permission to play on a community football team that he learned
about through a friend. . . . Ms. Taylor found the experience taxing and she
"pray[ed] that we don't have to do it again." (p. 66)

Lareau calls this narrative repertoire "the accomplishment of natural
growth." In contrast with the "concerted" part of the middle-class family
repertoire, the "accomplishment" part of this repertoire does not refer to
parents. Instead, it flags what working-class children do on their own. The
subject at the center of these upbringing narratives is, at once, more responsible for coming of age and less linked to parents as central characters
in their stories. The idea is that children naturally grow up, even while they
grow up in families. Children face the challenges that come with the territory, more or less on their own. As if to say, let nature take its course, family stories of children coming of age in working-class households feature
children removed from the parental scripting of their lives.

In the contrasting narrative environments of these families, children are
different sorts of subjects. While middle-class mothers and fathers repeatedly
produce scripts of parental responsibility for their children's success and
well-being, the working-class family's narrative environment promotes stories of children coming of age by getting through life on their own. The
moral horizons of the two narrative environments differ dramatically. If
middle-class parents blame themselves for their children's failures and
personally bask in their successes, working-class parents, black and white,
take pride in what children achieve by themselves. In this regard, consider
Ms. Taylor's responses to questions about the place of sports in Tyrec's
development. The child remains central to the story's theme of personal
accountability, even as his mother is prompted to include other factors.

Unlike middle-class parents, however, Ms. Taylor didn't see Tyrec's football
experience as crucial to his overall development. "I don't know how it's helped
him," was her reply to the question "Are there any ways that you think it has
helped him in other aspects of his life . . . Even in little ways?" Ms. Taylor's
first and most decisive point was that she could not think of any way that it
helped him. When asked "Were there any spillover effects that you didn't
expect—in some other areas of his life?" she generated this answer:

"Well, just the responsibility part, knowing that [mimicking Tyrec] this is
what I have to do and this is what I'm gonna do. They give him a routine of
his very own: I have to do this and then I have to do my homework and then
I have to eat, you know. So I thought that was good." (p. 79)

Lareau views these contrasting family narratives as operating reflexively
in children's upbringing. Don and Louise Garrett and other middle-class

parents blame themselves as much as the children for the children's growth and development. Ms. Taylor and other working-class parents account for their children's accomplishments with stories of the children's personal responsibility for getting through or not getting through life. True to the family tales, childrearing and coming of age both reflect and provide the basis for their narrative accounts.

Conclusion

If we figure that the smallest of social contexts are narrative environments, the analytic task is to discern patterns of similarity and difference within and across them. The important thing to keep in mind is that narrative work is as much at stake in the production of similarity and difference in these environments, as in larger, more formally organized settings. Listen, observe, and take systematic note of the ways participants in close relationships construct who and what they are, especially as this varies in time and social space. This is of special importance for close relationships, as these are so often viewed as homogenous in their storytelling. Orienting to close relationships and their accounts as embedded in members' perspectives and their varied narratives can tell us a different story.

11

Local Culture

From coffee shops, street corners, and neighborhoods, to shopping malls, playgrounds, and apartment buildings, public places comprise the mundane settings of everyday life. As casual or socially fleeting as these settings seem to be, we tend to expect little of them in terms of narrativity. Public places ostensibly are settings where the barest of expectations sustain the thinnest veneer of social life (Brekhus, Galliher, & Gubrium, 2005). But, time and again, researchers are surprised when they discover that public places have culture. As such, they are narrative environments that shape the little stories of habitués in relation to bigger stories of shared experience and accountability (cf. Bamberg, 2006; & A. Gubrium, 2006).

Orienting to Local Culture

When William Whyte (1943) described how he discovered the moral order of the Italian slum neighborhood he called "Cornerville," it carried an element of surprise. Because Cornerville was a "mysterious, dangerous, and depressing area" to the rest of the city, its complex moral order was largely hidden. It was widely believed that slums were public places without rules and regulation—jungles of untamed exchanges and social problems for society. To "respectable people," Cornerville was a disturbing part of town. It was a recognizable location certainly, but one without organized scripts, actors, and performances. It was a stage for living in name only, an amorphous habitat for denizens without stories.

Other researchers of neighborhoods and street life have been similarly surprised. Elliot Liebow's (1967) "study of Negro street corner men," the subtitle of his book *Tally's Corner*, was another eye-opening discovery of local culture. The area this time was a poor, inner city Washington, D.C., neighborhood. More than two decades after Whyte's book *Street Corner Society* was published, the public belief in the disorder of the slum persisted. Locations such as Tally's corner offered the merest sociability, hosting habitués to be sure, mostly men who hung around with little aim in life. To the general public, it was clear that the "limited lives [located there just] eddied and flowed" (p. vii). There were no noteworthy stories, the result of which is that the neighborhood held little or no human interest.

But, like Whyte and Mayhew before that, Liebow had a different, surprising narrative in store. The surprise begins as Liebow sets up the striking contrast between a mere location and local culture on the opening pages of the chapter titled "Men and Jobs." As he describes a commonplace scene in the area, it is evident that what appears be a set of fleeting encounters between "scavengers" (white employers) and "would-be prey" (black workers) is actually the tip of a bigger story. As if to say that something beyond shared racial and economic backgrounds binds together the men on the streets, Liebow begins to flesh out the local culture of Tally's corner. His description is worth quoting at length for the unexpected reversal of understanding presented in the second paragraph.

> A pickup truck drives slowly down the street. The truck stops as it comes abreast of a man sitting on a cast-iron porch and the white driver calls out, asking if the man wants a day's work. The man shakes his head and the truck moves on up the block, stopping again whenever idling men come within calling distance of the driver. At the Carry-out corner, five men debate the question briefly and shake their heads no to the truck. The truck turns the corner and repeats the same performance up the next street. In the distance, one can see one man, then another, climb into the back of the truck and sit down. In starts and stops, the truck finally disappears.
>
> What is it we have witnessed here? A labor scavenger rebuffed by his would-be prey? Lazy, irresponsible men turning down an honest day's pay for an honest day's work? Or a more complex phenomenon marking the intersection of economic forces, social values, and individual states of mind and body? (pp. 29–30)

If the first of these paragraphs presents characters as thinly storied, the characters will grow in narrative prominence as the book unfolds. Liebow identifies specific individuals and their particular stories. First there is Tally, who "is a brown skinned man, thirty-one years old"; second is Sea Cat, who is 27 years old; third is Richard, who is 24; and finally there is Leroy, who is 23. The increasingly visible social order and local culture of street life adds complex meaning to individual accounts, which at first appeared en masse, anonymous, and narratively mute. The individual accounts, in turn, enliven the place as a narrative environment. The outline of characters with stories to tell comes into view to reveal a social world. Their narratives of work, friendship, and family life lay bare the bigger story that surrounds them. These are stories the uninformed passerby would not imagine to be there.

A decade later, Elijah Anderson (1976) continues to surprise, this time with a focus on a neighborhood on the South Side of Chicago. Two paragraphs from the preface of his book, *A Place on the Corner*, provide contrast in this case between a mere locale and fleeting exchanges, and the larger narrative that makes for a meaningful whole. The first paragraph launches the contrast without specifying what Anderson discovers:

> Between 1970 and 1973 I engaged in participant observation at "Jelly's" bar and liquor store on the South Side of Chicago and gathered materials for this study. During this period I hung out with black working and nonworking men who spent a good deal of their time in the bar or "on the corner." At all times of the day and night and throughout the seasons of the year, I socialized with the people—drinking with them, talking and listening to them, and trying to come to terms with their social world. They carried on their business and talked about life, and they taught me much. In what follows I attempt to convey some of what I have learned. (p. ix)

The second paragraph, below, provides a glimpse of that meaningful whole. It teaches us the lesson that Mayhew's observations of London's humbler classes taught a century earlier. There is social order anywhere human beings talk and interact with each other, which, surprisingly perhaps, develops in the leanest of circumstances. As if to say that even "a place on the corner" (the title of Anderson's book) has a story, Anderson describes events that, with a tilt at the bigger story he is about to tell, offer a peek at local culture. As we read on, the culture comes into bold relief.

> After being around Jelly's neighborhood for a while and getting to know its people, the outside observer can begin to see that there is order to this social world. For example, the wineheads turn out to be harmless, for they generally do the things people expect them to do: they drink on the street, beg passersby for change, and sometimes stumble up and down the street cursing at others. One also begins to understand that what looks like a fight to the death usually doesn't come near a fatal end. Often such a "fight" turns out to be a full-dress game in which only "best friends" or "cousins" can participate—but at times even they can't play this game without its ending in a real fight. (pp. 2–3)

These studies of local culture suggest that the researcher apply two analytic guidelines in studying public places. The first one orients more to the spatial than to the narrative dimension of local cultures:

Guideline

Consider that no matter how seemingly informal or anonymous a public setting might be, its social interactions can lead to narratives of identity and interpersonal relations. Listen for, and document, accounts that reference roles and relationships, with the aim of constructing the bigger story to which accounts are linked.

Years later, Anderson (1999) expands his research on "decency, violence, and the moral life of the inner city," this time in Philadelphia. His book, *Code of the Street,* which we briefly took up in Chapter 6, adds a distinctive parameter to the narrative horizons of local culture. Attention turns directly to the relation between little stories and a larger story by the book's name—the code of the street. As Anderson makes clear, while there is a bigger story, it isn't one that frames all accounts of life on the street. As he shows, there are varied appreciations of the bigger story related to one's position and purpose in the setting (see Jimerson & Oware, 2006; Wieder, 1974). This again serves as a caution against narrative homogenization.

Anderson starts by noting that the code is the key cultural element of street life in the location. It is a shared understanding about the organization of interpersonal respect on the one hand, and is the leading way of accounting for the ongoing actions and infractions of street civility on the other. The big story the code represents reverberates with the continuing little stories about who and what particular individuals are and what that means for talk and interaction among them. Anderson explains:

> Street culture has evolved a "code of the street," which amounts to a set of informal rules governing interpersonal public behavior, particularly violence. The rules prescribe both proper comportment and the proper way to respond if challenged. They regulate the use of violence and so supply a rationale allowing those who are inclined to aggression to precipitate violent encounters in an approved way. . . . Everybody knows that if the rules are violated, there are penalties. Knowledge of the code is thus largely defensive, and it is literally necessary for operating in public. (p. 33)

Because the big and the little stories are reflexive, the code is practical. It is an integral part of the ebb-and-flow of street life. Anderson works with this everyday sense of local culture, whose code translates into the evanescent rules that are ever present in talk and interaction. The code does not stand over and above street life but operates in the ordinary acknowledgments and violations of deference and demeanor. If in some sense the code is an empirical abstraction, it is simultaneously epiphenomenal and practical—both an added sense of what is shared and something that transpires in ordinary usage. As the key principle of street conduct, it referentially stands over and above street life, as Berger and Kellner's (1970) *nomos* does in the regulation of talk and interaction in close relationships. At the same time, the code's modus operandi derives from the grounds of daily living, from the indigenous accounts or little stories that experientially feature the empirical abstraction.

In this context, Anderson rightfully needs to "loosely define" the code, since it operates in the exchanges of street life (for the same reason we asked the reader in the introduction to move ahead into the book with a commonsense understanding rather than a formal definition of story). The code is as loose as it needs to be in order to relate to all contingencies.

> At the heart of the code is the issue of respect—loosely defined as being treated "right" or being granted one's "props" (or proper due) or the deference one deserves. However, in the troublesome public environment of the inner city, as people increasingly feel buffeted by forces beyond their control, what one deserves in the way of respect becomes ever more problematic and uncertain. This situation in turn further opens up the issue of respect to sometimes intense interpersonal negotiation, at times resulting in altercations. In the street culture, especially among young people, respect is viewed as almost an external entity, one that is hard-won but easily lost—and so must constantly be guarded. The rules of the code in fact provide a framework for negotiating respect. (p. 33)

The extent of the code's application is well worth emphasizing. If the code is an empirical abstraction that everyone acknowledges and shares, its use relates to one's purpose in the circumstances. It can operate on the streets as the regulating ingredient of social relations, especially among young people. Many are unemployed and, as a result, have little else to secure their position in life. From their vantage point, the code is a living *nomos* sui generis, something whose seemingly separate and distinct rules they vigilantly monitor. When the key ingredient of respect is violated, it can generate focused and intensely emotional responses. For these young people, the big story of local culture seems to hover over every little story as a matter of principle, asserting its relevance time and again in imminently expansive ways. It is no wonder that street life is both tense and intense.

But, as Anderson makes clear, the code is not "the" applicable big story for everyone. While it is universally recognized, it is attended differently and has varied practical relevance for other members of the community. We soon learn that, young or old, the employed have other fish to fry, so to speak, even while respect is an important ingredient of the world they share with the unemployed. For the employed, respect is drawn from jobs in addition to the respect or disrespect of street encounters. "Decent kids" and "decent families," as Anderson calls them, bring middle-class sensibilities to the street and community, taking pride in other matters. This complicates the relation between the code's big story and particular little stories. The "old heads" add to the mix. These elderly men are the eroding male mentors to youth, and cast their own gaze at both local culture and the world beyond. Old heads put respect in broader perspective, diffusing its performative intensity in their own and others' lives.

These observations lead to a second guideline for narrative analysis in the context of local culture. Anderson found that in specifying the big story that regulates everyday street life in the inner city, he needed to continuously turn to how narratives work on the ground, in relation to different vantage points, circumstances, and purposes (also see Candida Smith, 2002; Modan, 2007; Narayan & George, 2002; Passerini, 1987; Portelli, 1990, 2003). Big stories relate to varied ordinary lives and their stories. Recall that Abu-Lughod (1993) similarly cautioned us not to take for granted the dominant place of patriarchy, one of the big stories in Bedouin society. Generalizing from these insights, it is important to keep in mind that if there is a big story in place, its little stories have a way of defusing and diversifying its presence in practice. This suggests the following guideline:

Guideline

Discern the big stories of local culture with a constant eye toward their individual articulations. Approach the big and little stories as reflexively related, not categorically distinct, dimensions of narrativity.

Into the Field

Whyte, Liebow, and Anderson provide intriguing glimpses of the street corners of public places. Others, such as Arlie Hochschild (1973), take us indoors. Hochschild's research setting is not a shopping mall, public restroom, or the like; it's an apartment building for the elderly. Merrill Court, which is the pseudonym she gives to the building, is located near San Francisco Bay. It is not in any sense a nursing home, but it does have organized activities for elderly residents. Hochschild worked there as an assistant recreation director when she did her fieldwork. The residents are independent, eat and sleep in their own units, and come and go as they please or are able. Most were born and raised in the Southwest and Midwest and moved to California in later life.

Merrill Court is a public place in the sense that it is like a neighborhood of individual homes, located within a single physical structure. Blocks are organized vertically as floors rather than contiguously at ground level. The streets—hallways in this instance—are traversed by any and all who come and go to the various apartment units along the way. Lobbies are versions of public squares, with pedestrian traffic composed of residents and a mix of outsiders such as tradesmen, visitors, and delivery persons.

The element of surprise for Hochschild derives from a common experience of living in urban apartment buildings. Such buildings typically house individuals unknown to each other. Certainly, some might in time become acquainted, but they are just as likely to come and go anonymously. Individuals housed in apartment units down the hall, or on the floor above or below, don't much matter in the daily scheme of things. As strangers, residents might regularly pass each other in the hallways or the lobby, or smile at one another in elevators. Otherwise, their encounters are bereft of sociability or accountability. The social tide might occasionally turn into something more complex when neighborliness or friendships form, setting the stage for *nomos*-building. But, in public places such as apartment buildings, this is rare and superficial. Or so it would seem.

Hochschild did not have the first guideline of this chapter in view when she began her fieldwork. Instead, she expected to find the anonymity associated with urban apartment living. She was looking for individual stories she might tap into and analyze, and did not expect there to be a big story tying things together in any particular way. Merrill Court, she originally figured, would be the site of little stories, individual accounts of persons coming of age somewhere else and winding up far from home as old people. The title of Hochschild's book, *The Unexpected Community*, flags the initial image and the subsequent surprise at what she found. Hochschild explains:

> This book is mainly about a group of forty-three old people who lived in a small apartment building near the shore of San Francisco Bay. However, many of the things I found there reflect on other old people in the United States as well. One reason I have written this book is that these forty-three people were not isolated and not lonely. They were part of a community I did not expect to find. Ironically, these conservative, fundamentalist widows from Oklahoma and Texas and other parts of the Midwest and Southwest are among the least likely to talk about "communal living" and "alternatives to the nuclear family" even while they have improvised something of the sort. (p. ix)

As Hochschild continues, she finds an environment ridden with local culture and thus abounding in irony. Accounts of roles and relationships overshadow tales of social isolation and anonymity. The performative dimensions of local narratives are captivating.

> The book tells about their community as a mutual aid society, as a source of jobs, as an audience, as a pool of models for growing old, as a sanctuary and as a subculture with its own customs, gossip, and humor. It tells about friendships and rivalries within the community as well as relations with daughters, store clerks, nurses, and purse snatchers outside. It goes into a good deal of homely detail about such things as the insides of people's living rooms, their refrigerators and photo albums, what they watch on television, whom they visit, and what they think of other old people. (p. ix)

A key element of the big story in this environment is what Hochschild calls "the poor dear hierarchy." It too is a type of code, one that relates to local culture and status. It centers on the expectation that, since the mostly female residents of Merrill Court are elderly, there's a good chance that one might become frail, infirm, or disabled. There's a persistent likelihood that someone will need to go to a nursing home for a spell and sometimes permanently. Those lucky enough to remain in good health, who are active and ambulatory, command considerable presence on the premises. They are visible in the lobby and other public spaces. The status associated with this becomes apparent narratively, in terms of residents' related use of the term "poor dear" for those less fortunate.

In rounds of fieldwork on the premises, Hochschild heard many and varied accounts of residents' conduct. They incessantly evaluated each other for their good or bad fortune, much of it related to the infirmities of aging. The words "poor dear" were used to describe those less able and, at times, the elderly in general, in comparison to more fortunate residents and outsiders. If much of this related to ill health, other disadvantages such as insufficient income were similarly storied. Amazingly, Hochschild soon found that the words had vast narrative applicability, extending to all manner of status distinctions. "Poor dear" did extensive status work and could be counted on to indicate where those who used the term figured they stood in comparison to others. "Poor dear" was a narrative key to a bigger story, one telling of hierarchy in the community. Referring to residents as poor dears was a way of assigning a lower position in the hierarchy of luck. It was an important part of how little stories related to the broader scheme of things. The term "poor dear" simultaneously figured as a moral indicator, specifying which residents were worthier and which less worthy than others.

Hochschild describes her emerging sense of the broad narrative relevance of this usage. We quote her book at length to illustrate the big story Hochschild inferred from accounts, one resonating throughout the unexpected community. But, once again, if there is a big story at Merrill Court, it is not the whole story. As Hochschild is careful to point out in the following extract, the social logic that words can flag comes in different versions and proportions in practice. While "poor dear" marks status, it does it by way of diverse invocations. Little stories can take the big story in many directions, in this most surprising of circumstances.

> At the monthly meetings of the countywide Senior Citizens Forum, to which Merrill Court sent two representatives, the term "poor dear" often arose with reference to old people. It was "we senior citizens who are politically involved versus those 'poor dears' who are active in recreation." Those active in recreation, however, did not accept a subordinate position relative to the politically active. On the other hand, they did not refer to the political activists as "poor dears." Within the politically active group there were those who espoused general causes, such as getting out an anti-pollution bill, and those who espoused causes related only to old age, such as raising social security benefits or improving medical benefits. Those in politics and recreation referred to the passive card players and newspaper readers as "poor dears." Old people with passive life styles in good health referred to those in poor health as "poor dears" and those in poor health but living in independent housing referred to those in nursing homes as "poor dears." Within the nursing home there was a distinction between those who were ambulatory and those who were not. Among those who were not ambulatory there was a distinction between those who could enjoy food and those who could not. Almost everyone, it seemed, had a "poor dear." (pp. 60–61)

Who would think that such narrative plenitude could exist in an unexpected community? Fleeting roles and relationships? Anonymity? What kind of local culture could be expected in this ostensible community of strangers? If Merrill Court has a recreation program and there is a recreation director on the premises, this alone doesn't explain the varied formulations of its big story. The program may bring the more able bodied and interested together for activities and, as such, serve as a source of social distinction communicated throughout the building. But this only provides the opportunity to mark difference. If stories of "poor dears" are borrowed from broader cultural usage, local application and its elaborations have been invented by the narrative work of the residents. As the preceding extract indicates, the use of "poor dear" narratives is artfully taken well beyond the premises into wider community affairs.

What is important to note is not that individual stories exist in public places. That's to be expected anywhere. As we pointed out previously in relation to J. F. Gubrium's (1993) study of the quality of life of nursing home residents, people bring life stories with them wherever they go. What is noteworthy, rather, is that little stories, as we call them in this chapter, become part of bigger stories, and do so in places we commonly think of as bereft of them. This is Hochschild's contribution in documenting the "unexpected community" at Merrill Court. This, of course, resonates with the discovery of local culture in other public places such as neighborhoods and street corners. Our first guideline accentuates this point. The second guideline encourages the researcher not to lose sight of the big story's smaller articulations.

Conclusion

Once again, it bears emphasizing that our guidelines point to narrative reflexivity. If public places such as street corners, neighborhoods, and apartment buildings have big stories, the stories return to storytellers to shape their own accounts and their identities, roles, and relationships. These identities, roles, and relationships, in turn, exemplify and ramify big stories. Diversely flagged by working codes or the use of words such as "poor dear," the narrative environments of local cultures are surprisingly fruitful venues for narrative analysis.

12

Status

S tatus is an explanatory workhorse of social science. Characteristics such as class, race, and gender are commonly said to affect how individuals think and feel about things. As we saw, close relationships and local culture provided statuses that related to stories in distinctive ways. Viewing status in this way makes visible how it operates as a narrative environment. At the same time, as before, taking account both of narrative work and of the influences of narrative environments requires a reflexive approach, one in which the narrative reality of status and story play out in relation to each other.

Orienting to Status

In orienting to status in this chapter, we take up the issue of the status of being a storyteller pure and simple, someone who is assumed to have the capacity to story experience. The capacity relates to the issue of agency—the possibility of actively entering into talk and social interaction to compose accounts. We aim to illustrate how a focus on the exercise of agency enables the researcher to document the storytelling status of anyone or anything, regardless of their clinical or objective presence in life. We also aim to show that storytelling status is a matter of narrative assignment. Status does not exist as a force that independently shapes the process and substance of storytelling.

Status can be viewed as organizing rights and responsibilities in communicating accounts. In this view, status determines storytelling. In the context of children's schooling, for example, it is common for mothers to be the parents who provide accounts of home life and other outside-of-school information in interactions with teachers. Fathers tend to remain in the background, except when mothers are absent and cannot participate. If fathers do exercise narrative rights, they are treated as exceptional and, for better or worse, what they contribute can be assigned extraordinary value or special status. Similarly, in the context of the traditional household, the adage that children should be seen and not heard reflects their narrative status in the domestic scheme of things. The adage suggests that parents, not their offspring, have the right to provide accounts of household affairs. The children are relegated to the status of observers or the recipients of accounts.

Whether located at the interstices of home and school, within the social relationships of a traditional household, or elsewhere, status shapes expectations, actions, and reactions to what is tellable, by whom, and what is hearable and by whom. In this context, exceptions to the rule are surprising, and are often consequential. Indeed, the surprise and consequences are likely to prompt meta-storytelling, developed in narratives that justify, disclaim, or otherwise contextualize the exceptional rights and responsibilities of those in question. A child, for example, may gain storytelling rights, but needs to work at it in this environment, as we saw in the discussion of narrative activation in Chapter 4.

Elements of Clifford Shaw's life history of Stanley lead to a more complex view. As we saw earlier, signal aspects of Stanley's account point to the reflexivity of status and story in relation to narrative rights and responsibilities. Stanley is aware that, contrary to determining the right to tell stories, status can be manipulated to take narrative rights and responsibilities into unexpected directions. At the same time, he also describes status causally in various passages of his story, reporting how status affects his own, his fellow inmates, and neighborhood friends' rights and responsibilities in storytelling. Some persons are taken to have the right to provide accounts and others have the responsibility to listen. In Stanley's world, higher status is accorded those who have had experience in crime and lower status to those who have not. Those without status are narratively silent and look up to those who have it. Clearly, Stanley both is affected by status and manipulates it for various purposes, the combination adumbrating a reflexive view of the relationship between story and status.

The more causal usage is palpable in the following part of an extract from Stanley's story previously discussed in Chapter 1. We annotate this part and the extracts that follow by inserting the terms "story" and "status" to track their co-presence and everyday reflexive relationship in the narrative process.

But deep in my heart I knew that I was only a kid [status] and couldn't be expected to have a reputation yet [status]. I couldn't tell about my charge [story], for it savored of petty thievery [status], and everybody looked down on a petty thief in Pontiac [status]. I felt humiliated in the extreme, so only listened [story]. (pp. 108–109)

Stanley reappropriates status–story causality as he describes his response to cell mate Billy's narrative prowess. Stanley, the petty thief, is the listener and not the storyteller in his relationship with Billy, the big-time criminal.

The prisoners all had the idea that "if you can't steal something big don't steal at all" [status]. So I kept quiet [story], happy enough to listen [story] to the thrilling stories of adventure [story]. (p. 109)

Equally important, Stanley also is aware that, in narrative practice, the relationship between status and story isn't unidirectional. The causal relationship can go both ways. He realizes that status can be narratively manipulated and shaped for various purposes, changing status and story's operating force in talk and interaction. At various points in his account, Stanley virtually tells Shaw and the reader that adroit storytelling can be used to enhance one's status, which reflexively then enhances one's stories' credibility and objectives. The following annotated extract, also quoted in Chapter 1, is instructive.

But Bill (my cell partner) talked all the time about himself and his crimes [story]. I talked, too, and told wild stories of adventure [story/status], some true and some lies [story/status], for I couldn't let Bill outdo me [story/status] just for lack of a few lies on my part [story/status]. (p. 104)

The relationship between story and status is reversed in this extract. The construction and application of particular stories, lies if need be, is expected to affect the status of the storyteller.

Similarly, the aging Bedouin grandmother, Migdim, who we met in Chapter 7 (see Abu-Lughod, 1993), does not construct the story of her "arranged" marriage as the straightforward consequence of coming of age as a low-status young woman. Instead, Migdim's account of her own and her father's decisions regarding marriage stands in complex relationship to status vis-à-vis storytelling. At one level, Migdim's is an account of arranged marriage in traditional society, in which the marital partners have little or no say. It is an account of the normal narrative silence of the low status storyteller. In the traditional scheme of things, those of low status have no right to script marital arrangement.

At another level, Migdim relates a story ridden with willfulness, displaying an assumed right (status) to script the arrangement on her own terms. Her account is not centered on her father's traditional status in the matter. Migdim is immediately more narratively active, storying who she would and would not marry as opposed to who she might have married if narratively silent. At this level, she informs her granddaughters, who are listening, that if the cultural narrative of status and story specifies particular (patriarchal) rights and responsibilities, these can be reconfigured by willful participants.

These examples suggest that, in practice, storytelling influences status as much as status determines storytelling. Analytically, the question becomes how is status constructed and sustained in the narrative work that conveys storytelling rights and responsibilities? On a practical level, both Stanley and Migdim recognized the issue and worked to increase or deflect the influence of status in their circumstances. If status presented an environment for storytelling in their worlds, it was an environment that was as much strategically put into place as it was an environment that asserted its preferences. The following analytic guideline applies:

Guideline

If the narrative environment of status asserts its impact on storytelling rights and responsibilities, be aware of how everyday relationships and their narratives can, in turn, influence the production of status. View the relationship between status and story as reflexive, and document both the effect of status on storytelling and the active shaping of status in the narrative process.

Into the Field

Storytelling commonly assumes that there is an active agent in place, an underlying narrative consciousness capable of accounting for experience. This is the notion suggested by McAdams (1993), Kenyon and Randall (1997), and others (see Chapter 1). Ultimately, they would argue, we are our stories. Storytelling documents who and what we are or could be. Social and historical influences aside, the stories of a petty thief, for example, are assumed in principle to derive from someone who is an experientially present petty thief. The stories of an aging Bedouin grandmother are taken to emanate from someone who is an experientially present grandmother. This would seem rather obvious. But what if petty thieves and grandmothers lost the ability to tell stories for some reason, or never achieved it in the first place? Would this affect their status as storytellers? Would the loss or incapacity put their narrative agency in jeopardy?

The analytic lens of narrative practice suggests a more complicated picture. We turn to two studies that problematize the matter by considering them in the context of everyday life. The first study, by Melvin Pollner and Lynn McDonald-Wikler (1985), examines the narrative practice surrounding one family's attribution of narrative competence to a severely retarded child, someone ostensibly unable to provide accounts of experience. The second study, by Jaber Gubrium (1986a, 1986b), considers the cognitive status of Alzheimer's disease (AD) sufferers in terms of the construction of everyday narration. The studies show how the narrative reality of status and story relates to the storytelling work operating in their respective settings. Both studies orient to the performative dimensions of storytelling, featuring the dramatic realization of narrative agency.

Before turning directly to these studies, we begin with an amusing anecdote from Gubrium's parenting experience. Its familiarity should help establish the everyday focus of the studies. Years ago, Gubrium and his young twin daughters delighted in chatting with "Mrs. Bird" as he prepared a chicken for roasting. Cleaning the chicken at the sink with the girls alongside, he would sit the bird on the rim of the sink, cross its legs as best he could, and hold it by the wings. Mrs. Bird was ready to share her feelings and views of life. Chuckling, Gubrium encouraged the girls to ask her questions. They eagerly did, wondering with delighted attention what Mrs. Bird would say.

The girls usually asked Mrs. Bird how she felt today. (It was understood that this referred to her thoughts and sentiments, not her butchered condition.) Gubrium would lean close to the chicken and, in a voice suitable to a narrating bird, squawk at length about how pleased she was that the girls were visiting her. This loomed into animated repartee. Mrs. Bird typically commented that she looked forward to coming out nicely roasted and very nourishing, mentioning the girls each by name. The chicken obviously admired the girls and they, in turn, were most pleased to have met up with her again. They rollicked with giggles when Mrs. Bird pointed out how smart and kind they were, which the girls reciprocated.

There were specific concerns as well. Questions prompted discussions of the passing scene, life in general, the hen's past, and her hopes for the future. There were rare moments of sadness that Mrs. Bird had lost her pretty feathers and her head, but this was tangential to the mostly inquisitive and informative chatter. Being very curious about Mrs. Bird's family, the girls especially wondered about her chicks, how many she had had, and most importantly whether she had had twins. Mrs. Bird proudly commented about all aspects of her life as a hen and mother of many.

Personhood was at play throughout. In their everyday dimensions, these conversations performatively realized the narrative agency of all involved, from Mrs. Bird to Gubrium and his daughters. As talk and interaction developed, so too did the narrative status of the participants, Mrs. Bird included. Each participant was an active storyteller with rights to speak authoritatively about particular issues. The narrative work in progress collaboratively constructed motivations for storytelling, accounting skills, and narrative status. As story and status worked their way into the conversations, so too did the inner lives and social worlds they more or less shared in common.

Pollner and McDonald-Wikler's (1985) case study of status and storytelling, of course, is not about chickens, but its narrative material is performatively similar. Status and story exist in equally complex narrative relationship in the case of the family's interaction with their severely retarded child. As the researchers show, the child's status both is constructed by, and in turn, guides the family's normal conversations with and about the child. All around, storytelling assigns narrative status, which reflexively spawns the active agency of the participants.

The case was brought to the researchers' attention when family members approached a large psychiatric institute for help with their 5 ½-year-old daughter Mary's "unusual behavior." The request was puzzling. Note the unassailable normality assigned to the child by family members despite the clinical facts of the matter.

> Family members stated that Mary was a verbal and intelligent child who malingered and refused to speak in public in order to embarrass the family. Extensive clinical observation and examination revealed Mary to be severely retarded and unable to perform at anywhere near the level of competence claimed by her parents and two older sibs. (p. 242)

The clinical report also suggested the diagnosis of *folie à famille*, which is a medical framing implicating all family members. But systematic observation from an everyday life perspective revealed a complex narrative relationship between family members and a set of interactional practices resembling the everyday work that constitutes stories and narrative status in general, whether participants are clinically normal or abnormal, dead or alive, animate or inanimate. For example, family members spoke of Mary's behavior as either public or private. They acknowledged the child's difficult, resistant public behavior, and it was for this that they sought treatment. Otherwise, at home in private, the family said Mary acted normally. For all practical purposes, she was narratively agentic both in public and in private, but this agency wasn't activated in public. The following lists some of the particulars from family members' perspectives.

Each of the four family members who lived with Mary agreed with this:

Father (aged 42):	She's really a fast child, if anything. Once she even read a note aloud that I had passed over to my wife not intending for Mary to see it.
Mother (aged 39):	She puts on an act of being retarded in public while acting normally at home.
Half-Sister (aged 18):	I've had 10-minute long normal conversations with her, but she won't talk in front of most people.
Brother (aged 12):	I don't know why she fakes it; she's like any other 5-year-old. (pp. 242–243)

Rather than seeking to corroborate or otherwise evaluate the clinical picture in their research, Pollner and McDonald-Wikler asked a different question, one centered on narrative agency and practice in the family context. Their interest was in the reflexive organization of status and story in the situation. The aim was to understand how the family, as a matter of practice, constructed Mary as bizarre in public but as an otherwise normal child at home. They asked, what interactional work was done to construct Mary's status as a competent storyteller?

> Our analysis of the available materials has been instigated by the following questions: How does the family do it? What sorts of skills, practices, and strategies are utilized to create and then [reflexively] "discover" Mary's competence? . . . The yield of our analysis has been a set of practices by which family members created Mary's "perfection." (p. 244)

The researchers describe six narrative techniques, the everyday applications of which constructed and sustained Mary's status as a normal child with the capacity to account for her conduct. These include *framing* whatever Mary did in the context of the home as normal; *postscripting* or storying whatever Mary did, after the fact, as reasonably motivated; and *putting words into Mary's mouth*. We describe material showing evidence of the latter technique because it parallels the same technique applied in the Mrs. Bird anecdote. From a clinical perspective, the application of such techniques might be construed as part of the folly of the family, as features of familial pathology. But when viewed through the lens of narrative collaboration, such techniques serve a performative function that works to assemble the reflexivity of status and story across the normal/abnormal divide.

The following three extracts from the researchers' transcripts illustrate the technique of putting words into Mary's mouth, literally cooperating to normalize Mary's accounts. In "documentary" fashion (see Garfinkel, 1967), the reciprocating content of exchanges between the mother, father, and Mary portray Mary as narratively competent (status). Mary's responses (story), in turn, are taken to be the practical accomplishments of her status as a normal child. The narrative reflexivity at play is palpable. If status is a narrative environment, it is one whose effects on talk and interaction are themselves produced within the accounts provided.

The first extract is part of a conversation between the father (Fa), mother (Mo), and Mary (M) about how Mary looks in a new robe.

1.   Mary is wearing a newly bought robe.

Fa: Want to see it in the mirror?

M: Gurgling.

Fa: She doesn't like it.

Mo: You don't like the robe? It fits you.

M: Gurgling.

Mo: What did you say about Daddy?

M: Mmmmmmmm, [gurgle].

Fa: She thinks it's too cheap! (p. 249)

Bracketing a clinical perspective for the moment, turn by narrative turn, the story that unfolds in this extract is about a little girl who is viewing herself in the mirror to see what she looks like in a new robe and who concludes that she doesn't like it. Taken to be a rational response, the mother asked why Mary doesn't like the robe; after all, it fits her. At first, Mary says something inaudible about her father. The girl soon explains that she doesn't like the robe because it's too cheap. So the story goes, in the collaboration between daughter, mother, and father. In narrative practice, Mary takes the role of, and performs as, a verbally engaged young girl with a presumed taste in clothing, who speaks her mind and explains why she thinks the way she does. In narrative practice, there's no doubt about her storytelling status and her associated right to speak and offer judgments about apparel. Interestingly enough, there is only surprise at her opinion, not at her ability to offer it.

The second extract is part of a conversation in which the parents encourage Mary to talk into a tape recorder. Mary's reluctance prompts the father to provide an incentive. Mary evidently is figured by her parents to be someone who will cooperate if offered the right terms. The parents would be satisfied if Mary simply stated her name and age. Mary's response ostensibly tells the father that his offer is insufficient. It's evident that Mary has the wits to bargain for more. The calculating young agent constructed in the process indicates her narrative rights in no uncertain terms. Again, the unfolding narrative collaboration documents Mary's competence and status as an active storyteller.

2.   Encouraging her to talk into the recorder:

Fa: OK, you tell me your name and age into that thing, and I'll give you $5 to go out and buy a present that you want to buy yourself.

M: [Gurgling].

Fa: Your name and age—

M: Goo ga [gurgle].

Fa: She's bargaining with me for more money! (p. 249)

A while later, as the third extract below indicates, another story develops, further implicating Mary's narrative status. The interaction continues to document the practical rationality of someone who knows her own mind. The exchange shows that there's a normative (not practical) limit to Mary's rights and responsibilities; those stop at matters of which Mother knows best.

3.   Later:

Mo: Time for your pills, Mary.

M: Mmmmm.

Mo: Time for your pills.

M: [Gurgling].

Mo: You don't think you need them.

M: Mmmmm, ga.

Mo: I think you need them. (p. 249)

If we hadn't known Mary's clinical status, we might have presumed that these accounts were, interactionally speaking, the responses of any young girl interacting with her parents at this stage of life. Turn by narrative turn and despite the clinical diagnosis, Mary and her parents collaboratively construct an accountable subject who has sensible judgment and distinct preferences. In practice, status and story operate reflexively to produce a narrative environment whose participants work to assemble the everyday sensibility of their membership in it.

Gubrium's (1986a, 1986b) ethnography of the everyday cognitive status of Alzheimer's disease (AD) sufferers provides further illustration of the reflexivity of status and story. In this case, status refers to cognitive capacity at the end of life. The narrative material presented below was gathered as part of research on how the AD movement, which began in the late 1970s, deployed a new subjectivity for cognitive impairment, replacing the normal senility associated with the aging brain with a medical, ostensibly curable disease.

The Alzheimer's Disease Association was at the center of the movement. It advocated for research and was a voice for the afflicted and their families. Among other activities, local chapters sponsored support groups for home caregivers. Gubrium participated and observed in many of these groups. The proceedings typically dealt with informational issues surrounding the manifestations, causes, and the course of the illness; matters related to caregiver stress; and the shared experiences of caregiving. There was a great deal of storytelling at these meetings, some recounting caregiving experiences since the last meeting, some bringing others up-to-date on the cognitive status of care receivers, and many simply offering support or advice for how to think and feel about what was happening to loved ones.

Of particular concern to participants was the point at which AD sufferers no longer recognized themselves or the caregiver, the latter typically a spouse or an adult daughter. It was a devastating experience and difficult to discuss, and it produced much emotional storytelling. Put in ordinary terms, the leading question was whether the AD sufferer was "still there," raising the issue of the sufferer's cognitive status, and, of course, narrative agency. Related terms and phrases keyed the issue and the status, such as whether the sufferer had become a "vegetable," the "mere shell of his [or her] former self," or had "lost his [or her] mind." Answers were figured in relation to the AD sufferer's storytelling capacity. No matter what the disease manifestations, if AD sufferers were construed as being able to convey their stories, as limited as those might be, they were viewed as still having a mind and a story worthy of being heard.

In practice, the question was whether story, in the sense of accountable responses, signified cognitive functioning. The relation between status and story was raised time and again in group meetings. The following extract (J. F. Gubrium, 1986b), drawn from the proceedings of one of the support groups, illustrates this concern in relation to caregiver Rita's husband. His mental status of late had begun to worry Rita. Once again, the extract is annotated for story and status components. Rita explains.

I just don't know what to think or feel. It's like he's not even there anymore [status], and it distresses me something awful. He doesn't know me [story]. He thinks I'm a strange woman in the house [story]. He shouts and tries to slap me away from him [story]. It's not like him at all [status]. Most of the time he makes sounds but they sound more like an animal than a person [story]. Do you think he has a mind left [status]? I wish I could just get in there into his head and see what's going on [status]. Sometimes I get so upset that I just pound on him and yell at him to come out to me [status/story]. Am I being stupid? I feel that if I don't do something quick to get at him that he'll be taken from me altogether [status]. (p. 41)

Rita virtually pleads for the storying of mind. All the old narrative signs—him knowing her, recognizing her presence in the home, sounding like a person—have vanished. According to Rita, nothing signifies her husband's old self as intact and functioning (status). Her husband seems bereft of recognizable accounts; he sounds like an animal, tantamount to making noise without narrativity. As Rita wonders whether "he has a mind left," she audibly links mental status to accountability. In the end, she worries that if he doesn't soon show signs of "being there," the disease will take him away from her altogether.

As elsewhere, as things go in AD support groups there are differences of opinion about what constitutes accountability. Just as Mary's parents viewed their retarded daughter differently from others, group members differ in how, and how soon, they draw conclusions about the links between cognitive status and accountability. The key issue in practice is similar: What is sufficient evidence of narrative competence to warrant assigning storytelling status to the cognitively impaired? As the next extract and extracts from related scenes of everyday life show, there is no definitive answer to this, only narratively practical ones. The next extract, which immediately followed Rita's comments, features caregiver Sara raising an everyday form of the epistemological question at the center of the relationship between status and story. How does one know someone's mental status when the capacity to provide accounts is not evident or unclear? Sara challenges Rita's reading of the situation and Rita's moral commitment in the matter. The extract again is annotated for its story and status dimensions.

We have all gone through it. I know the feeling . . . like, you just know in your heart of hearts that he's in there [status] and that if *you* let go, that's it. So you keep on trying and trying and trying [story]. You've got to keep the faith, that it's him [status] and just work at him [story], 'cause if you don't [story] . . . well, I'm afraid we've lost them [status]. That's Alzheimer's. It's up to the ones who care [story/status] because they (the victims) can't do it for themselves [story/status]. (p. 41)

The story/status connection referenced in Sara's declaration "that's Alzheimer's" is an example of a general principle operating in narrative practice throughout life, across the life course, and across the boundaries of the clinically normal and abnormal. As narrative collaboration and performativity do, "that's Alzheimer's" implicates everyone, spreading the responsibility for the narrative status of AD sufferers to all concerned. Studies of human–animal interaction show similar evidence of assigned narrative agency, where dogs, for example, are oriented to and interacted with as if they possessed storytelling status and capability. Dogs' accounts are provided by their owners or others and, in turn, serve as documents of the dogs' active mental status (see Sanders, 1999). Indeed, in the practice of everyday life, any object may be assigned storytelling status, supported and embellished, or withdrawn and eliminated, as the narrative work entailed facilitates it. The moral dimensions of narrative agency are in this sense universal, implicating everyone (cf. Callon, 1986).

Conclusion

The researcher should be vigilant regarding the everyday narrative process in matters of status and story. Systematic field notes, tape recordings, and do-it-yourself transcripts should be used to feature, step by narrative step, the way status and story reflexively unfold. In the matter of narrative agency, the researcher should put aside the philosophical question of whether mind "really" exists for subjects such as material objects, animals, the mentally retarded, the demented, and human beings in general. Then, in that analytic context, the researcher can take up questions that inspired Pollner and McDonald-Wikler's and Gubrium's research on the social construction of narrative status. What sorts of practices are utilized to assemble and reflexively sustain narrative agency, authority, and competence? How do accountability and storytelling fit into the equation? Such are the basic issues of agentic status as a narrative environment.

13

Jobs

What people do for a living reverberates throughout their lives. Jobs shape identity, locate people in social and economic hierarchies, and affect their physical and emotional well-being. Some spend most of their waking hours on the job; time spent in the workplace encapsulates them. For some, jobs provide credibility, authority, and credentials, what the jobholder is especially certified as being able to do. Jobs not only shape our lives, but offer platforms from which to story experience. They provide recognized means of characterizing and making sense of things, including important ways of accounting for oneself and others. Jobs, in other words, serve as significant narrative environments, which is the topic of this chapter.

Orienting to Jobs

There are many ways of categorizing jobs; we won't survey the variety here. Still, important distinctions bear mentioning in orienting to jobs as narrative environments. In distinguishing some jobs as occupations, accountable horizons spread beyond particular workplaces. Occupations transcend specific employers or work settings. Being part of an occupation gives people much to share with a wide variety of others, most of whom they will never meet. Shared skills, orientations, objectives, and outlooks provide members of an occupation with what amounts to a set of interpretive tools for making meaning.

Professions insinuate themselves further into workers' lives. We might say that a profession is an occupation with a highly developed, formal culture all its own. A profession is based on a systematic body of theory; requires command of specialized, abstract knowledge and skills; marshals authority based on expertise; is sanctioned by the community; has its own regulating and certification associations; and has a code of ethics. Professional work tends to be organized around the provision of services to clients and, as such, might be considered more altruistic than profit-oriented occupations (see Miller, 1981; Roos, 1992). Examples of professions include accounting, engineering, law and criminal justice agents, teaching, architecture, medicine, social work, pharmacy, finance, and nursing, and those who work or perform research in the various sciences. Contrast these with nonprofessional occupations like custodian, waitress, retail salesperson, and postal clerk, where privileged relations with clients are uncharacteristic. While there is no clear demarcation, professions tend to involve greater investments for membership, supply more highly developed and distinctive interpretive "toolkits" (Swidler, 1986), and impose themselves in the form of "lifestyle" more than do nonprofessional occupations (Åkerstrom, 1993).

Professions tend to provide recognized standpoints and pervasive interpretive conventions through which relevant issues are approached. They are sources of authorized practices that are brought to bear not only on work-related matters, but on the meaning-making process generally. Members of occupations and professions share regularized ways of assigning meaning and responding to things. They share disciplinary discourses—recognizable categories, familiar vocabularies, organizational mandates, job-related orientations, group perspectives, and other platforms for making meaning. Members are socialized into ways of seeing and speaking.

While we are not suggesting that jobs, occupations, or professions govern description, occupational and professional influence is profound because the regularities are broadly recognized and certified, quite often by law. Some have characterized occupations and professions as distinctive *social niches* (see Miller, 1978) or even *social worlds* of their own (see Unruh, 1983). Borrowing from the work of Michel Foucault (1965, 1975), as jobs, occupations and professions deploy "gazes" through which work and related activities are apprehended and monitored. These gazes "discipline" the way jobholders view their world and the persons who enter into it, as Foucault would have it. A disciplinary gaze is not only a way of viewing the world, but also a way of understanding, describing, and controlling it. Such disciplinary discourses result in characteristic narratives, leading participants to story things in special ways (see Sheridan, 1980).

Understood in this fashion, jobs, especially occupations and professions, serve as compelling narrative environments. Consider the difference a toolkit of this kind makes in storying an event. The variation between a layperson's description of a possible crime scene and the description formulated by a police officer out of ostensibly the same facts is instructive. The layperson, for example, might describe a contentious traffic stop by a police officer in roughly the following way:

> The cop walked up to the car and told the driver to get out. He wouldn't get out of the car, and when the cop told him to get out again, he started yelling at the officer. So the cop yanked the guy out and threw him down on the ground.

In contrast, in his official capacity, a police officer is likely to narrate the same scene in something like the following terms:

> Officer Smith approached the vehicle and ordered the suspect to exit the vehicle. The suspect failed to comply and became verbally uncooperative. The uncooperative behavior escalated, and the suspect became verbally abusive and threatening. In light of this, and for officer safety reasons, Officer Smith physically removed the suspect from the vehicle and placed him prone on the ground in accordance with departmental use-of-force policy.

On the surface, these might seem to be simply two different wordings of the same situation. One might say, for instance, that the officer's narrative was couched in police jargon, implying that it is just an esoteric way of saying the same thing that the layperson might report. Their institutionalized bearings, however, are not equally consequential. Professional jargon is more than the distinctive language of a particular group. It is also a specialized vocabulary formulated to convey precise, job-specific actions that are especially germane to the collective work of the group concerned. In principle, police officers are held strictly accountable for their on-the-job activity. They need to formally report almost all of their professionally relevant decisions. In anticipation of the mandate to report, they are constantly preparing to justify their behavior. In turn, those with whom they work anticipate a particular type and style of narrative, which, in turn, allows them to do their own jobs.

For one thing, the reports are expected to make fine-grained distinctions between different classes of activities and persons that correspond to legal statutes and professional guidelines. They require formal justification (causes and motives) for decisions made and actions taken. Consequently, officers both see and say things differently than laypersons. They recognize "suspects" and "complainants" as particular categories of people with whom they routinely deal, to whom sets of distinctive traits and expectations are attributed. They narrate actions such as "take people into custody" and "transport them to detention" in order to convey professionally adequate, not personalized, descriptions that resonate with legally defined and defensible meanings.

For professional and related legal and institutional reasons, occupational vocabularies construct different narrative realities, not just surface descriptions. They are not just gratuitous jargon; they have descriptive demands beyond turns of phrases. This is true to some degree for all jobs, the accountable functions of which play into narrativity. For example, a baseball coach might formulate a teenaged player's season-long slump in terms of a lack of "coachability," "will to win," or "team spirit." That same student's teachers might describe the student's classroom foibles in terms of attentiveness, study habits, or academic motivation. While there certainly are resemblances between the vocabularies of such accounts, the meanings implied by, the courses of action suggested by, and consequences of the alternate vocabularies align with their narrative environments. If "not studying the playbook" or a "lack of discipline" is implied in the context of athletics and teamwork, attention deficit disorder might be implied in the context of classroom learning. This is far from being a simple matter of word selection; it is morally implicative.

For those old enough to recall, the classic "Officer Krupke" scene in the Broadway musical and subsequent motion picture *West Side Story* is exemplary. In this scene, a gang member is variously and ironically described by a range of human service and legal professionals. While the point of the scene is humorous, it offers insightful commentary on disciplinary differences in the formulation of juvenile troubles. The gang member under consideration transforms from a "punk" to "psychologically disturbed" to "sociologically sick" and, finally, to "no good" as description shifts professional auspices.

As tempting as it is, however, we must resist the view that a job is a fixed set of narrative rules. The representational contingencies of work require a more practical approach. If professional gazes comprise relatively stable and distinct ways of storying experience, gazes nonetheless operate in the context of everyday life. While occupational or professional outlooks and language may constantly be at the ready, they must be incited and articulated with matters at hand in order to do narrative work. Nor is the purview of occupational or professional gazes a clearly defined geographic or social space. Multiple professional cultures may simultaneously occupy the same geographic, organizational, or institutional site. An individual may simultaneously occupy different professional worlds (the school or police psychologist, for example). Or the relative salience of professional membership may vary from situation to situation, even within the same setting. An accountant, for instance, may be "all business" on the job, but when "speaking as a friend" to a client about a divorce settlement, his talk may be straight "from the heart," not "from the head."

Once again, ethnographic sensibilities and observational techniques provide access to this dimension of narrative reality. The following analytic guideline highlights these concerns:

Guideline

Observe job circumstances surrounding narrative production to identify the work-related resources and orientations that shape accounts. Listen for and record narratives with the aim of showing how they are characteristic of occupations and professions, taking note of how formalized categories are used to "certify" or "authorize" descriptions and accounts within and beyond the work setting.

Into the Field

Occupations and professions do not necessarily speak for their members, but they provide orientations, resources, and motivations that constitute narrative reality. Ethnographic research reported in *Caretakers* (Buckholdt & Gubrium, 1979), a study of a residential treatment facility for emotionally disturbed children, provides vivid examples of how professions operate as narrative environments. A distinguishing feature of this facility was the active participation of professionals from different disciplines in the facility's treatment programs. Their accounts allowed the researchers to compare the actionable consequences of narratives that centered ostensibly on the same persons, experiences, and treatment outcomes.

Treatment at the facility, called "Cedarview," was officially based on behavioral principles. In broad strokes, children's problems were interpreted as a calculus of inappropriate activities or exchanges, not as configurations of deep meaning. Behaviors, not symptoms, were the focus of attention. What children did was officially of more concern than the inner psychic forces that might motivate their behavior. Behavior modification, with various programs of reinforcement and sanctions, was the preferred treatment modality. Together with a token economy, this encouraged narratives of visible behaviors and "consequences." Staff members officially "stayed out of children's heads," an admonition to adhere closely to behavioral indicators.

Staffed by special education teachers, social workers, speech therapists, administrators, and psychological consultants, among others, Cedarview brought multiple professional perspectives to bear on the problems children presented. While most of the staff was trained in, and committed to, behavioral principles, several key members—particularly the psychological consultants—brought different professional outlooks to the mix. Through months of systematic participant observation, the researchers were able to watch staff members interact with children and with each other. They participated in various activities where different professional outlooks simultaneously came into play. In the process, they documented the numerous ways that the staff members' narrative activity constructed the disturbances in view.

One such activity was known as the semiannual "psychiatric staffing," where children's problems, programs, progress, and prognoses were discussed by multidisciplinary teams consisting of teachers, child care workers, social workers, supervisors, and psychological (or psychiatric) consultants. Competing professional narratives were especially likely to be heard in staffings, particularly when a child psychiatrist or a nonbehavioral psychologist attended. Their narratives tended to work against the official behavioral vocabulary. Just as the earlier police and lay accounts served to story events differently, the various staff members offered competing characterizations of the children and their actions, the accounts of which could be traced to the professional backgrounds of those involved.

For example, contrary to Cedarview's behavioral philosophy, one consultant's deep psychiatric gaze encouraged narratives highlighting early childhood disturbances, deep feelings, and hidden motives, rather than institutionally preferred, behavior-centered accounts. Contrasting professional narratives are apparent in the following annotated (do-it-yourself) transcript of a staffing in which one of the children, Kim Carmichael, was the subject of discussion. As is apparent in the following extract, narrative shifts abound as the deep psychological gaze of the psychiatric consultant repeatedly and almost jarringly alters the otherwise behavioral drift of the proceedings. The meeting was attended by a social worker (SW), the child's teacher (Te), the Cedarview principal (Pr), a county liaison officer (LO), and a psychiatric consultant (PC). The liaison officer doesn't speak in this particular extract, although she is present throughout the meeting and does talk at other points.

SW: We're going to staff our "no problems" child. [She elaborates Kim's background.]

Te: She's just the kind of child that responds to programs [Cedarview's behavior modification programs]. Ya put her on one, and she really follows along. She's just all smiles and loves every minute of it.

SW: Anyway . . . she's up to here in programs.

Pr: She's the type of kid who'll always be on programs.

SW: She was referred for eating nonedibles. She has a history of doing anything to get punished. [Kim's punishment history is detailed.] She has a low IQ . . . which is probably not accurate. On the Peabody [individual achievement test], she tested out at 67. We're dealing with a really low child. She's really tuned into both tangible and nontangible reinforcement. [Kim's reinforcement is exemplified.] She's peculiar in that she'll do anything for paper. She's into pica [a craving for unnatural food]. [Several utterances follow regarding the pica.]

Te: She'll repeat what other people say . . . over and over. Always repeats. She never comes up with an original idea. That's our Kim.

PC: I remember . . . maybe . . . that she's not affectively tuned into what's going on around her?

Te: I don't know about that.

PC: She doesn't respond to anything abstract.

Te: Oh . . . like that, you mean [Pauses.] I guess so. She reminds me of a slot machine. You put all you can into it, and she never gives you anything back.

PC: Sure! You never hit the Jackpot? [Eagerly] What is her object permanence? Is she, you know, out of sight, out of mind?

SW: She remembers dates.

Te: Yeah . . . especially things that she's highly interested in. Like she'll come in everyday and ask me when this, when that. Sometimes I can't shake her. She really gets onto something like that. She's a real cutie though.

PC: I guess the thing I want to do is look at her cognitively. How does she attend in class?

Te: Her attention is poor, and her retention is low.

Pr: She's very low in visual perception and auditory memory. Her Bender [a visual/motor integration test] came out very low.

PC: Under what conditions does she remember well? Emotional memory, you know, is tied into the existential. What does she build on in terms of her own experiences?

SW: She does very well on the specific concrete things she's being programmed for.

PC: Ahem! Then she does integrate! That the thing . . .

Te: [Kim's teacher describes Kim's habit of eating her pencils and putting Kim on a program for not eating pencils. Everyone laughs.]

PC: I'm concerned about her lack of memory. Her data bank just isn't working. Is she blocking? Is she lesioned out? Or what?

Te: Maybe she just likes programs. I don't know.

SW: She used to be the sort of child who never cried. Now she's more genuine. Like she was coming out of Children's Hospital and fell and she really cried. I reinforced her immediately.

PC: Good! That takes a lot of insight.

SW: She has a lot of stimulus deprivation in her background.

PC: [The consultant now asks several questions about Kim's affect, and her sensory faculties, and the teacher responds, finally moving to visual skills.]

Te: She observes things that other people are getting attention for.

PC: So she's good at modeling! Modeling really seems to be her thing then, huh? [The consultant proceeds to elaborate the psychology of modeling. He refers to a variety of theories of modeling and relates each one to Kim. The consultant then changes the subject somewhat after a few staffers take issue with the modeling idea.]

PC: She does seem to have a history of someone who lacks organic integrity, though. It's just a hypothesis, though. You may know better on that one. Apparently she doesn't discriminate between all these things she loves to eat. [Staff members begin to pick up on the organic integrity suggestion and recount evidence in support of it, whereupon the consultant elaborates his organic integrity theory. Eventually the evidence recounted and comments made by staff members become humorous. But the organic theory is dwelled upon and reinforced by all.] (Buckholdt & Gubrium, 1979, pp. 213–218)

The staffing continued for another 30 minutes, touching on a number of additional matters. Staff members continued to center their comments and questions on behaviors and issues of social learning, typically in specific relation to Kim and her troubles. But, as we see above, at various junctures the psychiatric consultant offered both case-specific and general formulations and hypotheses suggesting neurological disorders, chromosomal damage, genetic counseling, internalization, organic disorders, and deep cognitive effects (later, "If you want to get Piaget-y about it."). The narrative drift was clear: The consultant articulated accounts of internal disorder, while the others narrated Kim's troubles in behavioral terms.

Of course there are many possible reasons for the different accounts of Kim's problems, their causes, and solutions. Some are simply a matter of managing the children in residence. Staff members have to deal with children in specific, concrete terms. As far as this is concerned, their interest is not theoretical and their experience with Kim is far from abstract. On the other hand, the psychiatrist knows Kim mainly by way of secondhand reports and has not been responsible for managing her in residence. He can afford to approach Kim "theoretically" and tends to speak in broader psychiatric generalities. Indeed, that's part of his professional and occupational role in the staffing. House staffers, on the other hand, don't have the luxury of theorizing much; they need to respond to Kim in relation to dealing with her around-the-clock on the premises.

In addition, of course, the institutional treatment philosophy shapes the conversation. Staff members at Cedarview have been trained in, and talk, the principles of behavioral therapy. They practice its treatment tenets on a daily basis, in and out of staffings. Their orientation is to visible conduct, sanctions, and consequences. Their official working language centers on what children do, how staff members react, and how the children, in turn, respond to reinforcement and behavior modification programming. They have an institutional incentive for doing so, as they work with and for other staff members who deploy the same principles. And, of course, they are accountable to each other and to outside agencies for documentation that speaks this language.

In contrast, the consultant, trained as a child psychiatrist, deploys psychiatric principles. His institutional ties to Cedarview are more limited. He is professionally committed to seeking diagnoses and offering treatment strategies in terms of inner psychological disorder, not external activities. In the preceding extract, recall how frequently staff members report instances of Kim's behavior, whereas the consultant immediately seeks to appropriate the reported behaviors to the child's inner life, related theoretical formulations, symptoms, or etiologies. While he applies psychiatric terminology to the behavior-centered accounts offered by staff members, it is much more than simple jargon. It constructs a gaze, which has implications for actual practice. The extract ends with the psychiatrist formulating the case in terms of what is called "organic integrity theory," something at once nonbehavioral and of limited application in Cedarview's official scheme of things. If, over the course of the staffing, staff members and the consultant are not exactly involved in an interdisciplinary dispute, they are clearly on different narrative "pages" much of the time.

Yet, systematic observation shows that the psychiatrist, like the other consultants, does serve a purpose. He completes the mental health team and provides the required psychological consultancy. He is credentialed and is viewed as offering the kind of understanding considered to be appropriate for emotional disturbance. His accounts embody professionalism. He displays expertise, command of a specialized fund of theory and knowledge, and is fluent in the language of his discipline. His accounts and formulations of Kim's problems and circumstances distinctively reveal his professional moorings, and distinguish his narratives from those preferred by his behaviorist but less highly credentialed colleagues. If the narratives that staff members and the psychiatrist offer reflect contrasting descriptive habits, whose interpretive resources and repertoires are part of their professional interpretive tool kits, together they present the gamut of expertise that justifies a multidisciplinary approach. Any resulting narrative dissonance, which is minimal in practice, is overshadowed by the credentialing and institutional functions being served.

Researchers should be alert to the variety and nuances of occupational and professional environments. Their traces may be found in narratives of all sorts, not just person-descriptions. Occupational gazes mediate the broad range of social forms constructed in narrative reality. Consider, for example, how job orientations shape characterizations of the family during involuntary commitment proceedings. As a practical matter, when legal and psychiatric personnel consider committing a person for psychiatric treatment, a critical issue is the "tenability" of the candidate patient's proposed community living circumstances (see Holstein, 1993). If the individual in question can be released into a situation that reliably provides for his or her food, clothing, shelter, health care, and ongoing psychiatric treatment (including medications), there is a strong chance the individual will not be hospitalized. If no tenable living arrangement is available, commitment is likely to result. In tenability discussions, the presence or absence of family as "caretakers" is often the crux of the matter.

In the following (do-it-yourself) transcript, two professionals—a judge and a psychiatrist—vie with each other in storying tenability (Holstein, 1988). The exchange transpires between a community mental health center psychiatrist, Dr. Conrad, and the judge of an involuntary commitment hearing. In arguing for the release of his patient, Tyrone Biggs, Dr. Conrad asserted that Biggs's therapeutic program would be completely disrupted if he were hospitalized. Conrad claimed that Biggs was able to function adequately in a community setting and should not be committed. Conrad oriented to a preferred therapeutic environment, one with familial contact. The judge, in contrast, was concerned about the tenability of Biggs's living arrangements, which led to the following exchange:

Judge: Where's Mr. Biggs gonna stay while he's being treated?

Psyc: Tyrone lives with his family. They have an apartment in Lawndale.

Judge: I thought Mr. Biggs was divorced last year?

Psyc: He was, your honor. But he's moved in with his girlfriend and their two children. They share a place with her aunt. He really seems to be getting along fine.

Judge: Now who is it that takes care of him? You say these two ladies are going to be able to keep him out of trouble. How long has he lived with them? What happens when he gets delusional again?

Psyc: We're hoping that's under control. . . . I think it's important to understand that being close to his family is extremely important to Tyrone's [treatment] program. His family wants him there and they make him feel like he belongs. He needs that kind of security—the family environment—if he's ever going to learn to cope and he's not going to get it from anyone but his family.

Judge: That may be so, but you still haven't told me who will keep him under control. Who's going to make him take his medication? . . . I just don't see any family there to look out for him. You say this is his girlfriend and *her* aunt? How old is this woman [the aunt]? How are they going to handle him? I'm sorry, doctor, but this just isn't the kind of situation I can feel good about. I really don't see much of a family here. If I thought there were people there who could really be responsible for this man, it might be different. (Holstein, 1988, pp. 272–273)

The judge and the psychiatrist view this case from different angles, with different professional concerns and unfolding stories of the circumstances. They both have the same general objective: finding the best possible situation for Mr. Biggs to get the care he needs. The doctor, however, had Mr. Biggs for a client; Biggs's psychological welfare—viewed within a psychiatric framework— is his primary concern. The judge, in contrast, also is concerned with Mr. Biggs's welfare, but in addition worries about the safety of the community. Biggs would make trouble for others around him if the family can't handle him. For the judge, the family is construed as something that can or cannot manage Biggs. The judge draws strong links between the family, community safety, and psychological status. For the psychiatrist, the family is construed as something that is part of Biggs's treatment, the community being mostly a background feature of the matter. Accordingly, the strong linkages he draws are between the family and a treatment regimen. Family is storied quite differently in the context of contrasting professional concerns.

Professional purposes come forth dramatically. In the exchange, Dr. Conrad uses the language of therapy, focusing on how he hopes to improve Mr. Biggs's mental health. He describes family in terms of support for psychiatric treatment. From that perspective, those who provide a supportive environment are family. The judge, however, is concerned with monitoring and controlling the trouble that he anticipates from Mr. Biggs, because he believes Biggs is mentally ill and likely to behave erratically. The judge's primary orientation, at least for the moment, is managing trouble in order to avoid future problems related in no small part to the havoc Mr. Biggs's behavior poses for others. The vocabulary he applies invokes the language of custody and control more than the language of treatment. "Family" takes on its meanings in these terms, not so much as a support system but as a mechanism of containment. As the judge explains, for that particular purpose, "I really don't see much of a family here."

Conclusion

Job-related accounts are not always as clearly articulated as in these examples. The narrative effects of jobs are always situated and contingent on other matters, such as whether a professional, say, speaks from that perspective on all matters. We all wear many interpretive hats, so to speak, and alternately take one off and wear another in storying things. While jobs provide environments for encouraging particular kinds of narratives, jobholders play other roles in life. For example, most teachers, psychologists, police officers, doctors, judges, and other professionals go home at the end of the day. When dealing with their own children, they commonly end up "speaking as parents," discussing things in those terms, with parental concerns and domestic consequences at the tip of their tongues, so to speak. Such nuances can play out at work as well, when jobholders such as staff members and court personnel temporarily step outside of those roles and describe proceedings according to the rules of different narrative environments or contingencies. This is an important analytic issue for the researcher who focuses on narrative environments as mediators of storytelling. It is important to remember that the question in this case would be: Which job, role, or environment is at stake in the circumstances?

14

Organizations

J ust as jobs command much of our time, organizations increasingly house our daily lives and mediate our concerns. Contemporary life has come under the purview of countless establishments—schools, churches, hospitals, nursing homes, recreational clubs, sports leagues, and political parties. They provide particular ways of giving voice to, and dealing with, everyday matters. Many, such as recovery groups and correctional facilities, promote highly specialized ways of narrating experience, furnishing powerful, if delimited, frameworks of understanding. Other organizations are less formal and structuring. Borrowing a distinction used in Chapter 11, the present chapter considers how the big stories of these narrative environments relate to the little ones individuals bring with them and take away.

Orienting to Organizations

Everett Hughes (1984) thought of organizations and institutions as "going concerns." He was more interested in what organizations did than what they viewed themselves as being, using the term to characterize ongoing patterns of concerted action. For Hughes, going concerns could be as vast and formal as federal bureaucracy or as ordinary and informal as a group of friends who play golf on Saturday mornings. Large or small, formal or informal, each embodied a commitment to a particular moral order. Like local cultures and jobs, organizations provide participants with preferred ways of linking together and composing matters of concern to them.

Increasingly, narrative work is "organizationally embedded." We have used the term elsewhere to suggest that localized configurations of meaning and related narratives practices are mediated by organizations (see J. F. Gubrium & Holstein, 1997; Holstein & Gubrium, 2000b). Diverse organizations set the "conditions of possibility" for narrative production, as Foucault (1977) might put it. They have big stories to tell, which set the narrative agenda for the smaller, individual stories that follow along. Organizations establish general parameters for how narratives may be produced and who is authorized to produce them. They establish the foundation for what might pass in their purview as recognizable, legitimate accounts. Recall from Chapter 13, for example, that Cedarview offered a behavioral environment and vocabulary for storying children's disturbances. The staff and others generally thought and spoke in these terms, even while there always are alternative accounts in tow. In contrast, another facility might emphasize an in-depth psychological approach, which would likewise be apparent in the big and little stories composed on the premises.

Two studies orient us to the organizational embeddedness of accounts. Empirical material in both studies was obtained in two ways. The big story was discerned from interviews with staff members, from organizational documents, and from the way clients' narratives were shaped by staff members' responses to them in talk and interaction. The smaller individual stories were put together from listening to clients, taking notes of their accounts, and creating do-it-yourself transcripts, and from audio recordings of selected group meetings. It is important to point out that ethnographic fieldwork provides the opportunity to gather this broad range of empirical material.

The first study is a comparative ethnography of two family therapy agencies (J. F. Gubrium, 1992). The research focused on organizations that held similar goals, but drew from distinctly different understandings of troubled families. One agency, Westside House, viewed the family as a hierarchical authority structure. The big story there was that the functional family is one in which lines of authority are clear, distinct, and hierarchical. This supplied both staff and clients with particular narrative resources for evaluating domestic troubles. In contrast, nearby Fairview Hospital held a systemic understanding that emphasized pathological affective linkages between family members as the common source of familial dysfunction. The big story there was that the functional family is one in which there are open channels of communication, especially about feelings. Both agencies engaged in family therapy, in which counseling was undertaken with single families or with multiple groups of families, not with individual members.

When participants in the two organizations offered accounts of domestic troubles, the organizationally preferred narrative could be heard in the ways that family dynamics were described. For example, staff members at both agencies viewed physical posture, comportment, and the seating location of family members during therapy sessions as important indicators of domestic functioning. But these signs of functioning were interpreted in very different ways in the two settings. In observing a videotaped family therapy session, therapists at Westside might comment on a father's central seating position as a commanding location surrounded by various family members. As the language of hierarchy structured accounts, it was interpreted as an empirical indication that the father was rightfully in charge. This was a significant sign of positive family functioning and was reflexively related to further observation and description. The big story of an intact decision-making hierarchy resonated with this father's placement in the family grouping. Narratives of sound family structure and the father's fundamentally healthy sense of familial responsibility were usually forthcoming.

The same choice of central seating position was interpreted differently at Fairview. Here, the functional family was understood to be a democracy of emotions. If a father commanded center stage in a seating arrangement or otherwise drew too much attention to himself, it would incite narratives of paternal domination, foreclosed communication, or an unhealthy hegemony over family interaction. Staff members were apt to conclude that the father was distorting the family circle, drawing it out of balance communicatively by his overbearing presence. Forthcoming narratives of family troubles would cast the father as imposing himself in ways that prevented free and equal communication and the open display of feelings. Here again, the little stories about signs and specific families played out in relation to the bigger story and going concern.

Another study orienting us to the organizational embeddedness of accounts is Gale Miller's (1997) research on the history of a single therapy agency. Miller considered how a change in the narrative orientation (the big story) of a single agency affected how troubles came to be articulated (the little stories). The agency in this case was called "Northland Clinic." It was an internationally prominent center of brief therapy. For years, Northland employed an ecosystemic brief therapy treatment philosophy. That was its "coherence system" (Linde, 1993) for composing accounts of family troubles. This big story was told in systemic terms, emphasizing social context and the dynamic interrelationships of clients' lives and problems. In this narrative environment, therapists storied clients' problems as artifacts of malfunctioning systems of relationships that precipitated and sustained troubles. Staff members discussed problems in relation to the state of these systems, especially their lack of balance, and suggested solutions in terms of changing them to alter their dysfunctional dynamics.

For a variety of reasons, in time Northland shifted to a more construc-
tivist approach. Therapists began to practice solution-focused brief therapy,
which conceived troubles as distinctive ways of talking about everyday life.
This prompted staff members to orient to the therapy process as a set of
"language games," expressly drawing upon Ludwig Wittgenstein's (1953)
sense of the term. The big story now spoke of troubles as narrative constructions, ways of talking and related "forms of life." This transformed
clients from being passive victims of dysfunctional social systems to being
active narrative agents with the potential to formulate positive stories about
themselves and design helpful solutions for their troubles.

The lesson of these comparative and historical analyses of therapy
agencies is not to belabor the point that therapists or therapy agencies may
pursue their treatment objectives differently. Rather, the lesson is that
the organizational embeddedness of accounts leads to different therapeutic
objects and substantive outcomes for the "same" troubles. A family's
account of troubles in one organization is likely to become a different narrative of troubles in the context of an organization with a different story to
tell. As these organizations are going concerns, there is sizable institutional
momentum in place to keep storytelling going in relation to locally preferred
accounts.

Organizations are imbued with relatively stable narrative orientations
and resources. Their big stories are locally homogeneous, which of course
relates to the impetus toward organizational rationality. Analytically, this
suggests that researchers should listen carefully to individual accounts and
take note of the ways they reflect organizational groundings. At the same
time, it is important to pay particular attention to what is reproduced in
individual accounts and to note how biographical particulars and related
conditions provide variations in ongoing talk and interaction. Organizations
condition, but do not determine, locally articulated narratives. The following guideline applies:

Guideline

Attend carefully to the organizational embeddedness of accounts,
noting the organizational voices and preferences that are heard
in individual narratives. If possible, compare the organizational
narratives of various sites for differences and similarities in the
construction of individual accounts.

Into the Field

We move into the field by way of research projects dealing with contrasting
alcoholism treatment organizations. One is Norman Denzin's (1986, 1987a,

1987b) series of studies of Alcoholics Anonymous (AA). The other research is James Christopher's (1988) work on Secular Sobriety Groups (SSG; alternatively called SOS, which stands for Secular Organizations for Sobriety or Save Our Selves). Both organizations sponsor recovery groups. The big stories are different in the two organizations. Our aim is to provide guidance for analyzing how the difference resonates in the accounts of individual group members.

In his series of studies, Denzin observed three treatment centers that utilized AA principles, documenting narrative practices in over 2,000 open and closed meetings. Immersing himself in this environment, Denzin described the structure and interactions of AA, in the process documenting the array of narrative resources participants used to make sense of their lives and drinking experience. For our purposes, the most salient and significant aspect of AA is its language of alcoholism treatment and recovery. As Denzin was able to show, AA comprises a distinctive, comprehensive mode of storytelling.

Denzin traces AA's narrative tradition to its "Big Book" (Alcoholics Anonymous, 1976), which is the most important statement of the AA program and philosophy. The language of this tradition suffuses the AA literature as well as the formal and informal talk of AA leaders, lecturers, and members. The widely known "Twelve Steps"—typically found in the opening pages of AA texts—are key elements of the big story. Listed below, the steps serve as the primary resource for narrating the alcoholic experience in AA terms.

The Twelve Steps

1. We admitted we were powerless over alcohol—that our lives had become unmanageable.

2. Came to Believe that a Power greater than ourselves could restore us to Sanity.

3. Made a decision to turn our will and our lives over to the care of God *as we understood Him.*

4. Made a searching and fearless moral inventory of ourselves.

5. Admitted to God, to ourselves, and to another human being the exact nature of our wrongs.

6. Were entirely ready to have God remove all these defects of character.

7. Humbly asked Him to remove all our shortcomings.

8. Made a list of all persons we had harmed, and became willing to make amends to them all.

9. Made direct amends to such people whenever possible, except when to do so would injure them or others.

10. Continued to take personal inventory and when we were wrong, promptly admitted it.

11. Sought through prayer and meditation to improve our conscious contact with God *as we understood Him*, praying only for knowledge of His will for us and the power to carry that out.

12. Having had a spiritual awakening as the result of these steps, we tried to carry this message to alcoholics, and to practice these principles in all our affairs. (Alcoholics Anonymous, 1953, p. 2, italics in the original)

Denzin (1987a, p. 46) explains that the Twelve Steps deploy an ever-present working language for constructing accounts—terms, phrases, and meanings that "permeate as a threatening presence, every interaction that occurs between patients and their counselors." The following listing offers familiar narrative resources that are available for accountable use in the many settings where the AA philosophy is present. While the language is not formally imposed, its use is so pervasive that individual drinking experiences typically come to be articulated in its terms.

These Twelve Steps contain the following problematic terms and phrases: admitted, powerless, "lives had become unmanageable," restore, sanity, will, "lives," "care of God," "as we understood him," searching, fearless, "moral inventory," "admitted to God," "exact nature," "wrongs," "entirely ready," remove, "defects of character," "humbly," shortcomings, "persons we had harmed," "make amends," (direct amends), "injure," personal inventory, wrong, prayer, meditation, conscious contact, pray, "knowledge of his will for us," "power to carry that out," "spiritual awakening," carry this message, "practice these principles in all our affairs." (Denzin, 1987a, p. 45, punctuation as in the original)

Denzin goes on to describe these resources in use as he analyzes the production of individual narratives in AA groups. Participants, he shows, draw upon AA terminology and the Twelve Steps to consistently articulate a model of alcoholism, treatment, and recovery in what is now a widely recognizable form, even outside of AA. In these narratives, alcoholism manifests itself in physical deterioration, emotional illness, and moral or spiritual emptiness. Alcoholics are portrayed as having an obsessive craving for alcohol that produces an allergy-like reaction in their bodies. Among other things, this causes them to lose control of their drinking. As obvious as the symptoms may become, self-delusion and denial prevent the drinker from realizing that a problem exists. According to AA's big story—and Big Book—recovery requires complete abstinence from alcohol and an admission that one is powerless to resist it. A bedrock tenet of this narrative insists that one must turn one's life over to a power greater than one's self. The "alcoholic ego" must be renounced as the recovering alcoholic surrenders to a "spiritual" way of life (Denzin, 1987b).

Denzin explains that AA treatment and participation are largely about narratively reformulating the alcoholic self (little story) into an AA self (big story)—restorying the self according to the AA model. That is expressly linked to the AA philosophy as embodied in the Twelve Steps. The following self inventory offered by Jack, a member of an AA recovery group, is organizationally telling. Asked to share the meaning of his alcoholic experiences with the entire group of recovering alcoholics, Jack tells his story this way:

> Step One. I know I'm powerless over alcohol. I take one drink and I can't stop. My life must be unmanageable. I have bills up to the ceiling and the family is about to leave and I've been put on notice at work. Step Two. I want to believe in God. I used to but I got away from the Church. But this isn't the God of my church. It's different. I want a God of love and caring. I know I was crazy when I drank. The last time I went out, I ended up in a motel room across town under a different name. Now that's not sane! (Denzin, 1987a, p. 70)

The account is tightly composed in terms of the AA model, down to the sequential structure provided by the Twelve Steps. AA principles are the foundation of the way Jack's life is storied.

All individual AA narratives are clearly informed by AA tenets, even if they do not all virtually recite the Twelve Steps. Still, if participants' stories are organizationally embedded, they are not cookie-cutter accounts, as biographical particulars also come into play. Nonetheless, in their themes and concerted storylines, narratives emerging under AA's auspices end up bearing a strong family resemblance resonating AA doctrine. For example, consider the following portion of a classic story told by a recovered AA "luminary" in the Big Book. Known only as "Number Three," he reconstructs his experience of being hospitalized for intoxication for the eighth time in 6 months.

> I lay there on that hospital bed and went back over and reviewed my life. I thought of what liquor had done to me, the opportunities that I had discarded, the abilities that had been given me and how I had wasted them. . . . I was willing to admit to myself that I had hit bottom, that I had gotten hold of something that I didn't know how to handle by myself. So, after reviewing these things and realizing what liquor had cost me, I went to this Higher Power

which to me, was God, without any reservation, and admitted that I was completely powerless over alcohol, and that I was willing to do anything in the world to get rid of the problem. In fact, I admitted that from now on I was willing to let God take over, instead of me. Each day I would try to find out what His will was, and try to follow that, rather than trying to get Him to always agree that the things I thought of myself were the things best for me. (Alcoholics Anonymous, 1976, pp. 186–187)

Now, compare this with a housewife's account of her fight to quit drinking.

I had problems. We all have them, and I thought a little brandy or a little wine now and then could certainly hurt no one. . . . But from one or two drinks of an afternoon or evening, my intake mounted and mounted fast. It wasn't long before I was drinking all day. . . . I should have realized that alcohol was getting hold of me when I started to become secretive in my drinking. . . . I needed it and I knew I was drinking too much, but I wasn't conscious of the fact that I should stop. . . . I needed that alcohol. I couldn't live without it. I couldn't do anything without it. I couldn't do it [quit drinking] among my relatives, I couldn't do it among my friends. No one likes to admit they're a drunk, that they can't control this thing. . . . [After beginning to attend AA meetings] It was at that point that I reached surrender. I heard one very ill woman say that she didn't believe in the surrender part of the AA program. My heavens! Surrender to me has meant the ability to run my home, to face my responsibilities as they should be faced, to take life as it comes to me day by day. . . . Since I gave my will over to AA, whatever AA has wanted of me I've tried to do the best of my ability. . . . Life for me is lived one day at a time, letting the problems of the future rest with the future. When the time comes to solve them, God will give me strength for that day. (Alcoholics Anonymous, 1976, pp. 336–341)

While not identical, these narratives invoke similar themes and characterization. The first account practically relays the prototype alcoholic's story in precise AA terminology. While the second story draws less explicitly upon the language of AA, it, too, is composed out of the big story AA makes available to its participants for understanding their lives. As we see, these resources do not precisely determine how AA experiences are storied, since biographical particulars and individual circumstances come into play. Narrative environments provide resources, not templates, for the construction of accounts. It is apparent that the narrative environment of AA is a significant factor in how these stories are crafted. According to Denzin, participants in AA cannot tell their own stories without telling AA's story at the same time. (See Holstein & Gubrium, 2000b, pp. 182–186, for further discussion of AA narrative conventions and variations.)

The extent to which organizations mediate participants' narratives becomes even more apparent when we compare AA accounts to that of another organization with its own alcoholic recovery groups. Storytelling in the secular sobriety groups described in Christopher's (1988) book *How to Stay Sober: Recovery Without Religion* provides a powerful contrast. SSG/SOS is an alternative recovery method aimed at alcoholics or drug addicts who are uncomfortable with the spiritual content of widely available 12-step programs. Founded in 1985, it was explicitly designed as an alternative to AA. SSG/SOS takes a secular approach to recovery and maintains that sobriety is an issue separate from religion or spirituality. SSG/SOS credits the individual for achieving and maintaining his or her own sobriety, stressing that this avoids reliance on any "higher power" (SOS Dallas, 2007).

SSG/SOS's big story is centered on personal cognition and responsibility. A "cycle of sobriety" replaces steps to recovery in the SSG/SOS model. In this model, the cycle of addiction can be successfully replaced by the cycle of sobriety. The latter cycle contains three basic components: acknowledging one's addiction, accepting the addiction, and prioritizing sobriety as the primary issue in one's life. The recovery process is said to require the exercise of a "Sobriety Priority" to arrest the cycle of addiction. The cycle of sobriety remains in place only as long as the sober alcoholic chooses to continue to acknowledge the existence of his or her arrested addiction (SOS Dallas, 2007).

While SSG/SOS eschews the 12-step formula of AA, it does offer a list of principles of its own, some of which are excerpted here:

- Although sobriety is an individual responsibility, life does not have to be faced alone . . .
- Sobriety is the number one priority in a recovering person's life . . .
- Honest, clear, and direct communication of feelings, thoughts, and knowledge aids in recovery and in choosing nondestructive, nondelusional, and rational approaches to living sober and rewarding lives.
- SOS encourages the scientific study of addiction in all its aspects. SOS does not limit its outlook to one area of knowledge or theory of addiction. (SOS Dallas, 2007)

The principles are linked to general "Suggested Guidelines for Sobriety":

- To break the cycle of denial and achieve sobriety, we first acknowledge that we are alcoholics or addicts.
- We reaffirm this truth daily and accept without reservation the fact that, as clean and sober individuals, we can not and do not drink or use, no matter what.
- Since drinking or using is not an option for us, we take whatever steps are necessary to continue our Sobriety Priority lifelong.

- A quality of life—"the good life"—can be achieved. However, life is also filled with uncertainties. Therefore, we do not drink or use regardless of feelings, circumstances, or conflicts.
- We share in confidence with each other our thoughts and feelings as sober, clean individuals.
- Sobriety is our Priority, and we are each responsible for our lives and our sobriety. (SOS Dallas, 2007)

By outlining the narrative resources and orientations deployed by the SSG/SOS, we can examine how a parallel organization's narrative environment shapes individual accounts of the alcoholic experience. Consider the following extract, which recounts a conversation between an SSG member and some friends. Note how the member assembles his story out of organizational resources, but crafts it in terms of his particular circumstances.

"What exactly is it you do to stay sober? I mean is it a state of mind, or what?" My two friends were interested in a new Secular Sobriety Group I'd recently started. . . . I explained as best I could that our priority is staying sober and that we met once a week in a friendly, informal candlelit atmosphere to share our thoughts and feelings as alcoholics living sober.

"As you know," I said, "I've never kept my alcoholism a secret. I'm proud of my sobriety. Some other things in my life I'm not so pleased with, but sobriety is my most precious asset, my priority, my life-and-death necessity. . . . Now, from a factual perspective, I am just as alcoholic as I was prior to achieving sobriety; that is, I must reaffirm my priority of staying sober *no matter what!* I go to the market, work, see movies, make love, eat, sleep—all as a sober alcoholic. I'm a person with an arrested but lifelong disease. I place my sobriety and the necessity of staying sober before anything else in my life. . . . Alcoholism results in the inability to control one's drinking. Sobriety requires the acknowledgment of one's alcoholism on a daily basis, and it is never to be taken for granted. I must endure all my feelings and experiences, including injustices, failures, and whatever this uncertain life doles out. . . .

"So," I continued, "in answer to your questions: I have my alcohol problem licked only on a daily basis and I continue to stay alive by protecting my conscious mind, by staying sober and avoiding the muddy waters of religion. I can't deal with reality by way of fantasy.

"A.A. and other groups fight demons with dogma or gods or the 'powers' of belief and faith. That's too scary for me. The more I stay in reality, in rationality, the better my chances. So, yes, my sobriety is a state of mind rather than mindlessness." (Christopher, 1988, pp. 87–88, italics in the original)

Clearly, SSG/SOS's stance on personal control shapes this narrative, which stands in stark contrast to those offered by AA participants. The most prominent difference in the narratives is the place and role accorded to spirituality. But other SSG/SOS resources are also significant in the way the alcoholic self is conceptualized. These resources comprise a vocabulary of self-reliance, individual responsibility, and rationality—the discourse of secular humanism. This translates into alcoholic narratives that have different moral contours from those assembled under the auspices of AA. As we can see in this extract, the self is conceived in terms of personal responsibility, unlike the AA self, which comes into its own only by surrendering to a higher power. Only in the wake of such surrender is personal improvement possible. In SSG terms, recovery rests in the hands of rationality and the human will, which stands in opposition to the resignation of will featured in AA narratives. In the SSG/SOS narrative, the "conscious mind" is the center of self-control, as opposed to AA's supplicant self, which abandons control to divine guidance. In SSG/SOS narratives, the self is firmly grounded in secular reality as opposed to the AA self, which centers itself in spirituality.

Conclusion

These and other comparative studies attest to the influence organizations have on participant narratives. We conclude with an important reminder to again preempt the notion that narrative environments determine the form and content of narratives produced under their auspices. While organized settings provide accountable modes of description, other contingencies may simultaneously affect storytelling, including the other narrative environments examined in this book. Participants in AA, for example, also have close relationships, different statuses in life, and hold various jobs, all of which mediate their stories and play into the mix of narrative accountability. Researchers should bear in mind that storytelling is a complex process that responds to multiple layers of resources and varied forms of narrative influence, contest, struggle, and control (see Vila, 2005). As important as they are in setting the narrative stage, narrative environments do not fully dictate narrative practice.

15

Intertextuality

N arrative environments are not discrete domains, separate and distinct
from one another. If they have characteristic stories, these can overlap
and merge with those of other environments. The intersections provide complex resources for storytelling. This is especially evident for accounts produced in relation to multiple environments. Intersections emerge in both
space and time. They not only are taken into account in the composition of
texts between environments, but also in relation to past and future texts in
the same environment. Yet, here again, the accounts are not straightforwardly drawn from these influences, but derive from the ways narrative
work incorporates their resources into storytelling. As Patricia Ewick and
Susan Silbey (2003) explain, "Narratives are fluid, continuous, dynamic, and
always constructed interactively—with an audience and within a context—
out of the stuff of other narratives" (p. 134).

Orienting to Intertextuality

Post-structuralist literary criticism provides a useful concept for orienting to
the complex relations between narrative work and narrative environments:
intertextuality. Applied to literary works, intertextuality refers to the ways
in which the meaning of a text is shaped by the meaning of other texts.
Loosely adapting the concept for our purposes, it is a way of saying that
individual accounts owe much of their structure and meaning to other
accounts. It is one more way of claiming that narratives are as much socially

constructed as they are individually composed. "Their own stories," as we continue to argue, are shaped by other stories and circumstances.

In the latter part of the 20th century, literary theorists including Mikhail Bakhtin, Roland Barthes, and Julia Kristeva revolutionized understandings of textual meaning along these lines. We needn't adopt wholesale any of these theoretical positions to find inspiration that applies to narrative reality. For example, Bakhtin (1981; see Todorov, 1984) questioned the assumption that a text had a specific or final meaning. Instead, he suggested that meaning depended upon how a text was read. Because the reading was as important as the writing, the author could not be the ultimate arbiter of meaning. The author, according to Bakhtin, was only one among many interpreters of his or her own work (Todorov, 1984).

Advancing this theme in a radical treatise aptly titled "The Death of the Author," Barthes (1977) further reduced the role of the author: "To give a text an Author is to impose a limit on that text, to furnish it with a final signified, to close the writing" (p. 175). For Barthes, the text was a "galaxy of signifiers" (1974, p. 5), susceptible to an open horizon of readings. Barthes argued that "a text's unity lies not in its origin but in its destination," suggesting that meaning derives from usage and reception (1977, p. 148).

Sharpening these arguments, Julia Kristeva (1973, 1980) coined the term *intertextuality* to suggest explicitly that texts drew their meanings from other texts, in an ongoing interplay of readings and interpretations. For example, an author might borrow from or adapt a prior text or a reader might reference another literary work in making sense of the text under immediate consideration. As such, meaning is not transferred directly from writer to reader but instead is mediated by meanings or codes suggested to the writer and the reader by other texts. A considerable portion of the modern Western literary canon is beholden for its meanings to biblical and Shakespearean texts, for instance. This is not to say that all texts are likewise derivative, but rather that knowledge of Shakespeare and the Bible informs much of how modern literature is written and received.

Referring specifically to books, Michel Foucault (1972) offers a similar argument:

> The frontiers of a book are never clear-cut: beyond the title, the first lines and the last full stop, beyond its internal configuration and its autonomous form, it is caught up in a system of references to other books, other texts, other sentences: it is a node within a network. (Foucault, 1972, p. 23)

But Foucault makes clear that something can be deciphered over and above the influence specific texts have upon each other. He points to the broad context within which intertextuality arises. A text is a "node within a network." Beyond any one text's relation to another text, the landscape of textuality becomes a discernible configuration of influences, in other words, that bear on the meaning of texts. This observation points to the diverse narrative environments that mediate meaning making.

Borrowing selectively from Foucault and the literary theorists, and generalizing from written texts to accounts of all sorts, we can orient to everyday narratives as themselves nodes within networks. Analyzing such narratives as intertextual productions means that any episode of storytelling should be viewed as sharing the empirical stage with other stories. Narratives need not take the form of written texts to be intertextually influenced or influential. All forms of accounts can be reflexively related to prior narratives—written or unwritten—as well as to future narrative horizons, as this chapter will show. The researcher is encouraged to examine a story in relation both to its immediate environment and to other domains of storytelling. In the context of narrative practice, this means developing intra- as well as interorganizational sensitivities. It means looking within situations as well as trans-situationally for the ways in which narrative auspices—past, present, and anticipated—shape accounts.

Robert Emerson's research on social control decision-making and accounting processes offers valuable insights into everyday intertextuality. Looking at how discretion is exercised in a variety of rule-bound law enforcement and legal venues, Emerson argues that decisions and their accounts are not discrete, atomistic actions. Instead of conceiving the field of social control activities in terms of individual cases or settings, Emerson suggests that social control decisions and accounts should be viewed holistically. They are part of a larger organizational gestalt (Emerson, 1983, 1991; Emerson & Paley, 1992). While his attention has explicitly focused on social control complaints and decisions, Emerson's work is suggestive for narrative analysis more generally because it turns our attention to how narrative work proceeds intertextually, in relation to concrete networks of organizational concern.

As Emerson explains, decisions and accounts made in one setting typically consider prior decisions, accounts, and actions from other settings (i.e., organizational histories), and anticipate the impact of current decisions and accounts on anticipated actions and settings (i.e., organizational futures). Decision makers not only work under the auspices of organizations of which they are participants, but they also craft decisions and accounts in light of previous narrative formulations on the broader organizational horizon (Emerson & Paley, 1992). At the same time, decisions and accounts anticipate the reception they might receive in other organizations, so that they are crafted to be useful or accountable in an imagined future. Decisions and accounts are therefore both retrospectively and prospectively composed.

Emerson (1991) highlights the retrospective intertextuality of social control accounts in his discussion of the "real reasons" for making and accepting referrals for criminal prosecution. On many occasions during his fieldwork in courts, district attorneys' (DA) offices, school counselor's offices, and with the police, Emerson found that reports were not literally taken at face value. Rather than assuming bad faith or unprofessional practices were going on, Emerson paid close attention to how reports, case filings, referrals for prosecution, and other organizational records were read in relation to sources and destinations. In reading reports of cases sent forward by police for prosecution, for example, Emerson noted that deputy DAs read the reports in light of what they knew about the process of formulating those descriptions as well as knowledge of the officers who made the referrals. Rather than taking accounts literally, they understood them in terms of what they knew to be the history of the particular case in question, as well as in relation to their stock of knowledge about this sort of case more generally.

For example, deputy DAs come to know that certain police officers or units file for prosecution only when they have extremely strong or serious cases. Lesser cases are disposed of without formal prosecution. We might say that the narrative relevance of accounts has retrospective dimensions. It is known implicitly that the act of formally filing a case indicates that extensive and rigorous screening has already taken place, and the filing officers think the case is worthy of prosecution. Read in light of such knowledge, a request to prosecute a case is thus taken to be a legitimate request for the prosecution of a serious crime. This reading isn't given to all case filings, though. Other cases from different units, from unfamiliar officers, or from officers known to be less judicious in their filings are read differently and treated accordingly.

Alternatively, some generally rigorous officers may occasionally send forward cases that appear on the surface to be "weaker" than other cases for which prosecution is sought—particularly when dealing with juveniles. At first glance, one might expect the DA's office to apply a standard reading of a case from a known-to-be-reliable officer, which would lead to filing charges. This would follow normative expectations, based on a presumed case of this type. But knowing that particular officers also use the threat of prosecution to scare youthful offenders or to extract defendant cooperation prompts DAs to give a different close reading to some cases. Their prior knowledge of police practices and accounts helps DAs discern alternate meanings that keep them from immediately filing or dismissing charges in such cases.

In both instances, the case (text) at hand is read in relation to interorganizational relevancies. The meaning of a current case description is obvious only in light of knowledge of past cases and prior narrative practices. Thus, the meaning of a particular case and its accompanying accounts is not fixed in relation to what "actually happened," or even in relation to what was ostensibly apparent in reports of the case. Rather, a case and its meaning are "institutional objects" embedded in, and understood only by reference to, the organizational processes and narratives that predate any particular reading of the case (Emerson, 1991; Emerson & Paley, 1992).

The anticipatable futures of a case also shape how it is read and processed. Emerson demonstrates the relevance of the possible future receptions of decisions and reports in his description of how social-control decision makers consider the "downstream consequences" of their actions (Emerson & Paley, 1992). He reports, for example, on a conversation with a deputy DA regarding a police arrest report and subsequent decision to pursue prosecution. The DA first describes the case from the police report:

> The defendant sneaks into a building, breaks into eight or ten offices. Someone discovers him, they call the police. They [the police] bring a dog in, there's a big scuffle. The guy [the defendant] got eaten [bitten] by the dog. At eight o'clock they [the police] interrogate him. He makes a confession. (Emerson & Paley, 1992, p. 241)

The deputy DA then describes his reading of the case, for which he is about to file criminal charges:

> There's a couple of issues we're concerned about. . . . First, the constitutionality of the confession. The ultimate question is always voluntariness. The guy made the confession, right after the dog ate him, and he might say 'cause he was under medication. He ended up in the hospital. There's two questions: One, was he confessing 'cause he thought he might get more of the same treatment? And, two, more likely, because he was under medication, it might influence what he said. That's what worries me. He might say he didn't know what he was doing. Except he made a statement about what a fool he was. I could argue that if he could be flippant he must have known what was going on. (Emerson & Paley, 1992, p. 241)

The DA's decision and account clearly take the "facts" of the arrest situation into consideration, but their meaning is read in conjunction with two possible future scenarios that the DA speculates might emerge. Anticipating how the defendant might formulate a defense in court, the DA notes that the defendant is likely to dispute his confession on the grounds that it was not voluntary. Such a reading results from the DA's stock of knowledge about confessions in general, and confessions given under duress, in particular.

Even though the issue had not yet been explicitly raised in relation to this case, the DA anticipates this possibility. He notes, first, that the defendant might argue that the dog attack could be presented as a way of coercing a confession (i.e., "'cause he thought he might get more of the same treatment"). Second, and more likely, the DA speculates that the defendant could argue that under the duress of the dog attack and subsequent medical treatment, the defendant's confession was not totally voluntary. It was given under the influence of medication, which, arguably, could have clouded the defendant's judgment and invalidated his confession.

Having constructed two possible organizational futures for the case, the DA then projects his possible future response. He can argue that the defendant made flippant remarks—which were apparently recorded in the arrest report—indicating that the defendant "must have known what was going on." The case, then, was read in light of the constructed downstream consequences of taking the case to court. The meaning of the police report was composed in anticipation of the possible future of this case in court.

It is clear from Emerson's work that institutional narratives are not discrete packages of information strictly reflecting their origins. They are more like currents in an interorganizational flow of meanings, understandable only in the context of the "upstream" history of narrative meanings and the "downstream" consequences of current actions. This applies to narratives more generally. The intertextual character of narrative meaning depends on how both the past and the future are read in relation to the narrative work at hand. We offer the following analytic guideline for considering the intertextuality of narrative production:

Guideline

Scan the domain of retrospective narrative influences, both proximate and distant, for how research subjects construct and interpret accounts. Be alert as well to the prospective considerations that can influence narrative production, taking note of meaning making as it relates to downstream consequences.

Into the Field

Field procedures for studying intertextualilty are much the same as those discussed in previous chapters. The key in this case is to be attentive to how research subjects refer or allude to other narratives and other narrative environments, to make sense of the accounts in question. Take note of the extent to which research subjects are explicitly aware of intertextual contingencies.

Consider, for example, how a physical therapist is described as crafting progress reports on her clients in an ethnography of a rehabilitation hospital (see J. F. Gubrium & Buckholdt, 1982; J. F. Gubrium, Buckholdt, & Lynott, 1989). Describing the contingencies shaping the reports and completed forms filed by hospital staff members, the researchers explained that many of the staff's written accounts were "worked up" in terms of descriptions contained in previous case material. Staff members often turned explicitly to earlier reports in order to show consistency in current documentation. The practice related to the broader need to appear organizationally rational. As one physical therapist explained,

> You check what you've said already to make sure you're connecting what you said now with what you said before. You'd look pretty stupid if you say the patient has never made progress and in the note you wrote two weeks ago, you said he was making progress. It'd sound real dumb. . . . It's a pain, but you can't just say what's happening. You've got to show some kind of progress—like it's happening, or it's not happening, or like it's always been happening, but like, maybe we just found out about it. So you kind of try to connect things back with what you said before. (J. F. Gubrium, Buckholdt, & Lynott, 1989, p. 210)

In this instance, the physical therapist carefully considers the intra- not the interorganizational history of the client before adding to the record of the client's progress and present condition. The therapist's orientation is primarily retrospective, as she seeks to align her present remarks with what had been previously reported. Her aim is to assemble a report that is consistent with prior accounts "so that things jibe together." Note, however, that her orientation is also implicitly prospective in that she wants to assemble a present-time narrative that, in conjunction with past reports, presents a trajectory of patient progress into the future, or the lack of it, as the case might be. She is concerned with the downstream consequence of looking "pretty stupid" to future readers—colleagues, superiors, regulatory agents—if her report were inconsistent.

There is an important lesson here for the kind of narrative analysis that is focused exclusively on texts. If the issue were the consistency of stories, we would evaluate comparable texts in terms of their internal organization. Depending on the degree of consistency, highly consistent texts might be distinguished from those that are inconsistent. Without knowledge of the conditions of narrative production, the differences would likely be attributed to the authors of the texts and explanation sought in background differences or variable competence or integrity among text writers. But viewed in terms of the accounts' intertextuality, we have a basis for understanding consistency or inconsistency in terms of situational or institutional imperatives. To use Garfinkel's (1967) phrasing, there might be "good organizational reasons" for the consistency or inconsistency of accounts. In this regard, textual consistency has as much to do with texts' organizational embeddedness as it does with a patient's actual progress or the author's accuracy in representing it.

Donileen Loseke's (1989, 1992) study of social problems work in a shelter for battered women provides further illustration of the intertextual production of accounts, this time in relation to a contingent background of unwritten texts—commonly told narratives about battered women. Loseke conducted 2 ½ years of participant observation in a shelter she called "South Coast." Her fieldwork gave her access to shelter workers' and administrators' conversations as well as to shelter documents. In the following discussion, note how ethnographic attention to documents in the context of staff's narrative work on the premises casts intertextual light on the everyday meaning of organizational records.

The most important document was the shelter logbook, a continuing worker-written commentary about life inside the facility. Among other things, the log provided a means for shelter workers to communicate with one another, especially across revolving shifts of workers who rarely saw one another. The log was compiled by workers for an audience of other workers. It was designed to keep staff members mutually informed about consequential happenings that could affect work on other shifts. Many logbook entries described encounters with women applying for shelter services. Such narratives would typically detail the prospective client and the encounter, and then account for whatever decision the staff member had made about admission.

Understanding log entries, however, is not a matter of straightforwardly reading the text. In surface readings, entries often seemed cryptic and inconsistent. Related admission decisions would appear arbitrary to a reader unfamiliar with the shelter. Loseke's fieldwork provided her with background knowledge similar to that of the other shelter workers, so she had indigenous insight into how cryptic log entries were constructed and how they were read in practice. Her ethnographic knowledge helped her decipher their implicit, organizationally embedded meanings, particularly those constructed in intertextual relation to locally prominent, yet generally unwritten, understandings of the practical definition of a battered woman.

Loseke's intimate knowledge of the shelter's working definition of the battered woman was especially important in this regard. On the surface, it may seem obvious that a battered woman is someone who has experienced physical violence or abuse at the hands of someone else, usually an intimate male partner or family member. What Loseke observed, however, was that shelter workers formulated organizationally relevant "battered woman gestalts" appropriate to individual cases as needed. The gestalt served as a practical, fluid, open-ended model of the type of woman for whom the shelter's services were appropriate and, conversely, of the type of woman for whom services were inappropriate.

Like most shelters, South Coast did not have the facilities or resources to serve every woman who requested services. Most prominently, they had a limited bed capacity, which forced shelter workers to be selective about whom they admitted for overnight stays. This limitation played a key role in how shelter workers came to view potential clients, independent of their stated needs. Staff members' working definition was not simply a woman who had been physically abused. Rather, practical experience taught South Coast staffers that the appropriate client—the battered woman as an admissible *type*—displayed a constellation of institutionally relevant characteristics. These included, but were not necessarily limited to, displaying an immediate and pressing need for the shelter's services, appearing likely to benefit from those services, and giving good indication that she would be a good member of the shelter community. This battered woman type formed the working typification or gestalt in relation to which individual cases might be considered. Of course relevant characteristics varied depending on organizational contingencies, which also varied over time and in relation to applicant characteristics. The working rationale of log entries was thus embedded in an ethnographically discernible, but unwritten and fluctuating, institutional context.

The shelter's logbook contained hundreds of narratives of encounters with women seeking the shelter's services. Many of these included descriptions of potential clients and accounts for why services were delivered or withheld. Loseke examined these entries, seeking to understand the practicalities of how shelter workers justified and explained their decisions to admit some women and not others. The simplest form of entry was seemingly straightforward: "Brought in a new resident, battered woman" (Loseke, 1989, p. 183). This served as generally adequate justification for admission, a shorthand way of articulating client characteristics with admission criteria. Conversely, it was not uncommon for log entries to account for denial of services with entries like the following: "(Hospital) called. Wanted to dump LW on us because she had no where to go. She wasn't a battered woman" (p. 183) and "Woman called on crisis line, has not been battered but landlord threw her out . . . we should not let her in since she is not battered" (p. 183).

As Loseke studied the various accounts, it became evident that only narratives presented or read as resonating with the battered woman gestalt were viewed as justifiable admissions to the shelter. But resonance was an interpretive matter; it required narrative work in addition to organizational knowledge of admissibility. It was not sufficient for a log entry to simply say that a woman to be admitted had been physically or psychically harmed. Rather, accounts provided justification that could be read in such a way as to accord for the practical purposes at hand with the battered woman gestalt. This, of course, required prior knowledge of the gestalt, which was open ended, as well as information regarding the case in question. The following accounts, for example, were constructed about women for whom services were recommended:

(1) Call from G. She had just been very beaten up and requested shelter. Met her and brought her in—a very classical case and nice woman. I really enjoyed talking to her, she's pretty hip to the psychological trips. . . . She was at the shelter two years ago. This time the police took him away. (Loseke, 1989, p. 184)

(2) She has been mentally abused by her husband for about three years. Her doctor told her to get out before it's too late. She sounded like a very typical battered woman. She cannot do anything, has lost all her friends, is always at home living this way. Her doctor told her that her physical problems were due to stress and will get better when she leaves him. She's been warned not to tell him she's leaving. (Loseke, 1992, p. 88)

(3) She seems like a classic battered case. Had a long session with her, she was crying and very hurt. Absolutely no self-esteem, husband treated her like a child but she is still in love with him. . . . She feels very helpless and lonely. (Loseke, 1989, p. 184)

While these cases all sound compelling, other women also presented claims of violence and abuse, yet were not admitted to the shelter. The analytic task was, in part, to discern how differential decisions were justified. What kind of logbook narratives justified admission under the circumstances? How was the battered woman gestalt textually flagged? It is only by reading the log entries against shelter workers' practical concerns and the shelter's unwritten guiding typification that decisions make sense. A woman who is granted admission, Loseke argues, has a story that can be read as a close approximation to the "typical" battered woman, that is, a woman who needs the shelter, who could benefit from the shelter's services, and who would likely become an acceptable member of the shelter collective. The woman's story must resonate with the organizationally favored "formula story" (Loseke, 2001) of the battered woman—the shelter's "big narrative," so to speak.

It is only when the particulars of individual cases are read against the shelter's unwritten gestalt or organizational formula story that the logbook narratives make organizational sense. Informed readers, for example, can clearly hear shelter policy echoing in the background of each narrative presented above. To an outsider, the characterization of the client in account 1 as "nice woman," someone whom the staff member "really enjoyed talking to," might seem extraneous to determining if the woman had been battered. But an experienced shelter worker can hear "nice woman" or "enjoyed taking to" as evidence that the woman would become a good shelter resident. This is the type of woman adumbrated in the shelter's working policy of serving women who readily fit in with the shelter community. Read in that light, being a "nice woman" is organizationally integral to the assessment of whether an applicant should be admitted. Calling the woman a "very classical case" provides further instructions for how to read the other particulars of this narrative, signaling a type that, reflexively read, brings an organizationally suitable understanding to whatever else appears in the log entry. The intertextual reading imports meaning to each entry, making understandable the substantiation or denial of a woman's claim for services.

Entry 2 poses an interesting complication because there is no mention of physical abuse, yet the woman is admitted to the shelter. Again, an outsider might wonder why this case was more compelling than others where physical violence was prominently noted. Read in light of "a very typical battered woman"—which is explicitly cued—the presence of mental abuse, and the doctor's suggestion that the client's physical problems would get better if the client left her husband clearly suggest to shelter workers that the woman would benefit from the shelter's policy of providing alternative housing solutions to problems.

Similarly, in account 3, the client is described as "feels very helpless and lonely," which doesn't necessarily imply physical violence. At first glance, this would not appear to fit the criterion of the battered woman, if that criterion centers on physical violence. Yet, once again, reference to the "classic battered case" serves to intertextually compose the remainder of the account, so that other features of the applicant can be read as suitable admitting criteria. The phrase "classic battered case" signals to the reader that the woman being described in the entry is someone the shelter can serve. Such phrases reflexively document the meaning of the entry as a whole, even if what is written is largely the same as that which appears in log entries of applicants denied admission. Brought to bear in this case because the woman was admitted, the unwritten battered woman gestalt provides a working context for understanding the woman's admission, the appropriateness of which is further signaled by the reference to the classic battered case.

Loseke's study also documents the intertextualilty of log entries that justify the refusal of services. Consider the following account for denial of services to a woman who claimed to have been physically assaulted by her husband:

> Hotline call from Joyce, rather evasive, claims to battery (husband), has three children—husband has kicked her out of the house, to let her return. Joyce requested a place to sleep for 2–3 days. She's employed. I do not see an immediate need here—she has mother and friends here. (Loseke, 1992, pp. 86–87)

Loseke argues that despite surface congruities with those that characterize the battered woman, the shelter worker's interpretation of Joyce's situation didn't sufficiently conform to the shelter's battered woman gestalt to warrant admission. The log account highlights subtle, yet important discrepancies with the "classic battered woman." Joyce is said to have other resources to which she may turn for the help she requests (i.e., "she has mother and friends here"). Moreover, in the log narrative, Joyce was reported to have merely "requested a place to sleep for 2–3 days." She was not portrayed as wanting or needing shelter services—just a place to sleep. The log entry also indicated that the "husband has kicked her out of the house"; she is not trapped. She also is portrayed as "employed," hence she is not financially strapped. Nor is she socially isolated ("she has mother and friends here"). Especially noteworthy is the absence of the explicit label "classic [or typical] battered woman" from the log entry. The shelter's key coded term is replaced by "claims to battery," a significantly downgraded description of the gravity of Joyce's plight. This is read by other shelter personnel as an indication that Joyce is not really a battered woman. The log suggests at nearly every turn that Joyce doesn't quite fit the classic type—that her story is somehow at odds with the organizational formula story. The battered woman gestalt still applies, but its fluidity takes shape in relation to the case in question.

Reading the South Coast logbook is a complicated matter. The entries seem self-explanatory when terms such as "classic battered woman" are used. It flags admissibility despite the particulars listed in the log entries. But in some cases, the code is absent; the shelter's "big" narrative or formula story isn't so apparent. No matter. In admitted cases, the particulars of such cases are interpretively read so that they resonate in some fashion with a working version of the battered woman gestalt. For those denied admission, the particulars are read as inconsistent with the working gestalt, which of course justifies a refusal of services. Whatever the decision, unwritten wholes reflexively frame the relevant particulars providing meaning-making linkages. At the same time, the particulars coalesce into patterns that resonate with the unwritten whole. Either way, intertextual readings can make seemingly inconsistent texts consistent in practice.

Conclusion

Intertextuality need not refer to written texts, as Kristeva and others may have originally intended. Like literary texts, the interactional texts of everyday life are mutually referential. With this in mind, we reiterate that ethnographic examination of the narrative circumstances surrounding narrative work is essential for understanding how this work operates in practice. This is especially pertinent today, as organizations and their preferred narratives—both written and unwritten—are virtually everywhere. At the same time, as Gubrium, Emerson, Loseke, and others show, organizational embeddedness does not fully regulate intertextuality. Meaning is constructed at the confluence of sites of narrative production and the work of situated storytellers, listeners, and readers. Accordingly, it would be analytically naïve to think of personal accounts or records as merely "their own stories." While we are not implying the "death of the narrator," we do emphasize the need to look outside particular narratives (and their transcripts or records) to fully comprehend their practical meaning.

PART IV

Narrative Adequacy

Interactionally useful narratives are both skillfully crafted and circumstantially conditioned. Practically speaking, good stories and good storytellers are good enough, that is, up to the task at hand. This suggests the possibility of an everyday aesthetics of narratives. We might ask what, in practice, constitutes a good story? Who is a good storyteller? Once again, we turn to the work and environments of narrativity for answers. While formalized standards of evaluation (e.g., criteria imposed by social service providers, physicians, police interrogators, judges, literary critics, or researchers themselves) may be important guidelines for appraising accounts, these guidelines follow abstract principles that mean little until they are actually applied. Everyday narrative adequacy is judged within ongoing schemes of concern.

Our stance vis-à-vis narrative adequacy differs significantly from the position some researchers would assume. The social sciences have well-documented standards for what constitutes good data (see, e.g., Babbie, 2007); they orient to the quality and sources of the material to be analyzed, including narratives. These standards are signaled by an arsenal of criteria that are the evaluative cornerstones of research methodology. Terms like validity, reliability, and objectivity come immediately to mind. They embody the aim of applying abstract principles across the board, in a consistent, disinterested fashion.

Qualitative research approaches tend to be more flexible and contextual with respect to evaluative criteria, yet standards of evaluation implicitly resonate when the collection and analysis of "good" qualitative data are discussed. With respect to narrativity, we frequently hear that good stories are rich, complete, and insightful and that good storytellers (often called informants or respondents) are knowledgeable, honest, and forthcoming. Some add more specific criteria: Good stories have protagonists, inciting issues, and culminating events, for example (see Labov, 1972b, Riessman, 1993). In describing qualitative interviews, Carol Warren and Tracy Karner (2005, p. 144) comment that "the ideal interview is one in which rapport is established and a rich narrative emerges." Steiner Kvale (1996, p. 144) enumerates similar criteria. Good narrative responses should be "spontaneous, rich, specific, and relevant" (p. 145). Herbert and Irene Rubin (1995, p. 76) add that the best responses in interviews are "deep, detailed, vivid, and nuanced."

Two things are noteworthy about such criteria as far as narrative adequacy is concerned. First, they are impossible to specify in a context-free manner. Determining each depends on the situation. Second, these criteria echo popular standards for good stories that we might hear in the most commonplace circumstances. We note this without intending to be either ironic or critical. The point is only that research standards tend to mimic commonsense standards where narrative adequacy is concerned.

Rather than adopting such criteria and advising the researcher to apply them to narrative material, we take a different approach. In analyzing narrative adequacy, we suggest that researchers make commonsense criteria the *topic* of analysis, instead of adopting those criteria as their own standards (see Garfinkel, 1967; Zimmerman & Pollner, 1970). This means approaching narrative adequacy from the perspective of those producing and receiving accounts, documenting how *they* circumstantially determine what is or isn't a good story or a good storyteller, and how they *use* commonsense criteria in the process. The resulting focus of analysis is on the indigenous practices applied to produce and assess what are considered good stories and storytelling.

In the two chapters that follow, we take up the questions "What is a good story?" and "Who is a good storyteller?" in the context of narrative reality. We don't assume an omniscient stance. Instead, we ask the questions in relation to what is adequate for all practical purposes. Our intent cannot be to provide definitive or final answers. Rather, we raise the questions in this way in order to argue and to demonstrate that an everyday aesthetics of narrativity operates on its own terms, in the nooks and crannies and reflexive considerations of lived experience. An everyday aesthetics attends both to standards and to the operating conditions in relation to which standards are applied.

16

What Is a Good Story?

S tanley knew a good story when he heard one. For him, a good story suited the purposes. On some occasions, this meant accounts that raised his status among peers. On others, it led to narratives that enhanced his masculine identity. There undoubtedly were times when no story, or just a token response, was the best story. For Stanley and others, such criteria derive from everyday life, not from an external set of standards. Still, external criteria remain and they are applied to accounts of all sorts. What can we make of this in the context of narrative reality?

Orienting to Goodness Criteria

As we have noted, popular criteria for evaluating narrative material can invoke standards that do not apply in practice, if they apply at all. In Chapter 11, which dealt with local culture, we explained how Anderson (1999) took care to center his study and analysis of the organization of street life on indigenous criteria. In the context of street life, a good story is one that takes account of the code of respect. However thin or rich stories are, regardless of whether they have a beginning, a middle, and an end, or make a point, narratives are formed at the confluence of respect and sociability. Violence lurks in the background of perceived infractions. A simple nod or acquiescent response—as truncated and unstorylike as that might seem—can be narratively adequate in the circumstances, functioning to smoothly facilitate casual yet consequential interaction. Indeed, an account or response that accords with the popular understanding that a good story be richly detailed and have a point, say, could very well be taken as arrogant or impertinent. This infringes on the code of respect and can lead to confrontation or even violence. Stanley was well aware of this and shaped his stories accordingly. Such understanding provides a useful guideline for analyzing a good story:

Guideline

Document indigenous criteria for narrative adequacy. If the question is the quality of an account, address it in the context of participants' criteria, not external ones. Do not seek thick accounts when they aren't forthcoming; likewise, do not seek thin (briefer and more concise) accounts when detailed, seemingly pointless accounts, or accounts contrary to fact, are offered. Instead, aim to understand quality and other criteria in terms of what is circumstantially adequate.

This guideline may be self-evident after 15 chapters of discussion. We raise the issue, nonetheless, because of the perennial desire in qualitative research especially for rich data and thick description (see Brekhus, Galliher, & Gubrium, 2005). The problem is that producing rich, elaborate accounts can be at odds with good narrative practice, and this needs to be repeatedly underscored. Rich, true, compelling, and well-formulated stories might not function well in some circumstances. Their consequences can be disastrous. As Richard Candida Smith (2002) suggests in his essay on analytic strategies for oral history interviews, while exaggerated and repetitive accounts might not be good stories on conventional grounds, they can function to suit the purposes, say, of ethnic solidarity in difficult times. The lesson for oral historians, which applies to all narrative researchers, is not to proceed by seeking "true," consistent, or prerationalized versions of good stories. Rather, the lesson is to orient to goodness in terms of how stories work in everyday life and to identify goodness criteria from that.

Into the Field

We approach the question of what a good story is by way of two researchers' experiences in the matter. First is J. F. Gubrium's (1986a) research on the descriptive organization of senility, which relates more to the *whats* than to the *hows* of a good story. In his fieldwork, Gubrium heard many stories of "what it's like" to become senile and "what it's like" to care for a loved one who is losing a mind. Stories were continuously evaluated for various practical purposes. Among these were how well stories aligned with personal experience and whether the stories had points worth considering. Gubrium began his fieldwork with the popular notion that the fuller and more informative the account, the better. He found something more complicated, however. Circumstances, it seems, had an important bearing on what was considered a good story.

Gubrium's research was concerned in part with how personal stories of caring for cognitively impaired elderly were changing their moral tone. The early 1980s were a time of transition in understanding cognitive impairment. There was a sea change in the offing, from the view that "senility" was a normal part of aging, to the medical view that it was a disease as noted in Chapter 12. Stories told early in this period had dramatically different meanings and consequences than similar stories shared later on. In the narrative environment of normal aging, stories of senility were accounts of woe, inevitability, and acceptance. In the narrative environment of medicalization, there was woe to be sure, but it was combined with the search for a cure and the hope for recovery. As far as the caregiver was concerned, as the overall view of senility shifted, the meaning of caregiving itself changed from being something one simply did, to something that had phases of adaptation. This had a bearing on what a good caregiving story was, altering the substantive criterion from compelling and regrettable accounts, to stories that more or less accorded with the emerging understanding that caregiving was an experience with particular psychological parameters.

But there was more to the matter in practice. As Gubrium listened to caregiver talk and observed related interactions in support groups at local chapter meetings of the Alzheimer's Disease Association (ADA), it was initially apparent that full and compelling accounts led the way as far as good stories were concerned. Narratives that provided complete and accurate understandings of the aging process, the caregiving experience, and cognitive impairment were considered good stories. Caregivers actually took account of these criteria in sharing stories. Variously challenged to convey their stories, they responded in ways suggesting that a good story was one that rang true with others' experience, for example. Time and again, this criterion was referenced in caregiver support groups as well as in interviews with family members and significant others. Following frightening stories of encounters with demented spouses who, for the first time, failed to recognize their husbands or their wives, it was not uncommon for group participants to respond with comments such as, "Yes, that's exactly the way it was for me," "That's telling it like it is," and "That's what it is in a nutshell." This criterion for the good story was not surprising, as it resonated with the popular assumption that a good story aligns with the facts.

A second criterion of the good story centered less on what rang true than on whether narratives were compelling or entertaining. Truth in this instance could take a back seat to engrossment. A good story might be compelling because it rang true, but also because it conveyed caregiving experiences in a captivating or emotional way. Such narratives might or might not exactly align with the facts. It was not unusual, for example, for caregivers to offer hilariously engaging and embellished stories of "the funny things" that happen in the caregiving process, even if this was known to be idiosyncratic or otherwise exceptional. It was a good story, for instance, when 70-year-old Martha, a long-time home caregiver for her demented husband, told of the time when her husband tried to dress himself and inadvertently put her panties on over his trousers. "What a sight that was," recounted Martha, even though she later admitted to embellishing the details. Some caregivers told compelling stories that weren't funny but rather were grippingly tragic. There were many accounts of the strange and unexpected twists and turns of the disease in which characteristically stoic sufferers became violent or normally expansive personalities became withdrawn. The good quality of these stories took tellers and listeners along a different path, compellingly exposing the dark side of the disease process.

A third criterion related to listeners' need for detail. This was a criterion that Gubrium himself, like other interview researchers, was inclined to apply to interviewees' stories. On this count, some caregivers told good stories because the stories were so richly articulated. A brief response to a question about how a respondent felt the first time a disease sufferer failed to recognize him or her was less satisfying than an extended account of the thoughts and feelings experienced at the time. Most participants in the support groups and the interview respondents wished to know more, not less, about what care receivers and caregivers "go through," as they commonly put it. The good story, in this regard, provided two things: useful information for managing one's own thoughts, feelings, and planning in the matter, and a rich sense of understanding of the experience.

A fourth criterion ran counter to the third. In these cases, less was more. Narratives were judged not only for how usefully detailed they were, but were also evaluated for how well they "got to the point" or how well the storyteller would "get on with it, for heaven's sake." Gubrium tended to adhere to this ideal as well. There were times, for instance, when interviewees went on and on, seemingly endlessly, about matters such as lucid moments or clues to the onset of the disease, well beyond what would seem to be useful or interesting to anyone. In the support groups, some caregivers told stories in excruciating or repetitive detail, which could reap none-too-subtle responses such as "My God, will she ever stop," "We've heard that umpteen times already," and "Who can take in all that stuff?" Sufficient, not exhaustive, detail was the byword.

Yet, at the same time, in the here-and-now of tellings, did these criteria straightforwardly apply across the board? Gubrium soon found that a caregiving story that rang true in one support group didn't necessarily ring true in another. The received criterion applied in principle, but specific locales filtered this through their own views of the truth. At certain times and places (narrative environments), particular kinds of caregiving stories seemed factually sufficient or authentic, while at other times and places, the same stories—as otherwise truthful, engaging, and detailed as they might be—were considered inauthentic or not at all "the real story." Gubrium began to understand that the various settings in which individuals engage in storytelling required different kinds of truth. What was concretely said about dementia and the caregiving experience was not identically valued in all settings, no matter how detailed or engaging it was.

In time, the various support groups Gubrium observed, which eventually included non-ADA sponsored groups, struck him as quite different in this regard. How group members responded to the quality of stories about the progress of cognitive impairment or the flow of the caregiving experience depended on the group's local culture. While participants in all groups evaluated accounts in terms of the criteria described earlier—the good story, for example, being the one that rang the truest or was the most engaging—Gubrium also recognized that what was true or engaging in one group wasn't necessarily the same as it was in another one. This didn't result from groups specializing in the discussion of particular topics of interest or of participants bringing different concerns with them. Rather, regardless of who participated or the particular topics of interest, the groups were distinctive narrative environments regarding what was or was not adequate.

Some groups, especially those sponsored by the ADA, preferred highly formulaic renditions of the caregiving experience (cf. Loseke, 2001). The ADA distributed extensive promotional literature to local chapters that described the "features" of dementia and the "dimensions" of caregiving, which support group participants read and shared. There were other groups—more likely to be independent—in which no particular version of these matters was valued over another. In the former groups, what rang true was articulated in more or less detail according to the ADA formula. Compelling stories of the caregiving experience tended to follow a stage-like script of what one "goes through" in the process. This combined with a stage-like understanding of what happens through time to the care receiver. In contrast, in the latter groups, participants were generally satisfied to simply compare notes and experiences, learning from each other about themselves and about the progress of afflicted family members' disease. Storytelling in these groups transpired in terms of what social psychologists call a "social comparison process," where meaning making develops with the flow of individual comparisons rather than in terms of an overarching framework.

Violations of local understandings were telling. For example, on one occasion in one of the ADA-sponsored groups, a participant offered what Gubrium initially viewed as a rather detailed and engaging account of her husband's growing forgetfulness and her caregiving experience. This was followed by heartfelt comments on the need to be valiantly devoted to the care of Alzheimer's disease sufferers because of the disease's relentless ravages. Gubrium was absorbed by how true-to-life the story sounded. He could only think, "Yes, she's been through it; she knows what it's like firsthand. One could learn a great deal from her experience." But participants' responses showed that the good story in such groups doesn't necessarily take this shape, as seemingly truthful, engaging, and detailed as it otherwise seemed to be. What participants wanted to hear instead were truthful, engaging, and reasonably detailed accounts that accorded with a particular experiential timetable, one paralleling Elisabeth Kübler-Ross's (1969) popular stage model of the dying process.

For example, the caregiver whose account challenged the view that the caregiver "goes through stages of this thing" was considered to be "denying" the real story. In such groups' formulation of the good story, accounts of unceasing devotion were irrational—out of the question. The truth of the matter was that one was being infinitely more realistic about the caregiving experience if one admitted to oneself and to others that there were limits to devotion (a stage of the process). This meant that, in time, one needed to think about oneself, the burden of care on the family as a whole, and should seriously consider nursing home placement (another stage of the process). In these groups, this preferred composition was locally evident at virtually every turn, as one or another participant monitored utterances for how well they reflected the formula story surrounding what it meant to be realistic.

Such research findings inform us that answers to the question "What is a good story?" need to be figured in relation to local understandings. While popular understandings are taken into account, the good story cannot be evaluated solely in terms of general criteria. Truthfulness, engrossment, and detail don't tell us much in practice. Nor does the view that dementia and the caregiving experience develop in particular fashions, as some of the Alzheimer's disease self-help literature suggests, because unaffiliated groups especially figure accounts in their own terms. In narrative practice, the good (or the bad) story is not simply told or appreciated or discounted, but relates to situated background knowledge. As a result, there are endless possibilities for good stories and the moral dimensions of the experiences implicated by them.

In their own way, caregivers shared and understood this complexity. On one occasion in the field, a caregiver made a poignant and analytically telling remark that echoed delinquent Stanley's sensitivity to circumstances. The caregiver was a participant in one of the comparatively unformularized support groups Gubrium had been observing. Commenting on the support group she had attended across town and comparing it to the group she now attended, the caregiver asserted,

> I just can't bear to go there [across town] anymore. All I heard there was stage one, stage two, and take the next step. Here, the stories you hear sound more like what I'm going through. I learn more from that and it makes me feel better. (J. F. Gubrium, 1986, field notes)

In one narrative stroke, the remark pointed to the agentic interface of narrative work and its environmental specifications. As a result, storytellers can do something about the local understandings to which they will be held accountable.

The other research bearing on the question of the goodness of a story is D. Lawrence Wieder's (1974) study of the organization of talk and interaction in a halfway house for paroled ex-convicts. His concern was more with the *hows* of narrative adequacy than with the *whats*. Wieder also initially oriented to a popular understanding, in his case the idea that norms are standards that govern behavior. In the social world he was studying, of which the halfway house was a part, stories were ostensibly governed by what was called the "convict code," operating in much the same way as other codes allegedly do, such as the "code of the street" (Anderson, 1999). The good story—what to say and what not to say—accorded with the rules of the code. Wieder at first presented his findings from this normative perspective. To that end, he carefully documented the individual strictures of the code from the talk and interaction of both staff and residents. The code was of great importance, since adherence to its strictures was highly consequential; it could be a matter of life and death.

Hugh Mehan and Houston Wood (1975) describe Wieder's initial approach to how the code operated.

> The code instructed residents how to behave toward one another and toward officials of the penal system. It constituted a system of rules, and dictated a moral order. Not living up to the code was a sanctionable offense. As ex-convicts and ex-drug addicts, all the residents expected to someday return to prison. Beatings were administered there to those who broke the code. Knowing the code and following it was thus a matter of life and death. (p. 138)

Understood in this way, the code was tantamount to a set of rules for what to say and do to others, including residents, staff members, and other officials. In turn, what residents said and did was evaluated by the code's standards. It took a while for Wieder to discern the code, because, as with most informal standards, they weren't written down anywhere in so many words. But continued fieldwork at the halfway house eventually produced discernible criteria, which Mehan and Wood summarize.

> Wieder heard these and other things about the code in bits and pieces. He was able to provide the following coherence to these bits. They represented maxims of proper conduct for residents.
>   1. Above all else, do not snitch.
>   2. Do not cop out.
>   3. Do not take advantage of other residents.
>   4. Share what you have.
>   5. Help other residents.
>   6. Do not mess with other residents' interests.
>   7. Do not trust staff—staff is heat.
>   8. Show your loyalty to the residents. (p. 138)

The second half of Wieder's book tells a different story, centered on how the code was applied in practice. In the second half, it becomes evident that users were more in control of talk and interaction than what was suggested by the normative view of codes presented in the first half. Wieder makes clear that house residents use the code for different purposes and according to what they figure to be at stake in the circumstances. In this view, the code is more a set of narrative resources than its strictures are narrative regulators. The code is a source of claims and justifications, not simply a constraint on storytelling.

For example, it initially seemed that ex-cons whom Wieder befriended and talked with openly about resident life were violating the code. But it was clear, too, that on such occasions they had little to lose from this, and few others figured differently. At other times, however, mid-interaction with Wieder, a resident would stop short, invoke the code, alter his demeanor, and become silent or walk away. From this, Wieder realized that another kind of analysis was necessary, one that accorded more with this chapter's orienting guideline, focusing on indigenous usage. He began to realize that codes, like other standards, are enmeshed in practical actions, whose interpretive contingencies influence their importance and discern their applicability. Put in technical terms, the goodness of a story can be viewed as "indexed" by the circumstance of application. What is or isn't good is reflexively related to its operating utility. Mehan and Wood explain this in relation to the "do not snitch" stricture.

The maxim "Do not snitch," means that good residents do not supply information to staff concerning the activities of other residents. But defining the maxim in this *one* way necessarily glosses the multiple meanings it has in interaction. When "I don't snitch" or "Cons don't snitch" is said in the house, it is seldom offered as an abstract statement describing a part of the convict code. When staff or residents refer to this or any element of the convict code during the ongoing life of the house, they say it within a web of practical circumstances. The saying is offered as an index of those circumstances. It is a call for the hearer to organize the ongoing interaction in accordance with that part of the convict code which exhorts residents not to tell on each other. (p. 140)

What Mehan and Wood are saying is that the code comes into effect as a regulating force when it is called into action for that purpose. Its regulating force is occasioned, not automatic. This is the way it affects the narrative adequacy of accounts. But this raises an explanatory problem. As Mehan and Wood ask, "If rules do not appear independently of their particular ongoing invocations, how is it possible for staff and residents to treat them so?" (p. 140). How do rules exert the work of quality control in talk and interaction?

The answer lies in the place of rules (in this case the code) in the reflexive organization of everyday life. As Mehan and Wood explain, residents and staff in the halfway house do not orient to the code as an abstract set of strictures on conduct, but rather, like other rules and understandings, the code is part of the setting's practical business. In practice, rules don't so much govern life from above, as they are part of the fabric of life as that unfolds on the ground, part of the narrative accounting work of the setting. Again, Mehan and Wood explain:

Wieder's work illustrates that such rules are never invoked by residents for abstract or merely descriptive reasons. Rather, they do work. They are offered as means for particular interactants at particular times to do particular things. To say, "You know I don't snitch," accomplishes different things within different scenes. Said to a staff member the ex-convict hates, it can be a shout of defiance. Said to one that he feels is his friend, it can be an apology for an impossible situation. But in all cases, the power of the saying comes from the sense that not "just anything" has been said. The saying demonstrates that the code stands independent of the particular scene in which it is invoked. This is accomplished by every saying of the code. (p. 141)

If the code is at all an abstraction, the abstraction derives reflexively from references and acquiescence to its separate and distinct regulating force when and where it is invoked. The quality of related accounts is tied to the different purposes for which the code is invoked and to the variety of stakes and consequences in place. At the same time, it is used to guide responses to the endless particulars of social interaction. The lesson of this is that goodness criteria should not be viewed as operating over and above social relations, as if the criteria served as a kind of quality control in their own right for directing and evaluating the construction of accounts. Rather, as the second half of Wieder's book shows, codes and other standards of adequacy are resources for, not determinants of, the work of formulating quality control in narrative matters.

Conclusion

To expect a definitive answer to the question of what a good story is, is to expect the impossible in practice. Standards, generalized criteria, or codes are not the issue, even while they are perennially present in everyday life. Rather, the issue centers on the question, What is narratively adequate in the circumstances? Put in these terms, the answer requires a view to application, to something that is reflexively discerned. It requires an aesthetics of narrativity that draws inspiration from the relevancies and contingencies of everyday life, from operating purposes, from the functions of accounts, and from the consequences for those concerned. To say "that's a beautiful story" is as much a reflexive measure of its situated utility as it is a judgment of the story's narrative quality.

17

Who Is a Good Storyteller?

I f a good story is discerned in practice, who qualifies as a good storyteller? The evaluation of a story depends, in part, upon its teller. The most outlandish tale may be accepted at face value, for example, if it is told by a trusted friend or someone who is known to be an expert in the matter at hand. It can make a difference if a story is attributed to an adult as opposed to a child, a disinterested witness versus a party involved in a lawsuit, or a reliable source rather than a dissembling politician. Even the most plausible account is likely to be discounted if it comes from a known liar. In this chapter, we continue to consider the everyday aesthetics of narratives by turning to the practical adequacy of storytelling.

Orienting to Good Storytelling

As with stories, commonsense criteria for evaluating storytellers abound. We often hear storytellers described in terms of authenticity, honesty, being knowledgeable, and their entertainment value, to name just a few. Of course the application of these qualities depends on the nature of the story. Social science research tells us that credibility, expertise, and trustworthiness, among other attributes, are associated with effective communication in everyday situations (see Franzoi, 1996). Discussions of research methodology add to this, telling us that particular kinds of research informants are best suited to provide useful accounts. Kvale (1996), for instance, describes ideal research interview subjects as cooperative, well-motivated, eloquent, and knowledgeable.

They are truthful and consistent, they give concise and precise answers. . . .
They provide coherent accounts and do not continually contradict themselves.
Good interview subjects can give long and lively descriptions of their life situa-
tion, they tell capturing stories well suited for reporting. (p. 146)

At the same time, not every eloquent, coherent, cooperative narrator is
fully credible. Common sense tells us that people have myriad motives for
offering particular accounts or versions of experience. Not all of these
motives promote truthful reports. People evaluating accounts are always
skeptical, to one degree or another, of what they hear. As Goffman (1959)
explains, expressions *given*—that is, narratives themselves—may easily be
manipulated. Consequently, we look for expressions *given off*—actions that
are less easily controlled—to tell us about actors' actual motives and true
selves. For example, in a family therapy agency J. F. Gubrium (1992) studied, staff members sometimes completely discounted family members'
accounts of their relations with one another, instead choosing to read these
relations from the way family members positioned, arranged, and com-
ported themselves during therapy sessions. Staff trusted expressions given
off over clients' verbal accounts, which they figured might be crafted for
self-serving purposes.

Other sorts of narrative positioning also are matters of concern for social
researchers. Many ethnographic reports, for example, promote the credibility of their informants by touting the extent to which informants are "there,"
"on the scene" (see Geertz, 1988). "Being there" provides a figurative as
well as empirical anchor for description, supplying a basis for treating such
accounts as factual because their authors are in the know from firsthand
experience. Getting "inside" and "up close" even extends to emotional
realms. Jack Douglas (1985), for example, indicates that the best informants
are "emotional wellsprings" from whom "deep experience" can be extracted.
The claim to "being there" has always been strong rhetorical footing for
narrative adequacy (see J. F. Gubrium & Holstein, 1997).

Taken together, these views of the good informant highlight access, privilege, and authenticity as key criteria. We tend to consider the storyteller who
has direct access to the experience being narrated as a good storyteller. Those
with privileged knowledge are also regarded favorably. An authentic storyteller—that is, one who is in touch with his or her phenomenological and
emotional experience and who will reveal his or her own true experiences,
feelings, and self (see Vannini, 2006)—is often considered the best narrator.

While social researchers have placed a premium on getting rich reports from
authentic, knowledgeable informants, these standards are quite similar to
those asserted by ordinary storytellers and listeners themselves. As a practical

matter, the working criteria for adequacy in everyday storytelling don't differ substantially in research circumstances. As we noted earlier, however, there is an analytic danger in adopting commonsense standards and applying them as if they were objective or scientific criteria. To do so risks confounding the researcher's topic with his or her analytic resources (see Garfinkel, 1967; Zimmerman & Pollner, 1970). In studying narrative practice, we must be careful to clearly identify those processes and criteria that members of situations themselves use to designate adequate narrators. We should take care to maintain our focus on indigenous criteria of adequacy as objects to be described and analyzed themselves, and not adopt them as our own evaluative criteria.

We approach the question of who is a good storyteller by looking at how good storytellers are identified in everyday life. We focus on persons telling and receiving stories and how they determine who is a good, unreliable, truthful, or suspect storyteller. The goal is to describe how the good storyteller is determined in the course of narrative practice. In general, the guideline for analyzing good stories offered in Chapter 16 is applicable to analyzing storytellers as well; we encourage researchers to document the use of indigenous criteria. The following guideline applies:

Guideline

Look for the ways in which storytellers and listeners interactionally construct the adequacy of the storyteller. Identify indigenous criteria and document their uses and application in practice. Discern how storytellers are circumstantially authorized as adequate storytellers for the purpose at hand.

Into the Field

Discerning the good storyteller compels the researcher to look beyond individual characteristics. If the individual attributes of a storyteller are significant, they become so in relation to circumstantial and interactional criteria. As such, no single attribute or list of attributes will universally apply. The same is true for standards and criteria generally. While they exist and are used in both research and more ordinary situations, and therefore are important to identify, the way they enter into narrative reality is far from a matter of straightforward application. Their effectiveness, rather, is established through the machinery of practice.

In her article "'K' is Mentally Ill," Dorothy Smith (1978) analyzes how the teller of an extended narrative is authorized in practice to be a credible narrator of the experience of several college students and others in their social circle. It is a classic study of the social organization of a factual account. Smith's analysis focuses on a lengthy, detailed narrative prompted by the interview question "Have you ever known anyone you thought might be mentally ill?" The story that the interviewee—Angela—tells provides a series of anecdotally supported descriptions that portray a college-aged woman—"K"—as becoming more and more obviously psychologically disturbed. This transcript is more complex than most firsthand narratives in that it partly summarizes or paraphrases Angela's account, including commentary by the interviewer on the story being told. Angela, who Smith calls the "teller of the tale," is the ostensible narrator, but the interviewer also assumes that role from time to time. The material is thus both a narrative and a meta-narrative about K's mental illness. The interview transcript highlights several mechanisms through which the teller of the tale is performatively cast as a legitimate, trustworthy storyteller.

The transcript of the narrative about K is several pages long and cannot be reproduced here in full. To summarize the account in its broadest details, Angela begins her story by explaining that her recognition of K's mental illness was very gradual. She recounts a series of incidents that, taken individually, might not signify much, but when considered together, pose a picture of K as behaving in a way that Angela found "queer" and "completely out of touch." (The term "queer" appeared in a British context and does not have homosexual connotations.) The following is a partial list of the incidents or anecdotes cited in the extended narrative:

- Nearly every morning, K would cry in the car on the way to school.
- K would undertake casual activities with an intensity completely out of proportion to the circumstance, for example, turning casual afternoons at the pool or beach into lap-swimming marathons, or working in a friend's garden for hours when she was only asked casually to help out.
- K would speak childishly and offer inane remarks in the midst of serious adult conversation.
- K's college essays appeared to have been written by a 12-year-old.
- She would get up and leave in the middle of conversations.
- K was uneasy in conversation with young men.
- K acted peculiarly at the breakfast table when staying as a guest at Angela's home.
- K would bathe or wash dishes fastidiously, but leave a mess in her wake.
- She made impractical purchases, overspending the household budget.
- K had "food fads," eating whole containers of ketchup, tinned fruit, and honey at a single sitting.
- She would fix separate meals for herself, even though her roommates were cooking communal meals.
- K couldn't do two things at once, such as watch TV and knit.

Smith's interest in analyzing this narrative was not to establish whether or not K was, indeed, mentally ill. Parallel to the position Pollner and McDonald-Wikler (1985) took in Chapter 12, Smith was decidedly indifferent to this issue and to the actual character of the events that were recounted. Rather, she was interested in unpacking how the narrative was produced and organized as a "factual account" by the persons engaged in it. Part of the work involved in constructing the facticity of events was establishing the narrator—Angela, "the teller of the tale"—as a believable, credible, authoritative storyteller.

Smith argues that "for any set of actual events, there is always more than one version that can be treated as what has happened" (p. 33). She notes that the credibility of a storyteller is central to the authorization of any particular version. It is an ongoing practical challenge for storytellers and listeners to determine who is allocated the "privilege of definition" (p. 33). Smith proceeds to describe how Angela's believability is built up as both Angela and the interviewer formulate the story.

Smith begins her analysis by discussing the way the reader/listener is "instructed" in how to read/hear the story about K and how Angela is "authorized" as the privileged teller of the tale. Clearly, there is serious narrative work involved in the process. Angela's first statement in the narrative provides a cornerstone for all that is to come: "My recognition that there might be something wrong was very gradual, and I was actually the last of (K's) close friends who was openly willing to admit that she was becoming mentally ill" (p. 32). Smith points to two very important features of this statement. First, it introduces a set of internal "embedded instructions" within the description itself that subtly explain and guide how listeners are to understand and appreciate what they are hearing.

Angela's opening claim is that K was "mentally ill," which frames what follows, as Goffman (1974) might put it. Angela treats this as an unequivocal fact, something that is simply there as a feature of K, a feature that was always available for Angela and others to notice. K's mental illness is portrayed as existing prior to Angela's own recognition or formulation of it. It is a separate and distinct condition, which Angela presents as having been progressively noticed by herself and others. This has profound narrative consequences because, as Smith points out, the fact "that we are told at the outset that K is mentally ill authorizes the version of those who realized or came to admit the fact of her illness" (p. 34). These first few words, Smith explains, position Angela as a credible observer and reporter on the situation because she is ostensibly in touch with the reality of the case. It further instructs listeners to hear and understand forthcoming descriptions and accounts in light of the "fact" of K's mental illness.

Angela's first statement also begins to build her credibility as a chronicler of K's troubles in another related way. Recall that Angela said that she was slow to recognize that something was wrong with K. She admits that she "was actually the last of her (K's) close friends who was openly willing to admit that she was becoming mentally ill" (p. 32). There are two important features to this claim. First, Angela says she is K's "friend." Indeed, this "fact" has already been introduced in an extended "preface" to the actual story, in which the interviewer provides considerable background information about K and Angela. Smith notes that, from the very outset, Angela is described as a "friend" who was "full of admiration" for K. Throughout the narrative, Angela and other observers are repeatedly referenced as "friends." This is important, Smith suggests, because Angela's credibility as the storyteller rests in part on the motives that might be attributed to her as she portrays K in this particular fashion. Establishing that Angela is K's friend essentially protects Angela from accusations of having malicious or nefarious intent when she characterizes K as mentally ill. To the contrary, it accentuates Angela's credibility because Angela (as a friend) is predisposed to resist unflattering portrayals of her friend. She could be expected normatively to try to portray her friend in a positive light. Hence, her description of K as mentally ill must be motivated by the "facts" of the situation, further enhancing Angela's credibility.

Second, Smith also points out that Angela claims that she was reluctant to acknowledge that something was wrong with K ("My recognition that there might be something wrong was very gradual . . . I was actually the last of her close friends . . . to admit that she was becoming mentally ill"). Several times, Angela reiterates her reluctance: "Slowly my admiration changed to a feeling of bafflement" (p. 29); "I still tried to find explanations and excuses—refused to acknowledge the fact that there was anything definitely wrong with K" (p. 29). Through these narrative moves, Angela establishes that she is essentially sympathetic to K, that she is on K's side, so to speak. Aligned in this fashion, Angela is positioned as a storyteller who is unlikely to offer a gratuitously negative depiction of K. This further underscores Angela's credibility as the teller of the "true" tale.

Looking further at the text of the interview, Smith describes several other ways in which Angela is authorized as a good storyteller. For example, Smith identifies a set of practices that establish that Angela is credibly dealing with the facts of the matter at hand, and not merely passing along supposition, hearsay, or fabrication. Angela, for instance, is involved directly in several of the "incidents" that are reported. Thus, she has direct, insider knowledge of what had transpired, which privileges her views in comparison to outsiders. Angela thus establishes herself as an authority or expert on K's troubles by virtue of proximity and engagement. It is important to note that Angela uses this standard of credibility herself; it is an indigenous application of the criterion.

Angela also enhances her credibility by appealing to other sources for confirmation. Commonsensically, Smith argues, "facts" will appear to be the same to independent observers. Smith suggests that credibility may be established by displaying that actions and objects highlighted in a narrative would be seen and reported in the same fashion by any observer/teller. Here, again, the "same-fashion" criterion is an indigenous evaluative feature of the account. Smith proceeds to show that Angela often appeals to others to verify her own reports. In a series of discrete anecdotes embedded in her longer story, Angela refers to several individuals who had similar observations of K's bizarre behavior. By the end of the interview, five persons—Angela, Angela's mother, Trudi and Betty (friends of K's), and a woman friend of K's family—are introduced as witnesses to K's mental illness.

As a practical matter, these witnesses would be considered especially credible, since, like Angela, each is likely to be seen as sympathetic to K and without motive to disparage her. Angela, for example, quotes Trudi—a mutual friend who is a college English major—who says that "(K) writes like a 12-year-old—I think there is something wrong with her" (p. 29). Betty is paraphrased as suggesting that "something should be done" about K's bizarre behavior in social situations (p. 31). As the accounts from varying sources mount, they can be seen as a compilation of independent reports. Thus, Angela can be heard as a knowledgeable reporter of facts because the anecdotes she relates are corroborated from separate, friendly sources who make similar empirical observations on different occasions.

Smith also indicates that it is important to recognize that, in telling her tale, Angela systematically adds one account to the others, building a seeming "mountain of evidence." At the same time, Angela implies no connection between the various witnesses to the events. Angela thus marshals several apparently independent sources of the "data" in her narrative, again suggesting that she is an informed, credible reporter on the matter at hand. Smith notes, finally, that one of the independent sources Angela mentions is a psychiatrist, thus adding a hint of professional validation to the observations that Angela has herself reported.

Smith's analysis presents a variety of ways in which someone can bolster the claim to being a good storyteller. As we have pointed out, the account is not so much truthful on its own as it is replete with authorization devices and tropes of truth—narrative moves to establish the good and true storyteller. But storytellers cannot fully control how others perceive and respond to them. Despite the narrative work they may do to establish their credibility, authority, or appeal, they still must be heard and understood in a positive light. A good storyteller is one who is so received by listeners. On this count, it is not uncommon for the adequacy of one's storytelling to be a matter of contention, if not open dispute. Angela's narrative above was presented in tape-recorded, then transcribed, form. It was elicited as a response to an interview question in a quasi-research situation. There was no opportunity for in situ challenges to Angela's status as authoritative storyteller.

This is a relatively uncommon storytelling situation in this regard. More typically, stories and storytellers must be authorized in the course of every-day interaction. Recall, for example, the ways in which the practical ade-quacy of the storyteller was tacitly brought to the fore in the "bad perm" account discussed in Chapters 8 and 9. In Chapter 8, we analyzed this story in terms of narrative collaboration, and expanded the interactional theme to narrative control in Chapter 9. The "bad perm" story involved several speakers, with the primary storyteller—Louise—eventually emerging only after several small conversational contests over who would get to tell it. We might consider these contests to be about who would be authorized as the primary storyteller—who would be considered the most adequate teller of the story of Jennifer's bad perm.

Let's revisit a portion of this conversation. Remember that Louise was attempting to tell a second story in the wake of a first "perm" story that Jean had been telling. Jean initially resisted, talking over Louise's bid to claim speakership, but Louise eventually succeeded in commanding the storytelling floor.

Louise: Remember [when—]

Jean: [It was] *terrible.*

Louise: Jennifer, the first time Jennifer had a perm when she came home, it was the funniest thing.

Jean: She put something on her head, a bag or something?

Louise: She wore her—

Annie: {laughs}

Louise: Well she wore her—

Helen: Hair ball, hair ball. Yeah because she—

Annie: She just always had this *hood* on, and she ran upstairs.

Louise: No. First she *threw* her bag up the stairs, almost *hit* me.

Annie: Oh, yeah.

Louise: Then, *bang*, the door slams and I'm like—I was on the *phone*. I was like "Ah I don't know. My sister just walked in. I think something's wrong." And [then she ran up the stairs.] (Norrick, 2000, pp. 154–156)

Once Louise had begun her story ("Jennifer, the first time Jennifer had a perm when she came home, it was the funniest thing."), Jean offered her tacit approval of Louise as the storyteller by contributing additional detail and extending the story. She even did this in the form of a question, further authorizing Louise to become the new storyteller. As Louise proceeded, Annie and Helen added details of their own, which could be heard as attempting to commandeer the role of storyteller themselves. Louise, however, directly contradicts Annie's contribution ("No. First she threw her bag up the stairs, almost hit me."), asserting both Louise's version of what had transpired and her right to tell the story. When she adds the observation that Jennifer "almost hit me" with the thrown bag, Louise further authorizes her version by placing herself at the scene of the incident, claiming firsthand, privileged knowledge. She also provides sound effects ("bang") and a direct quotation of talk from the scene ("Ah I don't know. My sister just walked in. I think something's wrong."). When Annie responds, "Oh, yeah," she concedes the facticity of Louise's account and implicitly grants Louise the right to continue with the story.

The point to be drawn here is that the good storyteller is not simply a characteristic of the teller, but is something that emerges in the context of a story's telling. Authorization and adequacy are not granted automatically. They are interactionally and situationally established.

This proves to be the case in even the most salient and restrictive narrative environments. Even seemingly obvious sources of authenticity or expertise need to be established in practice for the "good storyteller" to be acknowledged. Recall, for example, that we argued earlier that professional and organizational environments shape the narratives that emerge under their auspices. This does not mean that simply being a competent member of an organization or profession authorizes a person as an adequate storyteller where organizational or professional matters are concerned. As in other circumstances, adequacy remains a matter of practical application. As Barbara Czarniawska (1997, 1998) might put it, an organization is more or less realized through the authoritativeness of storytelling.

We can see how narrative authority is established in the highly professionalized environment of a mental health clinic in which Charles Suchar (1975) observed interactions between a variety of staff members and clients. We might expect that professional background, experience, and expertise would be especially valued in this realm. We would guess that members possessing the requisite professional and organizational credentials would be granted special authorization to narrate the pertinent details of matters of clinical interest in the facility. Indeed, Suchar characterized the clinic setting as deploying a "cult of expertise," meaning that the discourse of psychiatric knowledge, experience, and know-how was pervasive and locally powerful. Without denying Suchar's observation, a closer look at the narrative work going on in the clinic makes it evident that being a psychiatric expert did not necessarily or automatically authorize an individual to characterize clinical matters in his or her own terms.

Consider extracts from two extended conversations between a child psychiatrist, Dr. J, and the counseling staff at the clinic during psychiatric staffings. These meetings are very similar to staffings at Cedarview, the residential treatment center for children discussed in previous chapters. In the first extract, Dr. J, the child's counselor (Mrs. Star), and the program director are discussing the progress of a 9-year-old boy described as having "childhood psychosis of a chronic nature." The child has been in clinic programs for about one year, and Dr. J and Mrs. Star are evaluating his progress. The psychiatrist sounds optimistic, while the counselor is far less sanguine regarding the child's track record and future prospects.

Dr. J: I see something in him. I can smell it, something hopeful. Since he's rejected all avenues of pleasure, I don't think you should give him tasks to do. I think you're [Mrs. Star, the counselor] doing all right with him. . . . [To the program director:] I suggest we also begin seeing this mother and child together for a few visits for diagnosis.

Mrs. Star: The father's a jerk—he's too rigid. I don't know if he'd like that. Anyways, I don't know, he's [child] still twiddling [a major symptom]. It's so sad. . . . There's this kid in my neighborhood who's 20 and still does that. I don't know if [child] will ever change. It's so sad . . .

Dr. J: He [child] may do that at 20 also. He should have physical contact with someone. Mrs. Star, you're too pessimistic. . . . The hopeful thing with this type of kid is their opposition. I know. It takes experience with these kids to understand this. Once they give in and "yes" you all the time—they're cooked. Why don't you talk to him about his not talking? In time, he'll begin responding in a variety of ways, you'll see.

Mrs. Star: He *is* a great listener. I guess you're right. He knows what I'm saying. You can tell he knows. (Suchar, 1975, pp. 19–20, italics in the original)

Dr. J and Mrs. Star initially seem to be at odds over both the description of the boy and what to do with him. Their stories don't jibe. Dr. J's formulation is hopeful; she sees the child as "oppositional," but treats this as a good sign. In contrast, Mrs. Star sees the boy as the type who is unlikely to change. Attempting to legitimate her claim, Mrs. Star invokes her personal knowledge of another case, which she says is similar to the one under consideration. We might hear this as an appeal to specialized local knowledge. Dr. J responds by speaking of the typical biography of "this type of kid," who "in time" will begin to respond if the proper therapeutic steps are taken. Thus she invokes general psychiatric knowledge as bearing on the matter.

Throughout the discussion, Dr. J suggests that her description may have greater merit than Mrs. Star's because, as Dr. J claims, "I know" and "It takes experience" to understand these things, clearly implying Dr. J's superior, professionally grounded interpretive skill in such matters. Using a vernacular characterization, Dr. J invokes an almost mystical professional insight: "I see something in him. I can smell it, something hopeful." Taken together, the collection of small conversational moves to claim local narrative authority culminated in Mrs. Star's acquiescence. Dr. J's professionalism, experience, local knowledge, and credibility as the narrator of pertinent truths (her narrative power, in other words) did not simply emanate from her professional credentials. Nor did they just appear out of nowhere, as if her mere presence on the premises made the difference. Rather these components of practical narrative adequacy were skillfully marshaled within this clinical context to establish Dr. J's narrative authority.

We see something similar in another staffing, where Dr. J and a counselor-trainee, Mr. E, discuss a 12-year-old boy who has been diagnosed as borderline schizophrenic. Like the preceding case, the client has been in the program for about one year.

Dr. J: I'll tell you what he is, he's pervasively anxious, he's absolutely driven by his anxiety. [Addressing the boy's counselor, Mr. E:] If you really want to know what a hyperactive child looks like, you've got him. . . . Yeah, okay, he's begun to build controls for himself, but it was all built around his anxiety; all his activity is frenzy. . . . I think with him there is a vast split between what he says and what he feels. Most of what he says is garbage.

Mr. E: [Visibly angered by the psychiatrist's last statement:] But sometimes he does mean what he says!

Dr. J: But look, even from your material [progress notes written on a daily basis by counselors and submitted to the psychiatrist before the staffing] I get the feeling that what he verbalizes means nothing.

Mr. E: But one time for example, he told me "I miss you" and he meant it.

Dr. J: But that's different. Some things like that may touch him, but I'm still very dubious that words mean anything to him. I do not think words reach him at all. [The psychiatrist's tone of voice becomes more insistent and the counselor is still angered by the evaluation.] Look . . . Mr. E, I know what I'm talking about. I've seen cases like this before. It takes time to understand this. You must not kid yourself that what he says means anything. There's a lack of integration between his feelings and his words. (Suchar, 1975, pp. 20–21)

Here, Dr. J's narrative is initially quite negative, characterizing the boy as "pervasively anxious . . . absolutely driven by his anxiety," and referring to him as a "hyperactive child." Even though Mr. E disagrees with the psychiatrist's narrative, Dr. J eventually has the final say. Suchar argues that this is an example of the counselor-trainee encountering the clinic's coercive "cult of expertise," which, in effect, forces him to capitulate. But looking at the interactional moves involved in this exchange, we can see more subtle processes at work. It is certainly important that Dr. J is a psychiatrist, speaking in a clinical environment, and that her professional status far exceeds that of the counselor-trainee. But her professional expertise and experience still need to be accountably invoked for the psychiatrist's version of the story to prevail. Looking closely, we can see that Dr. J's narrative is a strong assertion from the start. She characterizes the boy as "pervasively anxious," then argues in circular but difficult-to-refute fashion that "If you really want to know what a hyperactive child looks like, you got him." She then offers a brief counterargument, which she summarily refutes. When Mr. E objects, Dr. J turns Mr. E's own words against him, arguing that Mr. E's own progress notes indicate that the boy is unable to verbalize.

Each of these moves hints at Dr. J's superior powers of observation and diagnostic acumen—her expertise—which are put on display in practice as she describes the boy's case. Finally, Dr. J explicitly speaks what has been implied in most of the foregoing discussion: "I know what I'm talking about. I've seen cases like this before. It takes time to understand this." The words echo what Dr. J told Mrs. Star in the preceding case: "I know." "It takes experience." Professional expertise and experience are rhetorically brought to bear to trump the opposition.

The key observation here, once again, is that expertise must be articulated for Dr. J to be authorized as the circumstantially superior narrator of the facts of this case. We should also note that the emergent sense of narrative adequacy may be confined to this particular context, at this particular moment. Mr. E acceded to Dr. J's version of the case in these circumstances. In the context of the clinic staffing, Dr. J was the "best" storyteller, but her superior experience or expertise did not automatically dictate this outcome. Nor would this ensure that on future occasions Dr. J would be accorded the same narrative status.

Conclusion

Narrative adequacy—in this case, who is a good storyteller—is locally constructed, albeit with the mediations of its narrative environments. The work entailed, however, suggests that a good storyteller on one occasion may be discounted or ignored on another. If Dr. J was circumstantially authorized to describe mental health clinic clients, her psychiatric outlook and expertise might be worthless in depicting alcoholics at an AA meeting or caregivers in Alzheimer's support groups. In such settings, Dr. J might be labeled as "in denial" or "out of touch" with local realities, and her storytelling status diminished as a result. Her stories might even be dismissed in her own clinic if particular contingencies—such as the constraint of producing a report with different purposes for a funding agency—were brought into narrative play. Narrative environments are major factors in shaping who might be considered a good storyteller, but they do not determine outcomes. Environmental priorities must always be actively articulated with the case and by those concerned, which is a matter of narrative work. The everyday aesthetics of storytelling demand as much.

Afterword

Stories Without Borders?

As we close our discussion of narrative reality, important questions persist. What are stories? Do they have borders? If narratives don't have borders or their borders are fluid, how do we identify them? Is a research activity called "narrative analysis" still possible? If the material of narrative analysis is transcripts or texts of accounts, and these texts reflexively circulate in a world of constructive actions, doesn't narrative reality leave stories without structure and substance? Most treatises on narrative analysis would have addressed these questions at the start, but we've waited until the end because our view of story resists a priori definition.

The notion of borders is key to these questions. An important commonsense understanding about narrative borders is that a story is an extended account about something. It has a discernible topic, even if the topic is unclear. That is a kind of border. Presumed topical continuity is what makes it sensible to listen and respond to stories—to attend to talk or text that is about something else. We just don't listen to gibberish. More accurately, one listens to gibberish only if it is taken for granted that beyond it there is something to know. A topic is a kind of border in the sense that, given the topic, other topics are either ruled out or treated as ancillary. Anything within the border of the topic is figural, so to speak. Other matters are just part of the background. Of course, topicality is subject to negotiation, but the topicality assumption still holds in principle.

Another important understanding establishing borders is that narratives are assumed to have a plot. This means that the topic develops in a particular way as a story unfolds. A skeletal sense of emplottedness is that stories have beginnings, middles, and ends. Again, this is the principle. Plots may be underdeveloped, change course, or be recursive. The "story" may even work against emplottedness, in which case the idea of a plot makes it sensible to form plotless stories. Otherwise, in commonsense understanding, without the notion and possibility of plot, storytelling is gibberish. (Gibberish is itself a recognizable account and, as such, is culture bound and establishes courses of action. See Jameson, 1972.) Some narrative researchers discern particular kinds of plotlines in addition to developmental order, including plots that are heroic, fatalistic, comedic, and tragic. All of these also establish a border, permitting the researcher to discern matters supporting the plot, contrary to the plot, or working at various levels in relation to emplotment, among other kinds of narrative organization.

A third common understanding bearing on the question of borders is the matter of themes. This is of particular interest to text-based narrative researchers. Themes are discerned beneath the surface text of stories. While it is possible for a story or storyteller to announce a theme, themes are usually identified by listeners or researchers as underlying patterns of meaning. Kaufman's (1986) goal, for example, was to identify themes of storytellers' own doing, patterns of meaning that didn't simply reflect age or generational experiences (see Chapter 5). Themes also set borders. What thematizes some life stories or historical accounts, for example, can be distinguished from what thematizes others. The researcher typically names (and codes) types of themes, adding procedural dimension to thematic borders.

All of these kinds of borders are commonsensically understood to be characteristics of stories, storytelling, and accountability. From our perspective, however, the topics, plots, themes, beginnings, middles, ends, and other border features that are assumed to be the defining characteristics of stories are produced through the operating components of narrative reality—of border making as an activity in its own right (cf. E. Gubrium & Koro-Ljungberg, 2005). Whether or not an account has a topic is determined in practice, within the occasioned give-and-take of those telling and hearing a story. Relatedly, if researchers or listeners are aware of the intertextuality of accounts, they can discern topics of interest well beyond what is topical in any single narrative or text. As we saw, the borders of a story's topic may extend retrospectively to what is known about the past contexts of an account, and prospectively to what is imagined about its future contexts. The researcher who orients to narrative practice can actually hear storytellers take these extensions into consideration in figuring the meaning of reports and testimony, for example. Such complex discernments of topicality are neither word games nor narrative wheel spinning, but can have serious consequences. Discerned topics and associated meanings can lead to incarceration, commitment, dismissal, or violence, among other dire outcomes of designated intertextuality.

The same applies to plots and themes. Listeners presume that plots and themes are in place when stories are under consideration. But plots and themes emerge through narrative practice, raising two important questions. In what way is a narrative socially organized, and how is a narrative made meaningful? In the context of Cedarview staffings, for example, the progress of a child's emotional control (topic) could be emplotted and thematized in different ways. The institutionally preferred way was to emplot emotional control in terms of overt conduct, behavioral indicators, programmatic restructuring, and sanctions. Preferred themes included present learning, behavior modification, and visible consequences. But, as we saw, in-depth psychological emplotment and thematization also were possible. In these less common instances, emotional control was emplotted as operating beneath visible manifestations, the themes of which dealt with psychodynamics. All of this interpretive work established borders that circumscribed stories, but these borders weren't necessarily discernible from specific accounts or texts alone.

Narrative environments themselves deploy borders for stories. The "same" account in one setting—with a particular moral understanding of the topic and related form of emplotment—can be deployed with radically different plots, themes, and courses of action in a setting with a different understanding. Close relationships, local cultures, statuses, jobs, and organizations can be viewed as border-making concerns, if not narrative sovereigns. They shape stories in locally preferred ways. Dotting the narrative landscape, such going concerns assemble, define, route, and reroute what is commonly assumed to be the features of all stories. Common assumptions notwithstanding, borders such as topics, plots, and themes are constructed in reflexive relation to the preferences.

Narrative work—the other operating component of storytelling—figures prominently in border making. It puts borders in place and supplies their elasticity. If Barthes, Bakhtin, and other literary theorists extended the interpretive borders of stories well beyond what authors intended in particular texts, narrative work takes us to the constructive activity of accountability. Here, again, the assumption that identifiable stories exist is not at stake. Rather, the issue of how borders are identified, formulated, and sustained in practice is center stage.

In explicating narrative reality, the question is not whether stories have borders. Instead, we ask how borders are established, and what those borders might have been, are now, and will be in the future. Viewed in this way, the borders that, say, the transcripts of stories establish are artifacts of textuality. The transcript of a life story often loses an important portion of the story's social dynamics and organization. Stanley helped us a great deal in this regard, showing us that what appeared in the text of *The Jack-Roller* was important but also should be taken with a grain of salt. It's not that what appeared in Stanley's narrative wasn't a proper story with discernible borders. Rather the account presented a version of Stanley's life, which Stanley articulated as much for Shaw's purposes as for his own. We were fortunate that Stanley occasionally stepped outside of his story to point that out.

What, then, are stories? From our perspective, stories are continuously unfolding accounts, whose extensions move in many directions. They are bound by conventional borders such as plots and themes, but these are the ongoing products of narrative reality's operating components. To capture the richness of narrative reality, analysis needs to focus on both the circumstantial variety and the agentic flexibility of stories, not just on the structure of accounts themselves. This combination not only points to existing texts but to the shape and meanings of accounts of all kinds. In today's world, the possibilities are more extensive than ever. There are more stories, told in more circumstances, about an increasing number of topics. There are more border makers emplotting and thematizing stories in more ways than a text-based approach could ever accommodate. The analysis of narrative reality spotlights this complex landscape.

References

Abrahams, R. D. (1977). Toward an enactment-centered theory of folklore. In W. Bascom (Ed.), *Frontiers of folklore* (pp. 79–120). Boulder: Westview Press.

Abu-Lughod, L. (1993). *Writing women's worlds: Bedouin stories*. Berkeley: University of California Press.

Åkerstrom, M. (1993). *Crooks and squares*. New Brunswick, NJ: Transaction.

Alcoholics Anonymous. (1953). *Twelve steps and twelve traditions*. New York: Alcoholics Anonymous Worlds Services.

Alcoholics Anonymous. (1976). *Alcoholics anonymous*. New York: Alcoholics Anonymous World Services.

Amit, V. (Ed.). (2000). *Constructing the field*. New York: Routledge.

Anderson, E. (1976). *A place on the corner*. Chicago: University of Chicago Press.

Anderson, E. (1999). *Code of the street*. New York: Norton.

Atkinson, J. M., & Drew, P. (1979). *Order in court*. Atlantic Highlands, NJ: Humanities Press.

Atkinson, J. M., & Heritage, J. (Eds.). (1984). *Structures of social action*. Cambridge: Cambridge University Press.

Atkinson, P. (1990). *The ethnographic imagination: Textual constructions of reality*. London: Routledge.

Atkinson, P. (1992). *Understanding ethnographic texts*. Thousand Oaks, CA: Sage.

Atkinson, P. (1997). Narrative turn or blind alley? *Qualitative Health Research, 7,* 325–344.

Atkinson, P., & Coffey, A. (2002). Revisiting the relationship between participant observation and interviewing. In J. Gubrium & J. Holstein (Eds.), *Handbook of interview research* (pp. 801–814). Thousand Oaks, CA: Sage.

Atkinson, P., & Hammersley, M. (1994). Ethnography and participant observation. In N. Denzin & Y. Lincoln (Eds.), *Handbook of qualitative research* (pp. 248–261). Thousand Oaks, CA: Sage.

Atkinson, P., & Silverman, D. (1997). Kundera's *Immortality:* The interview society and the invention of self. *Qualitative Inquiry, 3,* 324–345.

Babbie, E. (2007). *The practice of social research* (11th ed.). Belmont, CA: Wadsworth.

Bakhtin, M. M. (1981). *The dialogic imagination* (M. Holquist, Ed.). Austin: University of Texas Press.

Bamberg, M. (2006). Stories: Big or small, why do we care? *Narrative Inquiry, 16,* 139–147.

Barthes, R. (1974). *S/Z*. New York: Hill & Wang.

Barthes, R. (1977). *Image, music, text*. New York: Hill & Wang.

Bauman, R. (1972). Differential identity and the social base of folklore. In A. Paredes & R. Bauman (Eds.), *Toward new perspectives in folklore* (pp. 31–41). Austin: University of Texas Press.

Bauman, R. (1986). *Story, performance, and event: Contextual studies of oral narrative*. New York: Cambridge University Press.

Becker, H. S., & Geer, B. (1957). Participant observation and interviewing: A comparison. *Human Organization, 16,* 28–32.

Behar, R. (1993). *Translated woman: Crossing the border with Esperanza's story.* Boston: Beacon Press.

Behar, R. (1996). *The vulnerable observer: Anthropology that breaks your heart.* Boston: Beacon Press.

Bell, S. (1988). Becoming a political woman: The reconstruction and interpretation of experience through stories. In A. D. Todd & S. Fisher (Eds.), *Gender and discourse: The power of talk* (pp. 97–123). Norwood, NJ: Ablex.

Benjamin, W. (1969). *Illuminations.* New York: Schocken.

Berger, P., & Kellner, H. (1970). Marriage and the construction of reality. In H. P. Dreitzel (Ed.), *Recent sociology No. 2* (pp. 50–72). New York: Macmillan.

Berger, P. L., & Luckmann, T. (1966). *The social construction of reality.* New York: Doubleday.

Bertaux, D. (Ed.). (1981). *Biography and society: The life history approach in the social sciences.* Beverly Hills, CA: Sage.

Bloch, M. (1975). *Political oratory in traditional society.* New York: Academic.

Blumer, H. (1969). *Symbolic interactionism.* Englewood Cliffs, NJ: Prentice Hall.

Brekhus, W., Galliher, J., & Gubrium, J. F. (2005). The need for thin description. *Qualitative Inquiry, 11*(6), 861–879.

Brennis, D. (1978). The matter of talk: Political performances in Bhatgaon. *Language in Society, 7,* 159–170.

Briggs, C. L. (2007). Anthropology, interviewing, and communicability in contemporary society. *Current Anthropology, 48,* 551–580.

Briggs, C. L., & Bauman, R. (1992). Genre, intertextuality, and social power. *Journal of Linguistic Anthropology, 2,* 131–172.

Briggs, C. L., & Mantini-Briggs, C. (2003). *Stories in the time of cholera.* Berkeley: University of California Press.

Bruner, J. (1990). *Acts of meaning.* Cambridge, MA: Harvard University Press.

Buckholdt, D. R., & Gubrium, J. F. (1979). *Caretakers: Treating emotionally disturbed children.* Beverly Hills, CA: Sage.

Burns, A. F. (1983). *An epoch of miracles: Oral literature of the Yucatec Maya.* Austin: University of Texas Press.

Butler, J. (1990). *Gender trouble: Feminism and the subversion of identity.* New York: Routledge.

Callon, M. (1986). Some elements of a sociology of translation: Domestication of the scallops and the fishermen of St. Brieuc Bay. In J. Law (Ed.), *Power, action, and belief: A new sociology of knowledge?* (pp. 196–223). London: Routledge.

Candida Smith, R. (2002). Analytic strategies for oral history interviews. In J. F. Gubrium & J. A. Holstein (Eds.), *Handbook of interview research* (pp. 711–732). Thousand Oaks, CA: Sage.

Charmaz, K. (1991). *Good days bad days: The self in chronic illness and time.* New Brunswick, NJ: Rutgers University Press.

Chase, S. (1995). *Ambiguous empowerment: The work narratives of women school superintendents.* Amherst: University of Massachusetts Press.

Chase, S. E. (2005). Narrative inquiry: Multiple lenses, approaches and voices. In. N. K. Denzin & Y. S. Lincoln (Eds.), *The SAGE Handbook of qualitative research* (3rd ed., pp. 651–679). Thousand Oaks, CA: Sage.

Christopher, J. (1988). *How to stay sober: Recovery without religion.* Buffalo, NY: Prometheus Books.

Clandinin, D. J., & Connolly, F. M. (2000). *Narrative inquiry: Experience and story in qualitative research.* San Francisco: Jossey-Bass.

Clifford, J., & Marcus, G. E. (1986). *Writing culture: The poetics and politics of ethnography.* Berkeley: University of California Press.

Corsaro, W. A. (1997). *The sociology of childhood.* Thousand Oaks, CA: Pine Forge Press.

Cortazzi, M. (1993). *Narrative analysis.* London: Falmer Press.

Cosentino, D. (1982). *Defiant maids and stubborn farmers: Tradition and invention in Mende story performance.* Cambridge: Cambridge University Press.

Cressey, P. G. (1932). *The taxi-dance hall.* Chicago: University of Chicago Press.

Czarniawska, B. (1997). *Narrating the organization: Dramas of institutional identity*. Chicago: University of Chicago Press.

Czarniawska, B. (1998). *A narrative approach to organization studies*. Thousand Oaks, CA: Sage.

Daiute, C., & Lightfoot, C. (Eds.). (2003). *Narrative analysis: Studying the development of individuals in society*. Thousand Oaks, CA: Sage.

Darnell, R. (1974). Correlates of Cree narrative performance. In R. Bauman & J. Sherzer (Eds.), *Explorations in the ethnography of speaking* (pp. 315–336). Cambridge: Cambridge University Press.

Denzin, N. K. (1986). *Treating alcoholism*. Newbury Park, CA: Sage.

Denzin, N. K. (1987a). *The alcoholic self*. Newbury Park, CA: Sage.

Denzin, N. K. (1987b). *The recovering alcoholic*. Newbury Park, CA: Sage.

Denzin, N. K. (1995). *The cinematic society*. Thousand Oaks, CA: Sage.

Denzin, N. K., & Lincoln, Y. S. (Eds). (2005). *The SAGE handbook of qualitative research* (3rd ed.). Thousand Oaks, CA: Sage.

Donovan, F. R. (1920). *The woman who waits*. Boston: Gorham Press.

Donovan, F. R. (1929). *The saleslady*. Chicago: University of Chicago Press.

Douglas, J. D. (1985). *Creative interviewing*. Beverly Hills, CA: Sage.

Douglas, M. (1978). Do dogs laugh? A crosscultural approach to body symbolism. In T. Polhemus (Ed.), *The body reader: Social aspects of the human body* (pp. 295–303). New York: Pantheon.

Drew, P., & Heritage, J. (Eds.). (1992). *Talk at work*. Cambridge: Cambridge University Press.

Dundes, A. (1980). *Interpreting folklore*. Bloomington: Indiana University Press.

Eder, D. (1995). *School talk: Gender and adolescent culture*. New Brunswick, NJ: Rutgers University Press.

Egan, R. D. (2006). *Dancing for dollars and paying for love*. New York: Palgrave Macmillan.

Ellis, C. (1991). Sociological introspection and emotional experience. *Symbolic Interaction, 14*, 23–50.

Ellis, C. (2004). *The ethnographic I: A methodological novel about autoethnography*. Walnut Creek, CA: AltaMira Press.

Ellis, C., & Bochner, A. P. (Eds.). (1996). *Composing ethnography: Alternative forms of qualitative writing*. Walnut Creek, CA: AltaMira.

Ellis, C., & Flaherty, M. (Eds.). (1992). *Investigating subjectivity*. Newbury Park, CA: Sage.

Emerson, J. (1970). Behavior in private places: Sustaining definitions of reality in gynecological examinations. In H. P. Dreitzel (Ed.), *Recent sociology no. 2* (pp. 73–97). London: Macmillan.

Emerson, R. M. (1983). Holistic effects in social control decision-making. *Law and Society Review, 17*, 425–455.

Emerson, R. M. (1991). Case processing and interorganizational knowledge: Detecting the "real reasons" for referrals. *Social Problems, 38*, 198–212.

Emerson, R. M., Fretz, R., & Shaw, L. L. (1995). *Writing ethnographic fieldnotes*. Chicago: University of Chicago Press.

Emerson, R. M., & Paley, B. (1992). Organizational horizons and complaint-filing. In K. Hawkins (Ed.), *The uses of discretion* (pp. 231–247). Oxford, UK: Oxford University Press.

Ewick, P., & Silbey, S. (2003). Narrating social structure: Stories of resistance to legal authority. *American Journal of Sociology, 108*, 1328–1372.

Falassi, A. (1980). *Folklore by the fireside: Text and context of the Tuscan Veglia*. Austin: University of Texas Press.

Ferreira, A. (1963). Family myth and homeostasis. *Archives of General Psychiatry, 9*, 457–463.

Fish, S. (1980). *Is there a text in this class?* Cambridge, MA: Harvard University Press.

Foucault, M. (1965). *Madness and civilization: A history of insanity in the age of reason*. New York: Random House.

Foucault, M. (1972). *The archaeology of knowledge*. New York: Pantheon.

Foucault, M. (1975). *The birth of the clinic*. New York: Vintage.

Foucault, M. (1977). *Discipline and punish: The birth of the prison*. New York: Vintage.

Franzoi, S. L. (1996). *Social psychology*. Dubuque, IA: Brown and Benchmark.

Garfinkel, H. (1967). *Studies in ethnomethodology*. Englewood Cliffs, NY: Prentice-Hall.

Geertz, C. (1973). *The interpretation of cultures*. New York: Harper.

Geertz, C. (1988). *Works and lives: The anthropologist as author*. Stanford, CA: Stanford University Press.

Ginsburg, F. (1989). *Contested lives: The abortion debate in an American community*. Berkeley: University of California Press.

Glassie, H. H. (1995). *Passing the time in Ballymenone: Culture and history of an Ulster community*. Bloomington, IN: Indiana University.

Glassie, H. H. (2006). *The stars of Ballymenone*. Bloomington, IN: Indiana University.

Goffman, E. (1959). *The presentation of self in everyday life*. New York: Doubleday.

Goffman, E. (1961). *Asylums*. Garden City, NY: Doubleday.

Goffman, E. (1974). *Frame analysis*. New York: Harper.

Goodall, H. L., Jr. (2000). *Writing the new ethnography*. Lanham, MD: AltaMira.

Goodwin, M. H. (1989). Tactical uses of stories: Participation frameworks within girls' and boys' disputes. In S. Berentzen (Ed.), *Ethnographic approaches to children's worlds and peer cultures* (pp. 110–143). Trondheim, Norway: Norwegian Center for Child Research (Report No. 15).

Gubrium, A. (2006). "I was my momma baby. I was my daddy gal": Strategic stories of success. *Narrative Inquiry, 16*, 122–130.

Gubrium, E., & Koro-Ljungberg, M. (2005). Contending with border making in the social constructionist interview. *Qualitative Inquiry, 11*, 689–715.

Gubrium, J. F. (1986a). *Oldtimers and Alzheimer's*. Greenwich, CT: JAI Press.

Gubrium, J. F. (1986b). The social preservation of mind: The Alzheimer's disease experience. *Symbolic Interaction, 6*, 37–51.

Gubrium, J. F. (1988). The family as project, *Sociological Review, 36*, 273–295.

Gubrium, J. F. (1992). *Out of control: Family therapy and domestic disorder*. Newbury Park, CA: Sage.

Gubrium, J. F. (1993). *Speaking of life: Horizons of meaning for nursing home residents*. Hawthorne, NY: Aldine de Gruyter.

Gubrium, J. F. (1997). *Living and dying at Murray Manor*. Charlottesville, VA: University of Virginia Press. (Original work published 1975)

Gubrium, J. F. (2007). Urban ethnography of the 1920s working girl. *Gender, Work and Organization, 14*(3), 232–258.

Gubrium, J. F., & Buckholdt, D. R. (1982). *Describing care: Image and practice in rehabilitation*. Cambridge, MA: Oelgeschlager, Gunn, & Hain.

Gubrium, J. F., Buckholdt, D. R., & Lynott, R. J. (1989). The descriptive tyranny of forms. *Perspectives on Social Problems, 1*, 195–214.

Gubrium, J. F., & Holstein, J. A. (1990). *What is family?* Mountain View, CA: Mayfield.

Gubrium, J. F., & Holstein, J. A. (1997). *The new language of qualitative method*. New York: Oxford University Press.

Gubrium, J. F., & Holstein, J. A. (1999). The nursing home as a discursive anchor for the aging body. *Ageing and Society, 19*, 519–538.

Gubrium, J. F., & Holstein, J. A. (2000). Analyzing interpretive practice. In N. Denzin & Y. Lincoln (Eds.), *Handbook of qualitative research* (2nd ed., pp. 487–508). Thousand Oaks, CA: Sage.

Gubrium, J. F., & Holstein, J. A. (2002). *Handbook of interview research*. Thousand Oaks, CA: Sage.

Gubrium, J. F., & Holstein, J. A. (2008). Narrative ethnography. In S. Hesse-Biber & P. Leavy (Eds.), *Handbook of emergent methods* (pp. 241–264). New York: Guilford.

Gubrium, J. F., & Lynott, R. J. (1985). Family rhetoric as social order. *Journal of Family Issues, 6*, 129–152.

Haraway, D. (1988). Situated knowledges: The science question in feminism and the privilege of partial perspectives. *Feminist Studies, 14,* 575–599.

Harris, S. R. (2006). *The meanings of marital equality.* Albany: State University of New York Press.

Hawkes, T. (1977). *Structuralism and semiotics.* Berkeley: University of California Press.

Heidegger, M. (1962). *Being and time.* New York: Harper and Row.

Heidegger, M. (1967). *What is a thing?* Chicago: Henry Regnery.

Hendrick, C. A., & Hendrick, S. S. (Eds.). (2000). *Close relationships: A sourcebook.* Thousand Oaks, CA: Sage.

Heritage, J. (1984). *Garfinkel and ethnomethodology.* Cambridge, UK: Polity.

Heritage, J., & Maynard, D. W. (Eds.). (2006). *The communication of medical care: Interaction between primary care physicians and patients.* Cambridge, UK: Cambridge University Press.

Herman, L., & Vervaeck, B. (2005). *Handbook of narrative analysis.* Lincoln: University of Nebraska Press.

Hewitt, J. P., & Stokes, R. (1975). Disclaimers. *American Sociological Review, 40,* 1–11.

Hochschild, A. R. (1973). *The unexpected community.* Englewood Cliffs, NJ: Prentice-Hall.

Holstein, J. A. (1988). Studying family usage: Family image and discourse in mental hospitalization decisions. *Journal of Contemporary Ethnography, 17,* 261–284.

Holstein, J. A. (1993). *Court-ordered insanity: Interpretive practice and involuntary commitment.* Hawthorne, NY: Aldine de Gruyter.

Holstein, J. A., & Gubrium, J. F. (1995a). *The active interview.* Thousand Oaks, CA: Sage.

Holstein, J. A., & Gubrium, J. F. (1995b). Deprivatization and domestic life: Interpretive practice in family context. *Journal of Marriage and the Family, 57,* 607–622.

Holstein, J. A., & Gubrium, J. F. (2000a). *Constructing the life course* (2nd ed.). Dix Hills, NY: General Hall.

Holstein, J. A., & Gubrium, J. F. (2000b). *The self we live by: Narrative identity in a postmodern world.* New York: Oxford University Press.

Holstein, J. A., & Gubrium, J. F. (2003). A constructionist analytics for social problems. In J. A. Holstein & G. Miller (Eds.), *Challenges and choices: Constructionist perspectives on social problems* (pp. 187–208). Hawthorne, NY: Aldine de Gruyter.

Holstein, J. A., & Gubrium, J. F. (2004). Context: Working it up, down, and across. In C. Seale, G. Gobo, J. F. Gubrium, & D. Silverman (Eds.), *Qualitative research practice* (pp. 297–311). London: Sage.

Holstein, J. A., & Gubrium, J. F. (2005). Interpretive practice and social action. In N. Denzin & Y. Lincoln (Eds.), *The SAGE Handbook of qualitative research* (3rd ed., pp. 483–506). Thousand Oaks, CA: Sage.

Holstein, J. A., & Gubrium, J. F. (2008). Constructionist impulses in ethnographic fieldwork. In J. A. Holstein & J. F. Gubrium (Eds.), *Handbook of constructionist research* (pp. 373–396). New York: Guilford.

Holstein, J. A., & Miller, G. (Eds.). (1993). *Reconsidering social constructionism.* New York: Aldine de Gruyter.

Hopper, J. (1993). The rhetoric of motives in divorce. *Journal of Marriage and the Family, 55,* 801–813.

Hopper, J. (2001). Contested selves in divorce proceedings. In J. F. Gubrium & J. A. Holstein (Eds.), *Institutional selves: Troubled identities in a postmodern world* (pp. 127–141). New York: Oxford University Press.

Hughes, E. C. (1984). *The sociological eye.* New Brunswick, NJ: Transaction Books. (Original published 1942)

Husserl, E. (1931). *Ideas: General introduction to pure phenomenology.* New York: Humanities Press.

Husserl, E. (1970a). *The crisis of European science and transcendental phenomenology.* Evanston, IL: Northwestern University Press. (Original work published 1938)

Husserl, E. (1970b). *Logical investigations.* New York: Humanities Press. (Original work published in 1901)

Hymes, D. (1964). The ethnography of communication. *American Anthropologist, 66,* 6–56.

Hynes, S. (1997). *The soldiers' tale: Bearing witness to modern war.* New York: Penguin.

Jakobson, R. (1971). Shifters, verbal categories, and the Russian verb. In *Roman Jakobson: Selected writings* (Vol. 2., pp. 130–147). The Hague: Mouton. (Original work published 1957)

Jameson, F. (1972). *The prison-house of language.* Princeton, NJ: Princeton University Press.

Jefferson, G. (1978). Sequential aspects of storytelling in conversation. In J. Schenkein (Ed.), *Studies in the organization of conversational interaction* (pp. 219–248). New York: Academic Press.

Jimerson, J. B., & Oware, M. K. (2006). Telling the code of the street: An ethnomethodological ethnography. *Journal of Contemporary Ethnography, 23,* 24–50.

Josselson, R., & Lieblich, A. (Eds.). (1993). *The narrative study of lives* (Vol. 1). Thousand Oaks, CA: Sage.

Kaufman, S. R. (1986). *The ageless self: Sources of meaning in late life.* Madison: University of Wisconsin Press.

Kenyon, G. M., & Randall, W. L. (1997). *Restorying our lives.* Westport, CT: Praeger.

Kimmel, D. (1974). *Adulthood and aging: An interdisciplinary, developmental view.* New York: Wiley.

Kleinman, A. (1988). *The illness narratives.* New York: Basic.

Kristeva, J. (1973, October 12). The system and the speaking subject. *Times Literary Supplement,* p. 1249.

Kristeva, J. (1980). *Desire in language: A semiotic approach to literature and art.* New York: Columbia University Press.

Kübler-Ross, E. (1969). *On death and dying.* New York: Macmillan.

Kurz, D. (2006). Keeping tabs on teenagers. In J. F. Gubrium & J. A. Holstein (Eds.), *Couples, kids, and family life* (pp. 84–103). New York: Oxford University Press.

Kvale, S. (1996). *InterViews.* Thousand Oaks, CA: Sage.

Labov, W. (Ed.). (1972a). *Language in the inner city.* Philadelphia: University of Pennsylvania Press.

Labov, W. (1972b). The transformation of experience in narrative syntax. In *Language in the inner city: Studies in the Black English vernacular* (pp. 354–396). Philadelphia: University of Pennsylvania Press.

Lakoff, G., & Johnson, M. (1980). *Metaphors we live by.* Chicago: University of Chicago Press.

Lareau, A. (2003). *Unequal childhoods: Class, race, and family life.* Berkeley: University of California Press.

Lieblich, A., Tuval-Mashiach, R., & Zilber, T. (1998). *Narrative research: Reading, analysis, and interpretation.* Thousand Oaks, CA: Sage.

Liebow, E. (1967). *Tally's corner.* Boston: Little, Brown.

Linde, C. (1993). *Life stories: The creation of coherence.* New York: Oxford University Press.

Loseke, D. R. (1989). Creating clients: Social problems work in a shelter for battered women. *Perspectives on Social Problems, 1,* 173–193.

Loseke, D. R. (1992). *The battered woman and shelters.* Albany: State University of New York Press.

Loseke, D. (2001). Lived realities and formula stories of "battered women." In J. F. Gubrium & J. A. Holstein (Eds.), *Institutional selves* (pp. 107–126). New York: Oxford University Press.

Loseke, D. R. (2007). The study of identity as cultural, institutional, organizational, and personal narratives: Theoretical and empirical integrations. *The Sociological Quarterly, 48,* 661–688.

Luff, P., Hindmarsh, J., & Health, C. (Eds.). (2000). *Workplace studies: Recovering work practice and informing system design.* Cambridge, UK: Cambridge University Press.

Lynch, M. (2002). From naturally occurring data to naturally organized ordinary activities: Comment on Speer. *Discourse Studies, 4,* 531–537.

Marsiglio, W., & Hinojosa, R. (2006). Stepfathers and the family dance. In J. F. Gubrium & J. A. Holstein (Eds.), *Couples, kids, and family life* (pp. 178–196). New York: Oxford University Press.

Marvasti, A. (2003). *Being homeless: Textual and narrative constructions*. Lanham, MD: Lexington Books.

Mayhew, H. (1968). *London labour and the London poor* (Vols. 1–4). New York: Dover. (Original published in 1861–1862)

Maynard, D. W. (1980). Placement of topic change in conversation. *Semiotica, 30,* 263–290.

Maynard, D. W. (1989). On the ethnography and analysis of discourse in institutional settings. In J. Holstein & G. Miller (Eds.), *Perspectives on social problems* (Vol. 1, pp. 127–146). Greenwich, CT: JAI Press.

Maynard, D. W. (2003). *Bad news, good news: Conversational order in everyday talk and clinical settings*. Chicago: University of Chicago Press.

McAdams, D. (1993). *The stories we live by: Personal myths and the making of the self*. New York: Guilford.

Mead, G. H. (1934). *Mind, self, and society*. Chicago: University of Chicago Press.

Mehan, H. (1979). *Learning lessons*. Cambridge, MA: Harvard University Press.

Mehan, H., & Wood, H. (1975). *The reality of ethnomethodology*. New York: Wiley.

Miller, G. (1978). *Odd jobs: The world of deviant work*. Inglewood Cliffs, NJ: Prentice Hall.

Miller, G. (1981). *It's a living: Work in modern society*. New York: St. Martin's.

Miller, G. (1997). *Becoming miracle workers: Language and meaning in brief therapy*. Hawthorne, NY: Aldine de Gruyter.

Miller, G., & Holstein, J. A. (1996). *Dispute domains and welfare claims*. Greenwich, CT: JAI Press.

Mills, C. W. (1940). Situated actions and vocabularies of motive. *American Sociological Review, 5,* 904–913.

Modan, G. G. (2007). *Turf wars: Discourse, diversity, and the politics of place*. Malden, MA: Blackwell.

Mumby, D. K. (Ed.). (1993). *Narrative and social control: Critical perspectives*. Thousand Oaks, CA: Sage.

Narayan, K. (1989). *Storytellers, saints, and scoundrels: Folk narrative in Hindu religious teaching*. Philadelphia: University of Pennsylvania Press.

Narayan, K., & George, K. M. (2002). Personal and folk narrative as cultural representation. In J. F. Gubrium & J. A. Holstein (Eds.), *Handbook of interview research* (pp. 815–832). Thousand Oaks, CA: Sage.

Norrick, N. R. (2000). *Conversational narrative: Storytelling in everyday talk*. Amsterdam: John Benjamins Publishing.

Ochs, E., & Capps, L. (2001). *Living narrative: Creating lives in everyday storytelling*. Cambridge: Harvard University Press.

Ochs, E., & Taylor, C. (1992). Family narrative as political activity. *Discourse and Society, 3,* 301–340.

Passerini, L. (1987). *Fascism in popular memory: The cultural experience of the Turin working class*. Cambridge, UK: Cambridge University Press.

Patterson, W. (Ed.). (2002). *Strategic narrative: New perspectives on the power of personal and cultural stories*. Lanham, MD: Lexington Books.

Plummer, K. (1995). *Telling sexual stories*. London: Routledge.

Plummer, K. (2001). *Documents of life 2*. London: Sage.

Polkinghorne, D. E. (1988). *Narrative knowing and the human sciences*. Albany: State University of New York Press.

Polletta, F. (2006). *It was like a fever: Storytelling in protest and politics*. Chicago: University of Chicago Press.

Pollner, M. (1987). *Mundane reason*. New York: Cambridge University Press.

Pollner, M., & McDonald-Wikler, L. (1985). The social construction of unreality: A case study of a family's attribution of competence to a severely retarded child. *Family Process, 24,* 241–254.

Portelli, A. (1990). *The death of Luigi Trastulli and other stories: Form and meaning in oral history*. Albany: State University of New York Press.

Portelli, A. (2003). *The order has been carried out: History, memory, and the meaning of a Nazi massacre in Rome.* New York: Palgrave Macmillan.

Potter, J. (2002). Two kinds of natural. *Discourse Studies, 4,* 539–542.

Potter, J., & Hepburn, A. (2008). Discursive constructionism. In J. Holstein & J. Gubrium (Eds.), *Handbook of constructionist research* (pp. 275–293). New York: Guilford.

Propp, V. (1968). *Morphology of the folk tale.* Austin: University of Texas Press. (Original work published 1928)

Putnam, H. (1995). *Pragmatism: An open question.* Oxford: Blackwell.

Randall, W. L. (1995). *The stories we are: An essay on self-creation.* Toronto, Canada: University of Toronto Press.

Richardson, L. (1990a). Narrative and sociology. *Journal of Contemporary Ethnography, 9,* 116–136.

Richardson, L. (1990b). *Writing strategies: Reaching diverse audiences.* Newbury Park, CA: Sage.

Ricoeur, P. (1981). *Hermeneutics and the human sciences.* Cambridge: Cambridge University Press.

Ricoeur, P. (1984). *Time and narrative.* Chicago: University of Chicago Press.

Riessman, C. K. (1990). *Divorce talk.* New Brunswick, NJ: Rutgers University Press.

Riessman, C. K. (1993). *Narrative analysis.* Thousand Oaks, CA: Sage.

Roos, P. A. (1992). Professions. In E. Borgatta (Ed.), *Encyclopedia of sociology* (pp. 1552–1557). New York: Macmillan.

Rosenblatt, P. C. (1994). *Metaphors of family systems theory: Toward new constructions.* New York: Guilford.

Rosenblatt, P. C. (2006). *Two in a bed: The social system of couple bed-sharing.* Albany: State University of New York Press.

Rosenwald, G. C., & Ochsberg, R. L. (Eds.). (1992). *Storied lives: The cultural politics of self-understanding.* New Haven, CT: Yale University Press.

Rubin, H. J., & Rubin, I. S. (1995). *Qualitative interviewing.* Thousand Oaks, CA: Sage.

Sacks, H. (1992a). *Lectures on conversation, vol. I.* Oxford: Blackwell.

Sacks, H. (1992b). *Lectures on conversation, vol. II.* Oxford: Blackwell.

Sacks, H., & Schegloff, E. A. (1979). Two preferences in the organization of reference to persons in conversation and their interaction. In G. Psathas (Ed.), *Everyday language studies* (pp. 15–21). New York: Irvington.

Sacks, H., Schegloff, E., & Jefferson, G. (1974). A simplest systematics for the organization of turn-taking for conversation. *Language, 50,* 696–735.

Sanders, C. (1999). *Understanding dogs: Living and working with canine companions.* Philadephia: Temple University Press.

Schegloff, E. A. (1980). Preliminaries to preliminaries: "Can I ask you a question?" *Sociological Inquiry, 50,* 104–152.

Schegloff, E. A. (1984). Some questions and ambiguities in conversation. In J. Maxwell Atkinson & J. Heritage (Eds.), *Structures of social action* (pp. 28–52). Cambridge: Cambridge University Press.

Schegloff, E. A., & Sacks, H. (1973). Opening up closings. *Semiotica, 7,* 289–327.

Schutz, A. (1970). *On phenomenology and social relations.* Chicago: University of Chicago Press.

Scott, M. B., & Lyman, S. (1968). Accounts. *American Sociological Review, 33,* 46–62.

Shalin, D. (1986). Pragmatism and social interactionism. *American Sociological Review, 51,* 9–29.

Shaw, C. R. (1930). *The jack-roller: A delinquent boy's own story.* Chicago: University of Chicago Press.

Sheridan, A. (1980). *Michel Foucault: The will to truth.* New York: Tavistock.

Shuman, A. (1986). *Storytelling rights: The uses of oral and written texts by urban adolescents.* Cambridge, UK: Cambridge University Press.

Shuman, A. (2005). *Other people's stories: Entitlement claims and the critique of empathy.* Urbana: University of Illinois Press.

Silverman, D. (1998). *Harvey Sacks: Social science and conversation analysis.* New York: Oxford University Press.

Silverman, D. (2005). *Doing qualitative research* (2nd ed.). London: Sage.

Skidmore, W. (1975). *Theoretical thinking in sociology.* Cambridge, UK: Cambridge University Press.

Smith, D. E. (1978). "K" is mentally ill: The anatomy of a factual account. *Sociology, 12,* 23–53.

Smith, D. (1987). *The everyday world as problematic.* Boston: Northeastern University Press.

SOS Dallas. (2007). *What is SOS?* Retrieved May 29, 2007, from http://www.sosdallas.org/what_is_sos.htm

Speer, S. A. (2002). Natural and contrived data: A sustainable distinction? *Discourse Studies, 4,* 511–525.

Stoeltje, B. J. (1981). Cowboys and clowns: Rodeo specialists and the ideology of work and play. In *"And otherly neighborly names": Social process and cultural image in Texas folklore* (pp. 123–151). Austin: University of Texas Press.

Stone, E. (1988). *Black sheep and kissing cousins: How our family stories shape us.* New York: Times Books.

Suchar, C. S. (1975, April). *Doing therapy: Notes on the training of psychiatric personnel.* Presented at the Annual Meeting of the Midwest Sociological Society, Chicago.

Swidler, A. (1986). Culture in action: Symbols and strategies. *American Sociological Review, 51,* 273–286.

Tedlock, B. (1991). From participant observation to the observation of participation: The emergence of narrative ethnography. *Journal of Anthropological Research, 47,* 69–94.

Tedlock, B. (1992). *The beautiful and the dangerous: Encounters with the Zuni Indians.* New York: Viking.

Tedlock, B. (2004). Narrative ethnography as social science discourse. *Studies in Symbolic Interaction, 27,* 23–31.

Thomas, W. I., & Znaniecki, F. (1927). *The Polish peasant in Europe and America.* New York: Knopf. (Original published in 1918–1920)

Todorov, T. (1984). *Mikhail Bakhtin: The dialogical principle.* Minneapolis: University of Minnesota Press.

Turner, V. (1985). *Liminality, Kabbalah, and the media.* New York: Academic Press.

Turner, V. (1986). *The anthropology of performance.* New York: PAJ Publications.

Turner, V. (1995). *The ritual process: Structure and anti-structure.* New Brunswick, NJ: Aldine Transaction. (Original work published 1969)

Unruh, D. R. (1983). *Invisible lives: Social worlds of the aged.* Beverly Hills, CA: Sage.

Vandewater, S. R. (1983). Discourse processes and the social organization of group therapy sessions. *Sociology of Health and Illness, 5,* 275–296.

Van Maanen, J. (1988). *Tales of the field: On writing ethnography.* Chicago: University of Chicago Press.

Vannini, P. (2006). Dead poets' society: Teaching, publish-or-perish, and professors' experiences of authenticity. *Symbolic Interaction, 29,* 235–257.

Vila, P. (2005). *Border identifications: Narratives of religion, gender, and class on the U.S.-Mexico border.* Austin: University of Texas Press.

Walzer, S. (2006). Children's stories of divorce. In J. F. Gubrium & J. A. Holstein (Eds.), *Couples, kids, and family life* (pp. 162–177). New York: Oxford University Press.

Warner, R. L. (2006). Being a good parent. In J. F. Gubrium & J. A. Holstein (Eds.), *Couples, kids, and family life* (pp. 65–83). New York: Oxford University Press.

Warren, C. A. B., & Karner, T. X. (2005). *Discovering qualitative methods.* Los Angeles: Roxbury.

Weinberg, D. (Ed.). (2002). *Qualitative research methods.* Malden, MA: Blackwell.

Weinberg, D. (2005). *Of others inside: Insanity, addiction, and belonging in America.* Philadelphia: Temple University Press.

West, C. (1996). Ethnography and orthography: A (modest) methodological proposal. *Journal of Contemporary Ethnography, 25,* 327–352.

Whalen, J. (1992). Conversation analysis. In E. Borgatta (Ed.), *Encyclopedia of Sociology* (Vol. 1, pp. 303–310). New York: Macmillan.

Whyte, W. F. (1943). *Street corner society.* Chicago: University of Chicago Press.

Wieder, D. L. (1974). *Language and social reality.* The Hague: Mouton.

Wiley, N. (1985). Marriage and the construction of reality. In G. Handel (Ed.), *The psychosocial interior of the family* (pp. 21–32). New York: Aldine.

Wittgenstein, L. (1953). *Philosophical investigations.* New York: Macmillan.

Wooffitt, R. (2005). *Conversation analysis and discourse analysis.* London: Sage.

Wooffitt, R., & Widdicombe, S. (2006). Interaction in interviews. In P. Drew, G. Raymond, & D. Weinberg (Eds.), *Talk and interaction in social research methods* (pp. 28–49). London: Sage.

Woolgar, S., & Pawluch, D. (1985). Ontological gerrymandering: The anatomy of social problems explanations. *Social Problems, 32,* 214–227.

Young, A. (1995). *The harmony of illusions.* Princeton, NJ: Princeton University Press.

Young, K. G. (1986). *Taleworlds and storyrealms: The phenomenology of narrative.* The Hague, Netherlands: Martinus Nijhoff.

Zimmerman, D. H., & Pollner, M. (1970). The everyday world as a phenomenon. In J. Douglas (Ed.), *Understanding everyday life* (pp. 80–104). Chicago: Aldine.

Credits

p. 19–20, 41   Riessman, Catherine Kohler. 1993. *Narrative analysis*. Thousand Oaks, CA: Sage. © Sage Publications, Inc. Reprinted by permission.

p. 48   Gubrium, Jaber F., and James A. Holstein. 2000. Analyzing interpretive practice. In N. Denzin and Y. Lincoln (Eds.), *Handbook of qualitative research* (2nd ed., pp. 487–508). Thousand Oaks, CA: Sage. © Sage Publications, Inc. Reprinted by permission.

p. 62–63, 64–65, 66   Egan, R. Danielle. 2006. *Dancing for dollars and paying for love*. New York: Palgrave Macmillan. Reprinted by permission.

p. 83, 86, 87, 88, 89–90, 91   Abu-Lughod, Lila. 1993. *Writing women's worlds: Bedouin stories*. Berkeley: University of California Press. Reprinted by permission.

p. 93, 96, 104–105, 113, 219   Norrick, Neal R. 2000. *Conversational narrative: Storytelling in everyday talk*. Amsterdam: John Benjamins Publishing. Reprinted by permission.

p. 133, 134–136   Lareau, Annette. 2003. *Unequal childhoods: Class, race, and family life*. Berkeley: University of California Press. Reprinted by permission.

p. 166–168   Buckholdt, David R., and Jaber F. Gubrium. 1979. *Caretakers: Treating emotionally disturbed children*. Beverly Hills: Sage. © Sage Publications, Inc. Reprinted by permission.

p. 170–171   Holstein, James A. 1988. "Studying family usage: Family image and discourse in mental hospitalization decisions." *Journal of Contemporary Ethnography* 17: 261–284.

p. 178, 179   Denzin, Norman K. 1987a. *The alcoholic self*. Newbury Park, CA: Sage. © Sage Publications, Inc. Reprinted by permission.

Author Index

Subject Index